All Things in Common
A Canadian Family and Its Island Utopia

In the first decade of the twentieth century, a few closely related families established a utopian community in Canada's smallest province. Known officially as B. Compton Limited but described by a journalist in 1935 as "Prince Edward Island's unique 'brotherly love' community," this utopia owed its longevity to the cohesion provided by its communal organization, dense kin ties, and long-held millenarianism – and to a decidedly pragmatic approach to business.

All Things in Common demonstrates how "un-utopian" such a community could be while problematizing the contention that the inevitable end of all utopian experiments is a full-blown dystopia. Beginning with a compelling backstory and locating the Compton community in the historiography of North American utopias, the author goes on to explore the community's business endeavours; its religious, familial, and transgressive aspects; and its brief period of international fame before assessing the factors that led to its dissolution in 1947. Providing a strong narrative framework, *All Things in Common* draws on rich family and archival records and diverse secondary sources, concluding with a consideration of the community's legacy for its alumni and their descendants.

(Canadian Social History Series)

RUTH COMPTON BROUWER is a professor emerita in the Department of History at King's University College, Western University.

All Things in Common

A Canadian Family and
Its Island Utopia

Ruth Compton Brouwer

UNIVERSITY OF TORONTO PRESS
Toronto Buffalo London

Canadian Social History Series

ISBN 978-1-4875-0797-8 (cloth)   ISBN 978-1-4875-3729-6 (EPUB)
ISBN 978-1-4875-2556-9 (paper)   ISBN 978-1-4875-3728-9 (PDF)

Library and Archives Canada Cataloguing in Publication

Title: All things in common : a Canadian family and its island utopia /
Ruth Compton Brouwer.
Names: Brouwer, Ruth Compton, author.
Series: Canadian social history series.
Description: Series statement: The Canadian social history series |
Includes bibliographical references and index.
Identifiers: Canadiana (print) 20210164026 | Canadiana (ebook)
20210178701 | ISBN 9781487525569 (softcover) | ISBN 9781487507978
(hardcover) | ISBN 9781487537289 (PDF) | ISBN 9781487537296 (EPUB)
Subjects: LCSH: B. Compton Limited. | LCSH: Utopias –
Prince Edward Island – History – 20th century. | LCSH:
Collective settlements – Prince Edward Island – History – 20th century.
Classification: LCC HX660.B3 B76 2021 | DDC 307.7709717 – dc23

University of Toronto Press acknowledges the financial assistance to its
publishing program of the Canada Council for the Arts and the
Ontario Arts Council, an agency of the Government of Ontario.

This book has been published with the help of a grant from the Federation
for the Humanities and Social Sciences, through the Awards to Scholarly
Publications Program, using funds provided by the Social Sciences and
Humanities Research Council of Canada.

"How Memory Works" is reproduced from *Smallholding* courtesy
of the author and Fitzhenry & Whiteside.

Canada Council   Conseil des Arts
for the Arts   du Canada

ONTARIO ARTS COUNCIL
CONSEIL DES ARTS DE L'ONTARIO
an Ontario government agency
un organisme du gouvernement de l'Ontario

Funded by the   Financé par le
Government   gouvernement
of Canada   du Canada

Canada

In memory of Lydia Jardine Compton and Benjamin Compton.

How Memory Works

The frost heaves the past above ground – spoon, coin, stone blade.
Deep down things you'll not find by digging. Just so, there are memories
you couldn't reach even if you wanted to.

And then someone tosses you a phrase – small as a coin – and you're years gone.
Another epoch unfolding in your mind all because Aggie said *bread sandwiches*.

> A woman bringing a field-tea to the men at harvest time.
> Sandwiches wrapped in a damp cloth to keep them fresh –
> *bread sandwiches* – and tea in mason jars, the jars in wool sleeves.
> Tea the colour of a sedimentary river in spring time. The cups
> they're pouring it into are discards – railway dishware, creamy-white and
>   heavy
> Unbreakable. (The cup's weight, the thick lip of it.) Yes, but what else?
> They're sitting in the shade of the threshing machine. Chaff wandering the
>   air.
> One of them is eating apple cuts from the tip of a pocket knife.
> That'd be Uncle Ollie.
>   The thronged past you didn't know
>   until you were tipped off. All back. All back then.

Anne Compton

Contents

Acknowledgments

It is a pleasure to thank the many people who helped me with this book. I begin with my sister Anne Compton and my friend and fellow historian Marguerite Van Die, both of whom commented on an early draft and continued to provide good advice as I worked my way through several revisions. All of my siblings, and many of their children, contributed in one way or another. I am particularly grateful to my sisters Libbie MacKenzie (d. 2017), Isabel Dingwell, and Sophia MacLaren Clarke for digging deep into their personal memory banks in response to my questions about the final years of the Compton community. Ada MacDonald Compton provided some documents that I hadn't known existed. Without the careful Compton family genealogy compiled by Pamela Hatton Compton in the 1980s I would have had a great deal more difficulty in sorting out who was who among the many Prince Edward Island descendants of Loyalists William and Sarah Compton. Turning from my immediate family to an extensive network of kin, I am very much indebted to George H. Compton (d. 2012), son of Hector D. Compton, and to Sybil (d. 2019), Hector's daughter-in-law, for access to Hector's invaluable collection of papers on the Compton community. Russ Compton and Liz Salmis also shared documents as well as childhood memories of grandfather Hector in his post-community years. Others who because of their age or birthplace had no direct knowledge of the community era but who, in response to inquiries, reflected in writing on the lingering significance of their unusual family background in their own and their parents' lives included Danny Compton, Kent Compton, Scott Compton, Keith Gerrard, Judy Goodwin, Sylvia Hawkins, Debbie MacKenzie, Diane MacPherson, Karen Miller, Donna Morgan, and Ellen Rasmussen Pitcher.

For the resources, insights, and comparative perspective necessary to turn a family story into a scholarly monograph I am indebted to a great many archivists and fellow historians. At the Public Archives and Records Office in Charlottetown, John Boylan and his staff were unfailingly helpful, as were Simon Lloyd and others at the Archives and Special Collections Unit of the University of Prince Edward Island's Robertson Library. Other archives and historical associations from whose staff I received useful in-person or electronic assistance were the Beaton Institute/Cape Breton University; Croft House at Selkirk Park, PEI; Highland Village Museum, Cape Breton; Library and Archives Canada; Manitoba Archives; Maritime Conference Archives/United Church of Canada; Maritime History Archive/Memorial University of Newfoundland; Monmouth County Historical Association, Freehold, New Jersey; Public Archives of New Brunswick; Public Archives of Nova Scotia; and Quaco Museum, St. Martins, New Brunswick. Historians whose assistance went well beyond their published research include Harry Baglole (d. 2018), David Bell, Rusty Bittermann, Marian Bruce, Jill Campbell-Miller, Colin M. Coates, Marg Conrad, Ed MacDonald, John Reid, Ian Ross Robertson, and David Weale. In Toronto, Beth Moore Milroy shared her extensive knowledge of Canadian utopian communities, while on PEI Preston MacDonald provided help with photographs, and Jack Whytock shed light on aspects of the McDonaldite movement and its legacy.

Thanks to the good offices of Greg Kealey, general editor of the Canadian Social History Series at University of Toronto Press, I made my way back to UTP, where the efficiency and good humour of acquisitions editor Len Husband, especially as we entered the pandemic era, was beyond impressive. Two anonymous readers who evaluated my manuscript for the press provided the kind of thoughtful and supportive feedback that made me want to do everything I could to strengthen it. Stephanie Mazza and Robin Studniberg provided their expertise in the final stage of the publication process as did freelance editor Judy Williams, whose keen eye for stylistic errors and inconsistencies was much appreciated. As with my previous book Brian McLean patiently rescued me from several computer-related problems.

My apologies to any individuals and institutions whose contributions to this book I have inadvertently overlooked. As for any errors of fact or troubling interpretations, I alone am responsible.

All Things in Common

Introduction

In the first decade of the twentieth century, a small group of interrelated families on Prince Edward Island established their own utopian community. Its leaders were millenarian in outlook: Jesus would soon return; the old order would end. And yet very much engaged with the here and now: work must be done; income earned; order maintained. Thanks in part to their pragmatism, the community they directed was comparatively long-lived. With its tight communitarian social structure and strong if unchurched religious life, "Prince Edward Island's unique 'brotherly love' community"[1] had more in common with some of the numerous utopias established in the second quarter of the nineteenth century in the northeastern United States – their heyday in time and place – than with the back-to-the-land communes that briefly arose in late 1960s and early 1970s North America. Known officially as B. Compton Limited, Prince Edward Island's utopian community had its fifteen minutes of fame during the last half of the Great Depression, when its membership comprised about one hundred souls and enthusiastic accounts of its way of life briefly reached an international audience. Following its dissolution in 1947, former members and descendants of the community largely consigned their ancestors' utopian project to the recesses of the family memory bank and politely turned aside outsiders' requests to make it known.

Several decades ago, when I first started thinking about investigating this community, albeit in a fitful way and mainly to satisfy my own curiosity after reading about another long-lived and analogous utopia, I had no intention of seeking out a backstory beyond perhaps confirming the Loyalist origins of the Comptons. Long years later and more fully engaged, I recognized the need for a fuller consideration of

3

their pre-communitarian past: the journey that led up to their utopian experiment was a microcosm of larger regional patterns and thus
historically significant in its own right as well as essential to making
sense of the experiment's lineaments. The result is *All Things in Common: A Canadian Family and Its Island Utopia*. The first part deals
briefly with the Canadian founding family, New Jersey Loyalists William and Sarah Compton, before following one branch of the pioneering couple's descendants as they shifted around the Maritime colonies
and then, in the early nineteenth century, settled down on Prince
Edward Island. One or two generations on, some of them took to the
road again. Some of these movers-on settled permanently in distant
parts of Canada or (more often) the United States, but others, including the future utopia's founding figures, moved back to their Island
home. The first part of the book, then, engages with, and I hope illu-
minates, three familiar (and now fraught) topics in Canada's historical
narrative: Loyalists, settlers, and sojourners. By contrast, Part II, com-
prising four chapters on the life and legacy of B. Compton Limited,
deals with a subject still largely unexplored by professional historians:
Canada's experience with utopias and other intentional communities.[2]
   The field of utopian studies is sufficiently broad, international, and
vibrant to have had its own interdisciplinary scholarly journal since
1988, when *Utopian Studies* began to be published in the United States.
In Canada, utopian communities have so far remained primarily of
interest to popular historians, most notably in British Columbia. The
comparative neglect of such communities by scholars may reflect a
view that they have been too few, too ephemeral, and too far removed
from the main currents and themes of Canadian history to merit sustained attention.[3] Yet as *All Things in Common* shows, both in their
rise and demise utopian communities are products of particular historical and regional circumstances. However random and eccentric
they may appear to be, they are part of our country's development as
well as the products of their founders' vision. Their study can thus be a
fruitful source of new insights into several fields in Canadian history.
Both in its nineteenth-century backstory and in its utopian moment,
All Things in Common falls directly within the purview of historians
of the family, religion, and the Maritime region of Canada and the
transnational dimensions of those fields. The book also contributes to
a field that receives relatively little attention in contemporary scholarship: the history of Canada's long-lasting "rural majority," particularly
in its social dimensions.[4] The book tells a story of ordinary people
who sometimes behaved in unconventional ways, especially in their
pursuit of spiritual nourishment and family solidarity. In telling their

story I have provided details of their personalities and struggles and used their own voices as much as possible in an effort to bring them vividly to life.

All Things in Common is certainly not a monograph that I had in mind when I set out to train as a historian. Beginning with a doctoral thesis on Canadian Protestant women as Victorian-era overseas missionaries, initially suggested and subsequently supervised by Ramsay Cook, I became fascinated by Canadians who went to Asia and Africa and other parts of the developing world as religious and secular humanitarians. That fascination resulted in three books and drew me into a wonderful scholarly community whose networks and interests I still share. There is another reason, though, why *All Things in Common* is not a book I intended to write: the people in it are my ancestors. Until recently, it had seemed to me that historians who wanted to be taken seriously within the profession ought not to write about their own people. Was that not the terrain of genealogists and other practitioners of what writer and literary critic Alison Light, delving into the history of her own English family, feared might be dismissed as "history lite"?[5] Moreover, what little I knew about my ancestors' lives before I began this project, particularly about their unconventional religious and marital practices – both of which predated but became more pronounced during their utopian phase – had troubled me as a self-conscious teenager coming of age with a vague sense of otherness in a remarkably homogeneous society. Long after I had left my native Prince Edward Island and trained as a historian, there remained a remnant of that unease: perhaps my ancestors' unconventional lives *were* best left in the family history closet as the older alumni of the utopia had believed.

What changed was the kind of change that comes with retiring from an academic career with its real and perceived constraints: I felt free to investigate a family saga for which I had access to some rich sources, and a personal connection that inspired even more than the usual curiosity of the engaged historian. What also helped was my discovery early on of work by a small body of academic historians and other research professionals who collectively demonstrate that it is certainly possible to write about one's ancestors without writing "history lite." Among four books that I have found particularly useful in this connection, Richard White's *Remembering Ahanagran: Storytelling in a Family's Past* conforms least to the format one normally expects in a work from a professional historian. Internationally acclaimed for his books on environmental, Native American, and frontier history, White largely eschews such conventions as endnotes in *Remembering Ahanagran*. What he does not leave behind, though, in ruminating on his mother's memories of her native Ireland and her immigrant experience in the United States is his historian's sensibility ("I appreciate the case for memory, [but] I will still take the side of history"). White juxtaposes history and memory, testing memories that Sara Walsh and her kin claimed as part of their own lived experience against documented events in Ireland's past. *Remembering Ahanagran* is insightful about the kinds of things that people choose to "remember" and share about their own and their nation's past. But it is also helpful in other ways, such as in giving the reader a vivid understanding of the concept of transnationalism as lived, familial experience. Australian historian Marjorie Theobald and Alison Light employ a broader range of sources than White and delve further back in time, in both cases demonstrating how much can be learned about their ancestors (including some previously unsuspected religiosity), even in the absence of family papers, by working with census data and other public records. They also demonstrate that the experiences of the historian's own kin, even when those kin were mostly "common people" and "history's losers" (Light's terms), can provide useful insights into such big topics as emigration and industrialization. Canadian science journalist Carolyn Abraham uses DNA testing as well as such traditional sources as church records and employs a storytelling format to explore the exotic and long-hidden history of her family in *The Juggler's Children: A Journey into Family, Legend and the Genes That Bind Us* (it really did include a juggler). Different as it is from the kind of research conducted by White, Theobald, and Light, Abraham's work, like theirs, casts light on important historical themes – in her case, colonialism and global population movements – and provides evidence of family members' historic tendency to be selective and evasive about what they choose to share about awkward ancestors in the family tree.[6]

Like the books just discussed, *All Things in Common* is in part the product of a search for identity. Who were these people whose thick blood I shared, and how did their lives, life choices, and misadventures both reflect and deviate from familiar narratives of Canadian history before they surrendered their utopian otherness and became solid citizens of "liberal order" Canada in the last half of the twentieth century?[7] Personal searches of this sort have, of course, become the stuff of public and personal entertainment: one sees them enacted by prominent guests on PBS's *Finding Your Roots* and TLC's *Who Do You Think You Are?*; undertaken by ordinary people world-wide through for-profit companies like Ancestry.com; and promoted by direct-to-consumer genetic-testing companies whose seductive promises academics like Timothy Caulfield warn against. Most recently such searches have even become a boon for travel companies through the growth of "genealogy tourism."[8] Unquestionably, even when undertaken by trained researchers working far from the worlds of commercial genealogy and popular entertainment, the potential pitfalls of a history project driven in part by personal motives and a personal connection are many and undeniable. Nevertheless, I have endeavoured to make *All Things in Common* a work of solid scholarship and to hold myself to the standards of the historical profession.[9] I have also chosen, once beyond the Introduction, to keep myself largely absent from the pages of the book, except briefly at the end of Chapter 7 and in the Concluding Reflections.

Specialists in the field of Canadian family history would perhaps have written a very different book out of the raw materials at my disposal, one informed by different kinds of questions, more densely theorized, and freer from the risks of personal connectedness.[10] Yet that personal connectedness is what gave me an awareness of, and access to, the book's most valuable primary sources, in particular, the surviving papers of Hector D. Compton (1879–1970). Hector was the single most important figure in the utopian phase of the Compton family saga, not only the able secretary-treasurer of B. Compton Limited for most of its existence but also the stern and sometimes sorrowful guardian of what he thought its religious and communal life should be. Hector's penchant for letter writing and for making and saving copies is all the more remarkable and valuable for having continued into the long years of his retirement, when he shared frequent reminiscences about family history with one set of correspondents even as, with others, he pursued deeply problematic religious interests.[11] I make frequent use of his distinctive, sometimes gnomic, voice in writing about the utopian era. Primary sources were more difficult to come by for the period before the Compton family settled on Prince Edward Island and particularly before they established their communitarian utopia. Hence my appreciation for the rich array of relevant secondary sources on which I was able to draw for this book. They have provided muchneeded context for the fragments of information about my subjects available in, for instance, state documents on Loyalist exile and resettlement, wills, census data, and church records. Together, the primary and secondary sources on the period from the late eighteenth to the twenty-first century also provide context for information drawn from genealogists' investigations of these Comptons, most of them undertaken well before the internet era. Professional historians' scepticism about the findings of amateur genealogists is not unwarranted. When consulted by researchers on this family line, one certified American genealogist became so frustrated by their reliance on a genealogical bulletin called *Comptonology* that she pleaded for it to be used "only for CLUES!"[12] Nevertheless, at its best a carefully researched family genealogy can provide a springboard for, and a complement to, the work of the family historian by providing detailed information about such matters as lineages and locales, births, marriages, and deaths.[13] Indeed, as Christine Kenneally observes in her recent book on DNA and history, "Although genealogy is not widely valued in academia, it meshes perfectly with, and helps to explain, social history."[14]

For anyone writing about the history of one's family, Alison Light notes, "the feeling of belatedness is an occupational hazard."[15] In my case, that feeling is tempered by reality. Part of me wishes that I had started this project decades ago when there were still former communitarians available with deep and vivid memories of the utopian era and even of the decades preceding it. When I began work on the project in 2012, there *were* still a few people living who had reached adulthood during the community era. They included several men and women whose fathers had had leadership roles. But when I raised questions that they found uncomfortable (however innocuous some of the questions seemed to me), I encountered variations of what Carolyn Abraham encountered when she began asking about her family's past: "Why do you want to go into all that?"[16] On the other hand, I was able to tap into the memories of some Compton family members who were on the cusp of adulthood in the last years of the community. Their recollections provided insights – albeit necessarily subjective – into aspects of community living not touched on in Hector Compton's correspondence or in other written sources, or construed differently in those sources. Their memories also included family rumours about ancestors born in the mid- and late nineteenth century, ancestors recalled for the pathos of their lives, or for transgressive behaviour that had lasting consequences.

What neither memories shared by the still living nor the written records of the long dead can provide for most historians of the family is, of course, any adequate idea of the lives of its women. One of the ironies of family history is that even in the domain where women's lives supposedly counted for most, especially from the late eighteenth century when a powerful ideology about home and family as "women's sphere" began to emerge,[17] we know so little about what actually took place in regard to women's roles in family decision making.[18] Did women who became Comptons by birth or marriage share in decisions to move across national borders and from one colony and province to another, to take on a new religious identity, to be part of a patriarchal communal structure that prized solidarity (and fecundity) over personal autonomy? Did they even expect to share in such decisions? Did the strength of their own personalities and intellect or particular circumstances sometimes allow them larger roles? In this book, I speculate about such matters where possible. But as in all historical accounts of families, it is the men in the household who are most likely to be known to us by virtue of their presence in public and business records.

That said, most family members over time, irrespective of their gender, left few traces – sometimes no trace at all – in the historical record. This was especially true if they were poor, rural, and ill educated, and neither celebrated nor notorious, as was usually the case generation after generation in this family line. All this is to say that while *All Things in Common* was made possible by some rich sources, it is assuredly not without evidentiary gaps and lingering uncertainties. Despite these things, it is my hope that this book will succeed as an informative and thought-provoking account of a family whose members emerge over several centuries as both ordinary and "other." Living far from the concerns and power centres of nation building and commerce, they were a distinctive thread in a rural and regional landscape too often neglected or sentimentalized.

PART I

Unsettled Maritimers

1

Loyalist William and His Namesake in the Maritime Colonies: "Movement Became a Habit"

The Comptons' Canadian family story begins with their Loyalist ancestors. William and Sarah Compton were part of the first great wave of refugees to what is now Canada. As "liberty's exiles" – some sixty thousand in total – the refugees were tying their future to the continuing British Empire rather than opting, as most Loyalists ultimately did, to remain in the new United States of America.[1] In choosing exile, William and Sarah were pulling up deep roots. Comptons had been living in the New World from the early 1600s and in bountiful New Jersey from the 1660s. An earlier William Compton had been among the pioneer white settlers in Middletown, New Jersey, in that decade,[2] thereby becoming part of a settlement whose leaders believed they had created a kind of utopia, "a perfectly balanced, self-sufficient community" where they "desired to close themselves off from the rest of society."[3] This earlier William was also a founder of New Jersey's first Baptist church, a new sect that, like the Quakers, had become anathema to Massachusetts Bay Puritans for its perceived religious radicalism.[4]

Loyalist William and Sarah Sweed Compton – they married in Middletown in 1762[5] – had come to young adulthood at a time of religious and civic upheaval. The First Great Awakening had touched off a period of intense religious revivalism in colonial America. The evangelical fervour that roiled New Jersey paralleled and fed into conflicts with the colony's landed gentry and into property disputes whose ultimate effect was to increase rates of tenancy and even squatting. On the eve of the Revolution, New Jersey was already a colony "on the brink of collective violence."[6] Like most of New Jersey's Loyalists, William, a carpenter, was probably illiterate and thus could leave no written account of his revolutionary war experience or of the considerations that ultimately led him to loyalism and exile.[7] But thoughtful studies of Loyalist motivation and close-grained monographs on revolutionary Monmouth County, where William lived, provide context for his decision. When it came to choosing sides – and even switching sides – Ruma Chopra writes, "More than ideological commitments, the proximity of the British army and the threat of local coercion dramatically affected people's choices."[8] The observation seems particularly apt for William, who, at the time of the Revolution, was living outside Middletown at Compton's Creek near Sandy Hook Bay, where a large British fleet was anchored. The presence of the fleet helped to account for the unusually large number of Loyalists in New Jersey and particularly in Monmouth County. Even there, though, the majority of residents, Comptons among them, ultimately opted for the revolutionary cause. By choosing loyalism, William had made himself an outlier.[9]

During the last year of the war, William and his family lived in New York City on relief, classified in the records of British Commander-in-Chief Guy Carleton as "distressed Loyalists."[10] Under British military rule from 1776 onward, New York's civilian population had more than doubled as a result of the influx of desperate black and white refugees seeking safety from patriot vengeance. Although administrative policy towards them was more sympathetic under Carleton than it had been under his predecessor, refugees of poor and humble backgrounds had to accept the fact that the needs of New York's large military population and of elite Loyalists were prioritized, while they themselves lived in crowded and filthy conditions, regarded by British administrators as a burden and even as potential troublemakers.[11] If under these circumstances William and Sarah entertained any thoughts of returning to Monmouth County, a new organization was in place there to deter them: the Association to Oppose the Return of Tories, one of whose members was most likely a kinsman.[12] From the earliest days of white settlement, New Jersey had been known as the garden colony.[13] Now, the path ahead was exile from the garden. In the twentieth century, the Prince Edward Island descendants of William and Sarah would "remember" their Loyalist forebears proudly for unproblematic British loyalty. In truth, like many other Loyalists, William may not so much have chosen that path when the war began as stumbled into it.[14] Whatever the case, the result was the same: in 1783 he and his family joined an estimated thirty thousand Loyalist refugees from New York bound for the Maritime colonies of British North America: eighteenth-century boat people.[15]

Travelling from New York on the *Duchess of Gordon*, William and Sarah reached Saint John Harbour after a voyage that typically took about a fortnight and had their first glimpse of the bleak-looking land that was to be their new home. Another refugee, arriving as part of the same June fleet, would famously describe it as "the roughest land I ever saw."[16] The region was still part of Nova Scotia at the time; it would not be established as the separate colony of New Brunswick until a year later.[17] Although the Compton family came without kin, their fellow travellers on the *Duchess of Gordon* included many other Jerseyites.[18] The Comptons would have known some of them back in New Jersey and others during the hardscrabble months in New York City. Some would become neighbours in the new land. And, in a pattern that would last for another half-century, children and grandchildren of these and other Loyalist exiles would often become marriage partners for Compton offspring. Old associations and shared memories were doubtless a source of comfort and support as William and Sarah began a new life in Saint John. But it was not to be their final stopping point, for the bleak physical environment was only one of the discouragements that lay ahead. For William and Sarah and their descendants, as for thousands of Loyalists who went to more distant parts of the British Empire, "[m]ovement became a habit."[19]

The Saint John Years

Rough and wild it may have appeared, but Saint John was not a wholly unpopulated place. One estimate suggests that over four hundred people were living in the harbour area when the Loyalists arrived. More than one hundred of them were soldiers living in the fort that had been built in 1778 to fend off patriot raiders and their sometime Malecite (Wolastoquiyik) allies, the latter seeking in vain to hold onto their ancestral homeland.[20] Nor were the Loyalists facing exile without support. They had been transported at public expense, and Sir Guy Carleton had committed to the provision of further support in their new homeland: building materials and temporary shelters, food and clothing, and grants of land on which to settle and farm. Significant gaps between what was expected and what was made available, and inequities in distribution, led, inevitably, to hardship and early expressions of discontent. The promise of provisions for the Loyalists' first year in exile had to be extended for a further two years, with Fort Howe as the conduit for the victualling process. The most significant obstacle to timely self-sufficiency was the delay in getting the Loyalists settled upriver on land that they could farm, a problem exacerbated by a lack of administrative coordination. Meanwhile, they had to live somewhere, and that somewhere was the nascent settlements of Parr-town and Carleton, which in 1785 were united administratively as the new "city" of Saint John.[21] The pace of construction in the two settlements was remarkable. Already by mid-July 1783, about 400 framed houses were said to have been erected in among the tree stumps. By March of the following year, some 1,500 framed houses were reportedly built and some 400 temporary log dwellings.[22]

With his background in carpentry, William Compton could expect to be kept busy during this early building boom. He himself received two adjacent lots of land in Parr-town. Both were close to the harbour in the poorer area of Parr-town known as the Lower Cove.[23] William and Sarah had five children with them when they arrived in Saint John, three of them listed as ten or older. In addition to William's namesake, there was another son, Cornelius, probably the younger of the two, and three daughters: Phoebe, Elizabeth, and Catherine.[24] As a teenager or near-teenager, William, and perhaps even Cornelius, may have been able to contribute something to the family's livelihood.[25] But there was not much future for the family in Saint John, especially since they were part of the commercially disadvantaged Lower Cove community, looked down on socially as well as geographically by their "betters" in the Upper Cove. With the end of what pioneer Loyalist historian Esther Clark Wright called "the first boom days," even the city's carpenters were becoming redundant. The end of government victualling and the departure upriver of farm-bound families, especially as a proper surveying system was put in place in 1785, added to the city's slackening growth.[26]

As residents of Saint John, the Compton family would have been negatively affected not only by the city's declining economic fortunes but also by its fractious political culture and by the sharp class divides among Loyalists that had carried over from New York.[27] Nevertheless, it would have been the possibility of getting a more secure living somewhere other than Saint John with its hostile political and class culture that carried most weight in the family's decision to leave the city.[28] With the early boom days over, Loyalist William was one of a number of tradesmen who decided to try their luck elsewhere. Other Saint John Loyalists were also moving on, and not only to farms upriver. Some were departing for Upper Canada. Perhaps 10 per cent were returning to the United States, while still others were shifting around within New Brunswick and/or shuttling back and forth to communities in Nova Scotia.[29]

Quaco/St. Martins

Acting with another petitioner, Loyalist William sought land outside Saint John in 1785.[30] Ultimately, in or about 1796, he settled with his family in St. Martins (earlier called Quaco). A mainly Loyalist community some thirty miles to the east of Saint John on the Bay of Fundy, St. Martins would become important, indeed second only to Saint John, as a centre for building sailing vessels in nineteenth-century New Brunswick. The earliest Loyalist settlers in St. Martins were former members of a Loyalist militia, the King's Orange Rangers. It was through a former captain of the Rangers, John Howard, that William obtained land in the settlement. Writing from there in 1805 in one of his frequent petitions for land, Howard stated that Compton was one of four family heads to settle on land he had originally sought for himself some nine years earlier.[31] In the years after their move to St. Martins, the Comptons' economic and familial affairs would become interconnected with those of other early settlers in the area in addition to Howard. There were, for instance, the Morans and the Moshers; the Vails, who, like the Comptons, had come to New Brunswick on the *Duchess of Gordon*; and, most importantly for this book, the Vaughans, whose Planter background I discuss below.

Land in and around St. Martins provided abundant forest wealth for the future shipbuilding industry, while its marsh land was coveted – and quarrelled over – as a place for pasturing cattle.[32] But by the time William had obtained his two hundred acres, he was already on the cusp of old age and beyond the point of reinventing himself as an entrepreneur or successful farmer. No more than in Saint John would his life in St. Martins resemble the fanciful dream that more elite Loyalists had conjured with their talk of New Brunswick as sure to become "the envy of the American states."[33] Rather, his New Brunswick years seem to have been of a piece with the downward spiral that his life had taken after he cast in his lot with the British back in New Jersey. When he died in 1804 in the parish of St. Martins, still identifying himself as a carpenter, Loyalist William had little to leave behind. In the will he had made earlier that year, he divided his estate among seven persons: daughters Elizabeth, Phoebe, and Catherine, sons William and Cornelius, his wife, Sarah, and a granddaughter, also named Sarah. His executors were his son William, already married to Mary Vaughan, and his friend Philip Mosher, St. Martins's first justice of the peace. Mary's father, Daniel Vaughan, and Daniel's son Ebenezer are shown as witnesses to the will. In addition to the cow left to granddaughter Sarah, Loyalist William left five shillings to each of his children, sons and daughters alike. "All the rest of my estate, real and personal, I give and bequeath unto Sarah Compton, my well beloved Wife to be for her use and at her Disposal after my Decease."[34]

Within a decade, Loyalist William's son Cornelius was also dead, leaving behind a widow and four children. One of William's daughters is known to have married a Loyalist,[35] but nothing is known of the other daughters. As for his son and namesake William, and William's wife, Mary Vaughan, whose descendants are the focus of the chapters that follow, I have found no documents in their own words, but they turn up in a variety of historical records of the three Maritime colonies.

Mary's father, Daniel, had come to Nova Scotia from Rhode Island with his widowed mother and two of his brothers. The Vaughans were part of a movement of pre-Loyalist settlers, almost eight thousand people in total, collectively called Planters. The Planters had been encouraged to move north from New England in order to settle vacant and vacated lands as part of an imperial strategy for strengthening the British presence in Nova Scotia following the expulsion of the Acadians in the mid-1750s. Mary (1784–1866) was one of nine children born to Daniel Vaughan and his wife, Lydia Harrington, during the period when they lived in Chester. Now one of Nova Scotia's wealthiest playground communities, it was not then a propitious site for colonial settlement, though Daniel and his brothers may have built a sawmill and a gristmill while living there. In 1791 Daniel and his family left Chester and purchased a farm further north in Newport Township. In 1796 they made what was to be their final move, crossing the Bay of Fundy and settling down in St. Martins. There they would become, like the Morans and the Vails and several other interconnected families, well-known multi-generational shipbuilders.[36] Although the Vaughans' shipbuilding activity began with Daniel, its first significant commercial success came with the schooner *Rachael*, built by his eldest son. Nevertheless, Daniel's will, made in 1808, the year he died, and the inventory of his estate make it clear that Mary's entrepreneurial family had already achieved a good deal more material success than her husband's kin by the time of the two fathers' deaths.[37]

More than just a scarcity of marriage partners in the small community would have brought William and Mary together. Despite having come from two different American colonies and in two different waves of settlement, the families would probably have known, or known of, each other before arriving in St. Martins in the late 1790s.[38] And, importantly, they had Baptist backgrounds in common. The Vaughans were crucial figures in the early history of Maritime Baptists. In 1793

Mary's father and her uncle had signed the ordination papers by which the Reverend Joseph Dimock became minister of the first Baptist church to be established in Chester. Like the young Dimock, the Vaughans had been drawn to a radical group known as New Light Baptists, with roots in the evangelical teachings of the Rhode Island-born itinerant preacher Henry Alline (1748–1784), a larger-than-life figure in the religious history of the Maritimes. Alline had emphasized the necessity of a powerful conversion experience, a new birth such as he himself had experienced, rather than mere adherence to denominational forms, during his preaching years in Planter Nova Scotia. Following his early death, other preachers followed in his footsteps. One of them was Joseph Crandall, whose mother was a Vaughan. In 1811 another of Alline's largely unlettered preacher imitators, New Light Baptist James Innis, was jailed and fined after having solemnized the marriage of Daniel Vaughan's son Ebenezer to Hannah Brown two years earlier. In doing so Innis had violated the colony's Marriage Act, by which only Anglican clergymen could perform marriages. Not surprisingly, when the first Baptist church was established in St. Martins, the Vaughans were among its founding families.[39] This intense religious and familial milieu was part of what William Compton and Mary Vaughan Compton would leave behind when they moved on from St. Martins, at first temporarily and then permanently.

William and Mary as Sojourning Maritimers

Most of the children in the couple's large family were born in St. Martins, where William worked for a time as a ship's carpenter.[40] In 1810 he acquired two hundred acres of land as a result of a petition in the name of his brother-in-law Ebenezer Vaughan and twenty-four other petitioners. Seven years earlier he had been party to an unsuccessful land petition that had included his father, and in 1815 he would be part of yet another petition, also unsuccessful notwithstanding strong support from local justice of the peace Philip Mosher attesting to the petitioners' loyalty and their ability to fulfil settlement requirements. A note on the 1815 petition indicated that William and several other petitioners were or had been members of a company of the Saint John militia at St. Martins headed by Captain John Howard.[41] All these things would seem to suggest that William, even if not entirely successful in his economic life, was embedded in a network of personal relationships and community endeavours in St. Martins. But in fact by 1812 he had already sold off half of his land grant "on improvement" and with Mary had begun moving around in the Maritimes. During the second decade of the 1800s, the couple lived briefly in peninsular Nova Scotia and on Prince Edward Island before spending an interval of up to two decades in Cape Breton, followed, finally, by permanent settlement on PEI.[42] With the exception of their son William A. Compton, a youthful shipbuilder who remained in New Brunswick, working with and marrying into the Loyalist Vail family,[43] the children of William and Mary were part of their parents' journeying, and eventually all became settlers on PEI.

How is one to account for this couple's peripatetic existence? Among ships' labourers and marine craftsmen, there were good reasons for transiency in this era: quite simply, one went to where there was work.[44] In the early nineteenth century, PEI and Cape Breton were both on the cusp of having a robust shipbuilding industry, as was the Loyalist and Scottish community of Wallace, on the Northumberland Strait side of Nova Scotia, where Mary gave birth to daughter Louisa in 1810.[45] But why were William Compton and his sons not incorporated into the Vaughan family enterprise of shipbuilding and shipping as it grew and expanded through much of the nineteenth century on the basis of what was clearly a remarkable degree of kin involvement? "Fifteen or more members of the Vaughan family were builders, masters, sole owners, part owners or managing owners of vessels," Esther Clark Wright observes, and "four generations were involved; several wives and daughters owned shares; several sons-in-law were masters, builders, and owners." In time, Wright notes, the Vaughans had industrial and commercial involvements in Saint John and St. Stephen, and in Liverpool, England, as well as in St. Martins. There is, however, no indication that the Vaughans established business ventures in the several places to which William and Mary moved.[46] Did William lack the level of shipbuilding skill and steadiness of character that his St. Martins in-laws expected in a useful worker and partner? Were the problems with alcohol that would show up among later generations of Compton men also a problem for William? Excessive drinking did keep some skilled workers off the job in St. Martins shipyards, and doubtless other places, even when there was employment for them.[47] William, though, may simply have been something of a free spirit, determined to move on and make his way independently of his wife's people. Whatever it was, it did not bode well for a stable future for his family.

Mary gave birth to the last of her St. Martins children in 1817. Some two years later, during a brief initial residence on Prince Edward Island, the couple's second-last son was born.[48] The small colony provided an opportunity for some wage work: pine timber was being harvested for markets in the United Kingdom, and there was some early shipbuilding. But by the end of 1819 the Comptons had moved on again, this time to the Bras d'Or Lake area of Cape Breton, as other wage labourers from PEI had already done.[49] They would not have arrived friendless: in 1814, Eli Hume, a New Jersey Loyalist like William's father and, like him, a sometime resident of Saint John, had successfully petitioned for land in Cape Breton on which to settle his own family and other settlers.[50] The Humes were a family with whom two of the Comptons' children would intermarry and with whom there would be ongoing marital and religious connections on PEI into the utopian era. But while William and Mary may have spent some time with the Hume family when they first arrived in Cape Breton, they did not settle on Eli Hume's land. By the end of 1819, the couple and their still increasing family were living near Bras d'Or Lake at River Denys, where white settler occupancy was just beginning. William Compton of River Denys shows up in 1819 in the account book of Laurence Kavanagh, a wealthy and powerful Cape Breton merchant, as a purchaser of sundries, a broad axe, and a jacket. Kavanagh owed a good deal of his commercial success to a barter system that involved accepting local produce or workingmen's labour in exchange for such things as cloth, clothing, shoes, and rum. An entry for December 1823 showed William "& sons" being owed for seventeen days' work for Kavanagh. A more ominous entry a year later indicated that William – like many other settlers in the area – had become indebted to the merchant.[51]

William did not, however, remain entirely dependent on Kavanagh during his years in Cape Breton. In 1824 he built a sawmill and gristmill on Malagawatch Bay near River Denys, "a convenience greatly appreciated by the settlers." The sawmill was still operating some four years later when it supplied lumber for the first Presbyterian church in Malagawatch.[52] William may have had some help from the colonial government in completing or repairing his mills. In February 1824, Cape Breton residents petitioned for government funds for the repair of a damaged gristmill and the building of more such mills. The need was said to be particularly acute in a large area around Bras d'Or Lake, and "attempts were being made to build mills, even by 'persons whose limited resources ... prevented their completion.'"[53] In 1829, in another economic initiative, William became co-owner of a sloop, along with his son Daniel. Built by Daniel at River Denys and named the *Joseph*, presumably for the last, Cape Breton-born, son of William and Mary,[54] the sloop was lost at sea three years later. Given its small size and tonnage capacity, it was likely used for merely local purposes during its short life rather than for intercolonial commerce.[55]

During their years in Cape Breton, then, William Compton and, later, his older sons turned to a variety of economic activities in an effort to make a living. But they were in a colony where poverty remained pervasive, and where, even in the 1830s, half of the settlers were still squatters.[56] Many early settlers lived for years on Crown or "Indian" land without obtaining a title for their acreage. A short account of settlement in Cape Breton, written in 1820, referred to "two very inconvenient reservations," one of them near River Denys. The absence of effective surveying and other factors made it challenging to purchase or lease land in places like River Denys and many other areas of Cape Breton in this period, and in any case settlers who squatted often remained undisturbed, despite officials' occasional expressions of concern about protecting the interests of the Mi'kmaq.[57] There is no record that William Compton petitioned for land in Cape Breton. He was almost certainly a squatter.

In the long run, how the Comptons acquired the land on which they had settled and how they cobbled together a living was to be less important to the family's subsequent history than the fact that it was in this corner of Cape Breton that they became acquainted with the Reverend Donald McDonald (1783–1867). A minister of the established Church of Scotland (the Kirk), McDonald would dominate their religious lives and that of generations of their descendants when they moved permanently to Prince Edward Island.[58] Born in Scotland and trained at the University of St. Andrews, McDonald arrived in Cape Breton in 1824 as a self-appointed missionary. Despite having been properly ordained eight years earlier, he was dogged by rumours of having had a troubled relationship with the church back home as well as by stories of a drinking problem. During his two-year stay in Cape Breton, McDonald itinerated mainly in the Malagawatch area, living in a place that would later be remembered as Minister's Point.[59] While Cape Breton was slow to attract settled Protestant clergy, it was an open field for religious misfits like McDonald. Just a few years earlier, another renegade minister of the established Church of Scotland, Norman McLeod, had established a religious fiefdom in an isolated pocket of Cape Breton and there, for decades, exercised autocratic rule over his parishioners before persuading many of them to follow him around the world, first to Australia and then to New Zealand.[60] As for McDonald, especially given the few non-Indigenous people in the River Denys-Malagawatch region, it was not surprising that William Compton would have struck up a friendship with him despite their different denominational backgrounds and McDonald's reportedly infamous behaviour during this period as a drunkard who consorted with Catholics and Indigenous people rather than behaving as a proper Presbyterian man of God. A descendant of early Scots Presbyterian settlers in the area who were known to be deeply devout confidentially recalled ancestral memories of McDonald as "a trial and sore embarrassment."[61] William Compton, having no such shared ties of faith and ethnicity, may have bonded more comfortably with McDonald, and perhaps over rum as well as religion.

Sometime during the 1830s, William and his family left Cape Breton and returned to Prince Edward Island, this time to settle down. Absent from the Cape Breton census of 1838–41, they show up in the PEI census of 1841. Travel back and forth between eastern Nova Scotia, including Cape Breton, and PEI was far from uncommon in the early 1800s, part of the experience not only of poor and itinerant job seekers but also of merchants and preachers. One of the latter was the Reverend John MacLennan, pioneering minister from 1823 of the established Church of Scotland in Belfast, PEI, the district where the Comptons would settle. During the 1820s and early 1830s, MacLennan made preaching forays to the religiously ill served Presbyterians in Cape Breton, administering communion and performing baptisms in settlements that included Malagawatch, where he encouraged residents to build the church for which William Compton had supplied the sawn lumber.[62] MacLennan was particularly well positioned to let families like the Comptons know about the Belfast district, and PEI generally, as a place that now had more to offer than Cape Breton: marginally better served with roads and schools as well as arable farmland for its growing population. The small island colony was also described more favourably than Cape Breton in these and other respects by publicist and civil servant John MacGregor in 1828 in his *Historical and Descriptive Sketches of the Maritime Colonies of British America*. MacGregor cited the successful Scottish Selkirk settlement in Belfast where MacLennan ministered as an instance of industry quickly rewarded.[63] Family tradition, though, maintains that the main factor in bringing the Comptons back to PEI in the 1830s was not so much the prospect of greater economic security as a renewed connection with the Reverend Donald McDonald. Indeed, it was this motive and connection that some of the numerous descendants of William and Mary would literally have carved into stone in a monument erected to their forebears in 2006 in Brooklyn, PEI.[64]

McDonald had moved to PEI in 1826. A year later he had a conversion experience that largely eclipsed his previous reputation for drunkenness and turned him into a legendary preacher and revival-ist. Word of his marvellous transformation reached his former home in Cape Breton, where it caused great rejoicing, particularly among those he had formerly embarrassed.[65] Most of McDonald's followers on PEI were, like him, Gaelic-speaking immigrants from the High-lands and Islands of Scotland. The Comptons would also become "McDonaldites," albeit as outliers. In his 1902 biography of McDon-ald, Murdock Lamont, whose father, Ewen, was an early and ardent disciple, described a group he called only "The English." Arriving on PEI "between '35 and '40," they were, Lamont wrote, "the last consid-erable addition" to McDonald's followers: "They were descended from the English Loyalists who left the United States for British territory at the termination of the American War of Independence. Many of them had been Baptists and were well received by Mr. McDonald."[66] The group he referred to would have included the Humes and one other Loyalist family in addition to the Comptons. Not all of McDonald's Scottish followers on PEI were at first as willing as he to accept these cultural outsiders, Lamont conceded.[67] Nonetheless, William and Mary Compton and a large family, which by now included heads of their own households as well as still resident children, settled near the Scots, intermarrying with them and becoming fellow McDonaldite Presbyterians and at last putting down roots. At least for a generation or two, the days of moving on were largely over.

In her classic history of New Brunswick Loyalists, Esther Clark Wright downplayed the hardships of her subjects' early and frequent moves in their new homeland, suggesting that in fact "they moved around very freely, and with surprising ease, in canoe, small boat, schooner, or sloop, with little trouble in packing up their few and simple movable posses-sions."[68] Perhaps this was so if they moved locally. But especially for Mary, accompanying her husband as he moved between three colonies during her long childbearing years and over waters whose storms could blow travellers off course, or even into eternity, it would not have seemed easy. There was also the hard matter of the son left behind decades earlier in St. Martins, and undoubtedly wistfulness about separation from her Vaughan siblings as they raised families and prospered together during the golden years of shipbuilding. Good wives followed their husbands, though, and they made the best of things. This Mary evidently did in the long years that remained to her and William on Prince Edward Island.[69]

2

The Comptons and Colonial Prince Edward Island: Settlement and Spirituality

Did the Comptons fare better on Prince Edward Island than they had in New Brunswick and Nova Scotia? Eventually, yes. Indeed, in the early twentieth century, some of their descendants would create their own utopia, not just metaphorically but by establishing a robust material and spiritual community, one whose leaders aspired like Saint Paul and the early Christians to hold "all things in common." For much of the nineteenth century, though, the story of William and Mary Compton and their descendants seems to have been, like that of many other Prince Edward Islanders, a story of modest subsistence, surviving rather than thriving, rather like the colony itself. Settling on land they could not call their own, the Comptons seem not to have risen, even during the mid-century decades – the Maritimes' so-called golden age – to levels of prosperity and accomplishment that would result in local prominence and media-worthy success stories. The most salient aspect of their experience as nineteenth-century Islanders and the most crucial for understanding the millenarian dimension of their future utopia was not their material circumstances but rather their chosen new religious identity. Their ancestors had left England for the New World in the first half of the 1600s and, early on, become part of the new sect called Baptists. On Prince Edward Island as late-arriving Loyalists, they reinvented themselves religiously as McDonaldite Presbyterians. Captivated like many of their Scottish neighbours by the man they had first met in Cape Breton, an eccentric minister with only an arm's-length relationship to the established Church of Scotland, they became part of an ardent and close-knit body of believers. McDonald died in 1867, the same year as William Compton and a year after Mary. This chapter focuses on the intertwined material and religious lives of the Comptons during the long years when the pioneering couple and the minister were their ballast in the small island colony.

Their New Colony

Despite significant differences in their size and topography, Cape Breton and Prince Edward Island had a good deal in common at the beginning of the nineteenth century, both in terms of their histories of conflicting European claimants to their land and resources and in terms of an Indigenous presence already dramatically reduced in numbers and altered culturally as a result of contact with Europeans.[1] Known as Île St. Jean when it was a French possession, PEI fell permanently to the English in 1758, was annexed to Nova Scotia as the Island of St. John in 1763, and became a separate colony in 1769. Early efforts at settlement under British rule were not propitious. In the 1770s, a wealthy London businessman named Robert Clark made a strenuous but ultimately failed effort to establish a viable trading community for his fellow Quakers. A decade later, at the end of the American Revolution, the colony's population was augmented by the arrival of approximately 550 Loyalist refugees and disbanded soldiers. But their arrival did not signify a turnaround in the colony's fortunes. In fact, by the time it was officially renamed Prince Edward Island in 1799, some of the Loyalists had already moved on in search of better opportunities.[2]

A major source of frustration for would-be settlers was the colony's landholding system. Instead of a system of freehold land tenure creating many individual owners, a vexed system of proprietorial patronage-based land grants had been established in 1767. Virtually all of the land on the Island was divided into sixty-seven townships, or lots, awarded to about 100 proprietors or landlords. They not infrequently sold their lots without ever setting foot in the colony or endeavouring to attract tenants. In terms of early British settlement policy in North America, PEI was by no means an anomaly in having large blocks of its land granted to a few proprietors. What *was* anomalous was that in the island colony the landlord system survived well into the nineteenth century, seriously impeding satisfactory development. Such attempts as were made by the local colonial government to respond to periodic agrarian protests about the iniquitous system were vetoed by the powers that be in London.[3] Not surprisingly, the eighteenth century ended without significant population growth in the island colony, despite the arrival of emigrating Highlanders in the last three decades of the century.[4] A total of just 6,957 persons was recorded as the colony's population for the year 1805.[5]

Nevertheless, the first half of the nineteenth century saw a period of significant immigration to Prince Edward Island, particularly from Scotland and Ireland. The immigrants were both fleeing poverty and insecurity in their homelands and lured by glowing accounts of a better place in the New World. In his *Sketches of the Maritime Colonies of British America*, published in London in 1828, John MacGregor wrote enthusiastically of the Island, where he himself had lived for some years: "Almost every part affords agreeable prospects, and beautiful situations. In summer and autumn the forests exhibit a rich and splendid foliage … and the character of the scenery has at these seasons a smiling loveliness – a teeming fertility."[6]

In truth, early settlers faced immense hardships in the isolated colony, where, at intervals cut off from supplies from the outside world, even some senior government officials experienced near starvation.[7] Still, one group for whom the "agreeable prospects" had already become a reality by the time that MacGregor wrote his glowing account was the so-called Selkirk settlers, a group with whom the Comptons would become linked through geography and marriage. More than eight hundred in number, the Selkirk settlers were immigrants from the Highlands and Islands of Scotland whom Thomas Douglas, the Fifth Earl of Selkirk, sponsored in an 1803 settlement scheme in the Belfast district of PEI. To carry out his scheme, which attracted enthusiastic interest from such British intellectuals as Thomas Malthus, the earl had privately purchased several lots, making him one of the largest landed proprietors on the Island. Linked in some cases by kin ties to earlier Highland immigrants, the Selkirk settlers in turn inspired others to join them. Indeed, Selkirk historian J.M. Bumsted considers that the settlement established by the earl "helped to turn around a very depressed economic situation brought about by a lack of investment, commerce, and emigration" and contributed to "a spirit of confidence and enthusiasm for the Island's future."[8]

Like the British-era settlers who had preceded them, the Selkirk settlers and other immigrants to the Island typically undertook to establish farms, preferably near the shorelines. But farming alone could not provide a living, especially when densely wooded land could only slowly be cleared. Settlers also needed to engage in other activities, particularly fishing and harvesting the forests. These activities, in turn, and, later, coastal trade would eventually contribute to the development of the Island's significant shipbuilding industry.[9] By the time of the 1841 census, the colony had made noteworthy advances, and the local economy was supporting a population of 47,034 residents.[10] They included the Island-born children of the pioneer settlers' large families, as well as recent arrivals. Among the latter were the Comptons. As residents of Belle Creek in the Belfast district of Queen's County, the Comptons became neighbours of the Selkirk settlers and other Scottish immigrants. Notwithstanding Lord Selkirk's vision of viable self-contained "'national settlements'" for the transplanted Scots,[11] his settlers would quickly become interconnected by ties of faith and marriage with other ethnic groups.

Their Settlement: Belle Creek/Belle River

Five households headed by Comptons were shown as living in Belle River,[12] Lot 62, at the time of the 1841 census.[13] They were William and his sons Henry, Daniel (listed in the census as Donald), Wellington, and John, all married and, except for Wellington, with families of their own. Three younger siblings were still living in William's household, while Emily, the oldest surviving daughter, was already settled elsewhere in the Belfast area, linked by marriage, like her brother John, to a pioneering family of Selkirk settlers, the already prospering Martins.[14]

The arrival of these Comptons on the Island[15] coincided with a period of mass rural protest against the colony's iniquitous landholding system, the so-called escheat movement.[16] While there is no evidence that any Comptons became involved in the protests, the issues raised by the movement and its failure to resolve them directly affected their economic prospects. At the time of the 1841 census, only about a third of Island land occupiers had managed to achieve the status of small freeholders.[17] None of the five Compton households in Lot 62 was among them. The census showed William Compton holding one hundred acres in the category of "Occupants, being neither Freeholders or Tenants." Put plainly, he was a squatter, as he had almost certainly been during his years in Cape Breton. Son John's status was the same. Sons Henry, a shipbuilder, Donald/Daniel, a farmer, and Wellington, a carpenter, were described as holding their lands "by Verbal Agreements," although later that year Wellington did obtain a formal lease to his land.[18] These landholding arrangements did not bode well for the five families' future security and well-being.

William Compton *thought* he had obtained a clear title to land, according to a popular history of the Belfast area, and on that assumption built a mill on it, only to lose both land and mill "due to some misunderstanding." This explanation, which came from one of his descendants, may have been provided to deal with the perceived shamefulness of having an ancestor who was a squatter.[19] But since William was no stranger to the phenomenon of squatting, he may not have experienced his landholding status as a source of great shame. In any event, he had plenty of company: the 1841 census revealed that 11.6 per cent of the occupiers of Island land were squatters.[20]

The land William occupied was a standard-size farm of one hundred acres, ten of them cleared sufficiently for cropping. On this, in the year preceding the 1841 census, he had harvested 10 bushels of oats and 150 bushels of potatoes and kept two cows and one horse. Among his sons, only carpenter Wellington had no crops and, as livestock, just one cow. In making potatoes their crop of choice, these Compton men were part of an early and long-lasting Island pattern. Returning to PEI in 1804 to visit the settlement he had established a year earlier, Lord Selkirk had discovered that potatoes were "the principal part" of the settlers' crop. He observed that the quality and quantity were such as "would have been alone sufficient for the entire support of the settlement."[21] By 1841, some Island farmers were selling potatoes and oats and other surplus produce to Charlottetown or Georgetown or even to parts of Nova Scotia and New Brunswick.[22] But the Comptons as recent arrivals with still low productivity were hardly in a position to enter the market. A comparison with census data on several other families living in Lot 62 with whom there had been or would be intermarriage is revealing. James Munn, an immigrant from Scotland, had acquired one hundred acres by leasehold some twenty-one years earlier and by 1841 had thirty arable acres. On this, in the year preceding the census, he had produced ten bushels of wheat, one hundred bushels of oats, and four hundred bushels of potatoes. As livestock he had two horses, ten cattle, fifteen sheep, and eight hogs. He seems to have been the most senior of the several Munn families who were living in Lot 62 in 1841, but even those who had become heads of households more recently had somewhat more to report in the way of crops and livestock than the Comptons. Alexander Martin, another Scottish immigrant, owning eighty-seven acres in fee simple, more than half of them arable, was more productive than even the senior Munn in terms of crop yields and livestock. On the other hand, George and Thomas Bears, both coopers and, like the Comptons, recent arrivals from Nova Scotia, were worse off than they were: George had no livestock whatever and had produced nothing more than twenty bushels of potatoes on the land on which he was squatting, while Thomas had raised fifty bushels of potatoes and kept one cow on his sixty leased acres.[23] All other things being equal, how and how long a farmer had held his land in any given settlement was a significant factor in getting ahead.

Established farmers as well as newcomers like the Comptons were, of course, vulnerable to the vagaries of nature. In 1841 the census taker for Lot 62 reported rust in wheat crops, and livestock losses. Later in the decade, during several different years, there were potato crop failures on the Island. Inevitably, such occurrences bore most heavily on newer and poorer farmers. On Prince Edward Island, as elsewhere in the Maritimes, many of them turned to wage labour for part of their livelihood. The readiest prospect was to work part time for a better-off farmer, but there were also opportunities connected with shipbuilding, some of them within reach of Lot 62.[24] William Compton's son Henry shows up in the census as a shipbuilder in his own right, but he and his wife, Rebecca, may also have been boarding shipbuilding labourers or apprentices who were at or between jobs elsewhere. Twenty-seven people in total were listed in Henry's "family," a term that included servants and apprentices. Nineteen of the twenty-seven were shown as Island-born and were evidently not part of the conjugal family. The census taker observed in the adjacent "Remarks" column that "A few of the young men employed in the shipyards belong to other parts of the country [PEI] though they have been resident in the district for the last 8 or 9 months." That Henry and his wife could provide for nineteen extra people from their fifteen arable acres seems hard to credit, especially if the young men were apprentices and not paying for their keep, but it is possible that they *were* paying something for board or that Henry expected to profit from their labour if they could help him build a vessel for sale.

A chance at land security and early prosperity may not have been within reach, but what the Compton families did find in settling in Lot 62 was perhaps their first opportunity to get some consistent schooling for their children. Unless they had contrived to make private arrangements, William and Mary would have lacked an opportunity to provide regular formal education for their own children when they were young, either back in New Brunswick or later in Cape Breton. Even after the greatest challenges facing Loyalists and other early New Brunswick settlers were long past, there was a pattern of continuing indifference to providing publicly for education for the non-elite.[25] As for Cape Breton, reflecting back on the early days in the Gaelic journal *Mac-Talla*, Neil MacDonald/"Bartimaeus" had described the educational landscape as "very dark ... without school or teacher in all of inner Great Bras d'Or Lake." One John MacNeill did establish a school in 1831, MacDonald wrote, but left a few years later for PEI. Some Cape

Breton families, anxious to provide their children with basic literacy, were prepared to hire other families' literate children as teachers. William Macphail was one such youthful teacher, according to an evocative memoir written many years later by his son Sir Andrew Macphail. Young William's opportunity to teach in Cape Breton occurred while his then still unsettled Scottish immigrant family lived there before moving on to the Belle River area of Prince Edward Island in 1844.[26]

To be sure, things were not a great deal better on PEI in terms of schooling. John MacNeill – probably the former Cape Breton teacher – reporting on Island education in 1841 as inspector, found some schools and schoolmasters worthy of praise, as well as, overall, much to lament. In Lot 30, Ewen Lamont was teaching effectively in his native Gaelic as well as in English in a schoolhouse that was "one of the largest and most commodious on the Island." In Belle River, Lot 62, though, where William Lamont taught, the school, opened the previous year, was already too small for its forty-four scholars. But the fact remained that the community *did* have a school building and a teacher. Elsewhere, fewer than half of the colony's children were attending school, and illiteracy was widespread. It was a situation that the colonial government attempted to address in 1852 with pioneering legislation that provided for teachers to be paid out of the colonial treasury. If things were marginally better even before then in some settlements, it was because a few families were prepared to take on the cost of engaging a teacher, sometimes paying them in produce, and were able to find someone reasonably competent. For a time in the 1840s in Belle River, William Macphail, father of the Cape Breton boy teacher of that name, taught there, evidently succeeding William Lamont.[27] Macphail and Lamont were members of Scottish immigrant families who, like the Comptons, were devoted followers of the Reverend Donald McDonald.

Their Minister: The Doctrine and Drama of Donald McDonald

McDonald ministered on Prince Edward Island for more than forty years, eventually counting as followers some five thousand people, more than 10 per cent of the colony's Protestant population.[28] When he died in 1867, the *Summerside Progress* observed that "His influence was so great, and his individuality so peculiar, that notwithstanding he was a Presbyterian minister, his denomination seemed to be lost in the man, and hence his followers were known as 'McDonaldites.'"[29] They would not in fact be identified by that term in a census until 1881.[30]

In the 1841 census they were lumped in with those "in connexion with the Church of Scotland." While this phrase distinguished them from Calvinists enumerated as "Presbyterian, in connexion with the Presbytery of P.E. Island," it did not differentiate them from members of conventional congregations of the established Church of Scotland such as that of the Selkirk settlers in Belfast. Already in the mid-1820s, the Belfast congregation had built an impressive church and until 1849 had the eminently respectable John MacLennan as their minister.[31] Still, some of the Selkirk settlers also became part of McDonald's following, as did a great many later Scottish immigrants.[32]

McDonald's followers were most numerous in Queen's County. Orwell Head in the eastern portion of the county and DeSable in the west became the centres for large communion gatherings. By the time of his death, McDonald had followers in all three Island counties, served by some fourteen churches or preaching stations. Two intense revivals occurring a generation apart had increased their numbers and revivified the faithful.[33] Given the thousands of people who came under McDonald's influence, it was not surprising that, even as they disparaged his style of ministry, churchmen on either side of the so-called Great Disruption that split the established Church of Scotland in 1843 sought his support for their respective positions or worked indirectly to win his followers. Indeed, delegates from both the established Church and the breakaway Free Church reached out to McDonald's people in diverse ways during their visits from Scotland to PEI.[34] Similarly, in the sphere of Island politics, where religion played a significant role, it came to be recognized that McDonald "exerted a certain amount of political control over his people"; prominent Island politicians such as George Coles courted his support.[35]

McDonald attracted followers through his charismatic personality and speaking style, his millenarian theology, and the theatricality of his services. But a Sunday with McDonald often began with a report and commentary on contemporary events, followed by the singing of hymns before the beginning of the service proper. Composed by McDonald and some of his elders and often set to popular Gaelic tunes, some of these hymns would live on in the worship practices of the Compton utopian community and even in the repertoire of a few musically inclined evangelical Island families in the twenty-first century. As for McDonald's preaching style, writing a few years after his death, Island historian Duncan Campbell likened his "pulpit power" to that of John Wesley, George Whitefield, and Edward Irving, the latter, like McDonald, an alumnus of the University of St. Andrews and, like him, an ardent millenarian.[36] Dramatic physical manifestations of religious excitement occurred among worshippers who were moved by McDonald's impassioned preaching and his message that the Second Coming was both an imminent event and of particular significance for his own followers, who were led to understand that they were descendants of the so-called ten lost tribes of ancient Israel.[37] Although the extravagant physical phenomena – crying out in spiritual distress or ecstasy, falling about, weeping, clapping, etc. – were confined to a minority of his followers, "the works," as they were sometimes called, were the features of his ministry that contributed most to his notoriety among opponents and sceptics during and after his lifetime. Island author Lucy Maud Montgomery, who became the wife of a Presbyterian minister and who, both in her fiction and personal life, was an expert on the finer points of respectable Island behaviour, would be among the mockers.[38]

McDonald's brand of millenarian theology and the performative religious practices he sanctioned were perhaps particularly distasteful and embarrassing to his more sedate fellow Presbyterians. Yet McDonald was by no means unique in being a Calvinist who fostered revivals. Looking back from the perspective of the late twentieth century, historian John Webster Grant, who himself came out of a Presbyterian heritage, put McDonald's unorthodox ministry into perspective. He was, Grant wrote, "eccentric in his theology and extreme in his readiness to cultivate bodily manifestations," and yet "the ingredients of his revivalism were by no means novel and many of them would have been familiar to Scottish Highlanders."[39] Those ingredients would also have been broadly familiar to the older Comptons who became his followers, both from William's childhood days in a colonial New Jersey still bearing traces of the Great Awakening and from his and Mary's familiarity with latter-day Allinites and New Light Baptists in New Brunswick. William and Mary may not have heard McDonald preach during his dark days back in Cape Breton, but even there they had probably felt the force of what was later called his "great personal magnetism" and perhaps been the recipients of his legendary personal generosity. These qualities, and their own early familiarity with revival-style preaching, would have made them receptive to McDonald's style of ministry on Prince Edward Island and unlikely to be offended even by his published denunciations of Baptists' religious practices.[40] Furthermore, even if they had no access to religious or secular periodicals, they may have been aware, not least via McDonald himself, of a larger North American religious milieu in which many other preachers in the first half of the nineteenth century were attracting a mass following by propounding extreme forms of millenarian teaching.

The Millerites, followers of William Miller, and the Mormons, whose founder was Joseph Smith, both originating in the fertile religious ground of upstate New York, were just two such groups contemporaneous with the McDonaldites, albeit much better known, their influence extending even into Upper Canada.[41]

The Comptons and other McDonaldites perhaps took some pride in the fact that, unlike many millenarian and frontier preachers with a mass following, their spiritual leader did not personally adopt an anti-intellectual stance. Far from disparaging "learned clergy," as many of his non-mainstream North American contemporaries were doing in the first half of the nineteenth century, McDonald *was* learned clergy, a scholar as well as a preacher and, in the words of Sir Andrew Macphail, "an author of some repute." While most of McDonald's followers would have had limited schooling, particularly in the early years, he also attracted families who valued and fostered learning, the Lamonts and Macphails most particularly. Sir Andrew's father, schoolteacher William, edited and supplied a preface for the last of McDonald's three books, published after his death.[42] It was perhaps in part because he had the support of respectable families like the Macphails and the Lamonts, as well as the rough and unlettered, that bachelor McDonald was not dogged by public accusations of fostering or engaging in sexual improprieties such as were directed at many other preachers of his day who operated outside the mainstream.[43] And by continuing to present himself as a loyal minister of the established Church of Scotland, he could have some of the benefits of mainstream respectability even as he steadfastly resisted his church's polity.

Even if the Compton families did not move back to Prince Edward Island from Cape Breton exclusively because of McDonald, as family tradition had it, he was unquestionably important in their and their descendants' Island lives. In a world largely devoid of sources of interest and stimulation outside the workday round, worship with fellow McDonaldites offered a rich spiritual, emotional, and musical community. The highlight was the regional summer gathering that brought hundreds of people together for the preparation for and service of communion, an event that occurred over several days. For the Comptons, the communion gathering at Orwell Head would have been the closest. In August 1861 it brought 664 communicants together.[44]

Membership in the McDonaldite community involved more than just shared worship services. And McDonald himself was more than just an influential Sunday figure in his followers' lives. Although he could visit his scattered congregations only at intervals during the year, when he did arrive in a particular community it was to live in the households of congregational families for the duration of his stay. Despite the fact that the famously autocratic minister conducted himself as the undisputed master of the house during his visits, his arrival was "looked forward to with delight," according to biographer Murdock Lamont, and not only by the head of the family. "There is not one of his adherents with whom he does not converse face to face," wrote Lamont. Some of the "conversing" involved the bossy minister's admonitions and reflected his personal and political antipathies: Don't keep pigs, or hang pictures on your walls; don't keep your infant in a cradle; don't hire X as your schoolteacher, and don't vote for Y. Yet McDonald was also known and appreciated for his sociability and humour and his love of music. And when individuals and communities were experiencing hard times, he was reportedly generous with his own scant means (he had not even a home of his own) and adept at organizing relief for the most needy. Thus, when famine threatened in 1837, "Mr McDonald so arranged it among his followers that those older settlements who had abundance were enabled to minister to the necessities of others who were in want."[45]

McDonald's most influential relationships were those with the adult males within his congregations whom he single-handedly selected and ordained to eldership. More than one hundred men had been chosen for this role by the mid-1840s. For those singled out, there were opportunities for local leadership, notwithstanding McDonald's determination to keep his elders firmly under his control. In keeping with established Church of Scotland tradition, he forbade them to preach or administer the ordinances. But the tradition did authorize them to assist in matters of church government and communion and to read scripture and pray. The elders' importance in McDonaldite churches was signified by their being seated at the front, just down from the pulpit, facing the congregation, sometimes on an elevated platform surrounded by a rail. Here the elders could keep stern watch over the congregation and lead in the singing of the psalms. Particularly in the long intervals between McDonald's visits to his scattered congregations, there was considerable scope for them to enlarge on these roles.[46] After his death, elders in the McDonaldite remnant that remained outside official denominational structures had new and expanded opportunities for leadership. John Compton, a son of William and Mary Compton, would be one such elder. Such opportunities, however, also bred disputes. Presented publicly as theological differences, the disputes were also power struggles, sometimes affected by ethnicity. Such rifts would ultimately have life-changing consequences for elder John Compton and some of his closest kin, putting an end to their people's long and close personal relationship with other McDon-aldites and preparing the way for their turn to utopianism.

Their Not So Golden Age

Contemporary critics of extreme millenarian groups such as the Millerites were concerned that their belief in the imminent end of the world would cause them to neglect practical matters and give up on daily routines.[47] Although McDonald read some significance into the year 1850 in terms of biblical prophecies, he evidently did not encour-age his followers to invest strongly in a specific end-time date.[48] In any event, so far as the Comptons' economic circumstances are concerned, one does not need to look to millenarian beliefs to account for their failure to prosper their way into prominence even during the Mari-times' so-called golden age in the middle decades of the nineteenth century. The era was golden, scholars now recognize, only compara-tively and in regional mythology, while on Prince Edward Island, even during the best times, many Islanders continued to live hardscrabble lives.[49] To the extent that religion did play a part in enabling Islanders' successes, or in holding them back, it doubtless had more to do with related social and kin networks, cultural practices, and value systems than with specific theological beliefs.

An era of prosperity in nineteenth-century Atlantic Canada came to be strongly associated in the popular mind with the building, own-ing, and operation of wooden sailing ships during the great age of sail. It was a time when the Maritime colonies, despite their small size, had the means to establish direct connections with and achieve recogni-tion at the centre of the British Empire and in its far-flung outposts. In their history of the shipping industry in Atlantic Canada, Eric Sager and Gerald Panting write that the industry was indeed "impressive in its scale and its international dimensions" and "has rightly become part of the folklore and memory of our Atlantic peoples." But impres-sive as it was, "It lasted for little more than a generation."[50] Nor, to mangle a metaphor, did the brief rising tide of the shipping indus-try lift all Maritime family fortunes. As in other times and places and industrial contexts, there were winners and losers. And the chances were good that both groups would beget more of the same.

The building of large sailing ships on Prince Edward Island for car-rying cargoes – principally timber, agricultural products, and fish – and for sale in the British market rose dramatically in the course of the first half of the nineteenth century and reached a peak between 1840 and 1889, "the 'golden years' of the Island fleet." The construction that took place in many shore communities around the Island – more than 176 locations were involved – provided opportunities for farmers to cut and sell wood to area shipbuilders and for labourers and craftsmen to work in the building process. There was, however, a high concentration of ownership in the industry, with most large owners being merchants and men of commerce.[51] Many Islanders, of course, built small vessels for coastal trade or for their own fishing activities. James Compton was one of them. His *Dolphin*, a two-mast ten-ton schooner built at Wood Islands, near Belle River, in 1857, was co-owned by James's brother and his father, William (or possibly a nephew of this name). The *Dolphin*'s closure as a "wrecked" vessel was recorded in 1865 at St. Pierre and Miquelon, and perhaps by then it was under other ownership.[52] No other Comptons of this family line show up in the records as builders or owners of vessels until the early twentieth century and then under quite different circumstances.

Agricultural products were the Island's most important export during the mid-nineteenth-century decades, sold primarily to the other Maritime colonies during the 1840s and then, for about a decade from the mid-1850s, to a robust market in the eastern United States.[53] Although three sons and a grandson of the now elderly William and Mary Compton were farming in Lot 62 at the time of the 1861 census, they were not in a position to derive much benefit from these export markets: an examination of the crop yields and livestock numbers reported for household heads in the census shows that, though not the least productive, the Compton households remained, as they had been in 1841, at the lower end in terms of productivity by comparison with their neighbours. The crop production and livestock holdings of future McDonaldite elder John Compton, for instance, did not begin to approach those of his Scottish near-neighbour and co-religionist Alexander Martin, who had already held his acreage in fee simple at the time of the 1841 census.[54] In terms of the women's work of cloth-, butter-, and cheese-making, however, some of the Compton households were comparatively productive. It is possible that these activities occasionally provided something for barter or local sale as well as for the families' own needs.[55]

By the time of the 1861 census, some of the progeny of William and Mary had moved on from Belle River in Lot 62. Two heads of households, probably grandsons, were living in Lot 57, three lots to the north, where they practised the trade of joiner. Meanwhile the old couple's youngest son, Joseph, and another of their grandsons were farming slightly to the northeast on leased land in Lot 61. It was one of the least auspicious places in the colony in which to establish a residence: a "very miserable place," according to census taker Duncan Fraser, whose overview of the area for the colonial government was provided in the Abstract of Returns in 1861. "I did not see more than four or five good farms on the whole Township [Lot]," he wrote. In his study of the Tenant League, a grass-roots movement involving widespread tenant protest in 1860s PEI, historian Ian Robertson essentially concurred with Fraser's assessment, observing that it "probably presented as clear a case of combined poverty and insecurity as any township on Prince Edward Island."[56] The problems arising from the physical environment – swampy land and few roads – were exacerbated by the recalcitrance of Lot 61's absentee landlord. During the previous decade, the colonial government had begun purchasing landlords' holdings in order to resell the land to tenants or new settlers on reasonable terms. The Selkirk estate was sold to the government as part of this process in 1860. But not only did landlord Laurence Sulivan refuse to sell Lot 61 or any of his other extensive holdings on PEI but in 1864 his agent also sent a sheriff into the settlement to collect rents, despite reports of serious hardship among some settlers.[57]

Lot 61 was clearly an unpromising place in which to begin farming. What it did have was a strong McDonaldite congregation centred in the community of Brooklyn. The two Compton men who were trying to coax a living out of their third-quality land in Lot 61 at the time of the 1861 census, as well as other Comptons who began leasing land there during the 1860s, were most likely drawn by the McDonaldite connection. It was familial as well as religious: Brooklyn was home to George Bears, one of McDonald's foremost elders, an indefatigable preacher and hymn writer who, like the Comptons, had come to PEI from Nova Scotia and was linked to them through his marriage to a daughter of William and Mary Compton.[58]

As for the now elderly William and Mary, they no longer had an independent household at the time of the 1861 census and seem themselves to have been living in Lot 61 with son Joseph at the time of Mary's death. Mary died in Brooklyn in 1866 in her eighty-fourth year, "retaining her faculties unimpaired to the last." She was the first person to be buried in the new cemetery established on Joseph's property. Mary had given birth to eleven surviving children, all but one of whom had settled on PEI. Her obituary reported that she was grandmother to 112 grandchildren and forty-two great-grandchildren.[59] The 1881 census, the first post-Confederation-era PEI census taken after Mary's death, listed all family members, not just household heads. As such, it provides further evidence of this family's fecundity. It did not, of course, capture the many descendants of Mary and William bearing different surnames.

The 1881 census does, though, show that descendants bearing their name had by then spread not just to lots geographically near to Belle River, but across country to Bangor, a district some thirty miles to the northeast on the Morell River in Lot 40 in King's County. It may have been comparatively easy to obtain land in the area after the extensive holdings of proprietor Charles Worrell were acquired by the colonial government for resale to settlers in the 1850s. The Comptons who moved there did become farmers, but it is unlikely that the area's farming prospects were the main draw, since it was not deemed to be good land.[60] Here, as with Lot 61, religion was undoubtedly a decisive factor in the move: fellow McDonaldites, including MacDougall families, were also settling there. One of Mary's grandsons, John, and his wife, Annabella, had begun their family in Brooklyn, but by the time their daughter Margaret was born in 1874 they had relocated to Bangor. The adult Margaret would marry a McDonaldite minister from one of the MacDougall families in the district. And by 1893 there would be enough McDonaldite families in Bangor to undertake the building of a church.[61]

Census data and other sources such as the *Illustrated Historical Atlas of the Province of Prince Edward Island*, published in 1880, indicate that, occupationally, the Comptons remained mainly farmers throughout the nineteenth century. A number of others show up as tradesmen, and here there was a tendency to follow trades broadly related to woodworking, as their Loyalist forebears had done. Notwithstanding the census practice of listing a household head by just one occupation, there was in fact a good deal of occupational pluralism: for instance, operating a sawmill and farming, or serving as postmaster and farming, as several Comptons did in Lot 61.[62]

The income-earning activities of these Loyalist Comptons were both common and respectable. But the data available suggest that, overall, they failed to thrive and that their occupations did not serve as launching pads for generational upward mobility. One looks in vain for any of them achieving sufficient economic or professional success, even in the "golden" years, to figure prominently in contemporary Island newspapers or, later, in popular or academic historical studies. Even among Islanders named in 1880 in the "Patrons Directory" portion of the *Illustrated Historical Atlas*, only two Comptons likely to have been from this family line show up, both of them in building trades. Islanders listed in the Directory had paid $12.50 in advance to receive a copy of the *Atlas*. They were described collectively as "the principal professional and business men in the city, towns, and villages, [with] a description of their business, and of the principal producers of each lot who patronize this atlas." Since the list ran to thousands of names, it was far from being an exclusive club.[63]

Nor do these Comptons show up in accounts of late nineteenth- and early twentieth-century Islanders who, coming from pioneering settler families, made good elsewhere – often in the United States – in business, academic, or clerical pursuits. The Belfast district, where Belle River was located, took pride in its seemingly outsize contributions to these success stories: sea captains involved in international trade; a Presbyterian clergyman who presided over one of New York's most prestigious churches; a wealthy Boston widow who, starting out as Annie Griffin, a poor working girl, had the necessary chutzpah to acquire a string of lodging houses and other property in Boston's Hub, eventually becoming something of a philanthropist both in that city and in her native province. The Belfast district also produced pioneering women doctors, beginning in the late 1800s, and women who attended universities, including two sisters of the Orwell community's best-known native son, Sir Andrew Macphail. In *The Master's Wife*, his evocative memoir of his own family's life in the region, Macphail incidentally did much to provide insight into the ingredients of other local success stories, especially by showing the importance placed on education by high-achieving families and the doggedness demonstrated in pursuit of opportunities beyond the one-room school.[64] Such ingredients were absent in Compton lives.

Few Comptons seem even to have been subjects of obituaries in Island newspapers (Mary Vaughan Compton's obituary in 1866 stands out as an exception). Possibly I have overstated their economic and social marginality by making it sound exceptional: it is important, of course, to maintain perspective by keeping in mind that, as elsewhere in nineteenth-century Canada, the majority of Prince Edward Island's citizens would have been born and died in obscurity, often after a lifetime of struggle with adverse personal circumstances or the hardships of living in ill-favoured places like Lot 61.[65] Nevertheless, a perusal of the profiles of the comparatively numerous nineteenth-century Island men (and a few women) included in the *Dictionary of Canadian Biography* indicates that some of them – politician/reformer George Coles is a good example – overcame adverse early circumstances, including a lack of educational opportunities, and went on to achieve recognition for subsequent economic, professional, or political activities.[66] The Comptons, an outstanding demographic success story, were not part of this phenomenon. To the extent that their McDonaldite faith connections determined their movements in nineteenth-century Prince Edward Island and took them to unpropitious places, it helps to explain why they failed to prosper or to become prominent in other ways.

⁓

William and Mary had been much in motion from the days of their youth, beginning in William's case in Compton's Creek, New Jersey, and, in Mary's, in Chester, Nova Scotia. Their years in Belle River, beginning when their youth was already well behind them, marked the longest period of a settled existence. Their children, with the exception of their son William, who had remained behind in New Brunswick, and Henry, who temporarily returned there to marry his second wife, settled and stayed put in Prince Edward Island. It would be a different story, though, with the next generation. With the spiritual vacuum created by the death of the Comptons' revered minister in 1867, there would also, necessarily, be new religious paths.

3

On the Road Again: Sojourners and Religious Renegades in the Post-Confederation Era

The weakening of Prince Edward Island's economy in the years after Confederation would have touched all the descendants of William and Mary Compton to some degree. In the same period that some of them were putting down fragile roots in Bangor on the north side of the province, others were travelling much further afield in search of better opportunities: part of a province- and region-wide exodus. Meanwhile, with the passing of the Reverend Donald McDonald in 1867, they were confronted, like other long-time followers of the charismatic minister, with the need to make decisions about how to move forward in their faith lives. This chapter follows some of those descendants as they sojourned across provincial and international boundaries even as others remained on the Island and found new and inventive ways of being "McDonaldites." The latter preoccupation put them increasingly at odds with the tenor of the times, for Canada's post-Confederation decades saw the formation of important national denominational unions as part of the emergence of a mainstream Protestant consensus. For Prince Edward Islanders, the most significant of these unions was the one that took place within Presbyterianism when in 1875 the proudly national Presbyterian Church in Canada came into existence. Far from being attracted by the trend towards denominational unions, the Comptons became ever more separatist and anomalous in their religious practice, organizing for worship in modest little churches as a kind of spiritual family compact and making a virtue of their lack of professional religious leadership. Their physical and faith journeys took yet another turn from the 1890s when returning sojourners became part of a further reduced and now wholly unchurched religious kin group. Under the returnees' leadership, this close-knit and closely intermarried group would be transformed in the twentieth century into a prosperous millenarian utopian community.

Moving On and Moving Back

By the 1880s Prince Edward Island was well into the economic decline that beset the Maritime region in the decades after Confederation. While historians of out-migration are by no means in agreement about its specific causes, they depict the same broad features in the region's malaise, including the decline in shipbuilding and ship-owning and the loss of previously good markets for the Maritimes' primary products. And they agree that by the 1880s out-migration had reached "epic proportions."[1] The single most popular destination was the "Boston states," with young, single women and men in the lead. By the 1890s out-migration from Prince Edward Island was proportionately higher than in the other two Maritime provinces. Indeed, the 1901 census showed that PEI had suffered a net loss in population in the preceding decade despite the province's continuing high birth rate.[2] However heart-wrenching the departures of the Island's youth may have been for the families left behind, there was a philosophical acceptance of the fact that the young people would do better away and the expectation that the home folks would benefit from whatever assistance they sent back. The belief that moving away would make things better evidently became a kind of contagion. How else to explain the impulsive decision of the Gilman family of Malpeque to take their four children out of school and move to Maine in November 1887 with the family's wife and mother already ill with consumption? Lucy Palmer, the Malpeque schoolteacher from whose diary the Gilmans' story is taken, was considered very silly by her sister, a house servant for a well-to-do Massachusetts family, for not following her example and leaving the province.[3] Historian Alan A. Brookes looked closely at out-migration from the Island in this period and provided some numbers: Something over 31,000 people left in the course of the three decades. And this in a province whose total population in 1901 was just over 108,000. Married couples, even those with children like the Gilmans, became part of this exodus, and their destinations ranged widely across North America: "During the second half of the nineteenth century," Brookes writes, "an Islander might move to the American mid-West or Manitoba to farm, California or Colorado to dig for gold and silver, Gloucester to fish, or to cities such as Boston or New York to assume one of multifarious positions."[4]

Grandchildren and great-grandchildren of William and Mary became part of this story of continent-wide movement, both as permanent exiles and as sojourners. The fortunes of the permanent exiles are largely beyond the scope of this book. But the experiences of one group of sojourners bear recounting in some detail, since their movements and fortunes cast light on the denouement of the relationship between several close-knit Compton families and other McDonaldites in the decades following McDonald's death and figure importantly in the founding and operation of the Comptons' utopian community.

Some months after they had been counted in the PEI census in the spring of 1881, two married grandsons of William and Mary moved with their families to Brandon, Manitoba. John Henry Compton from Belle River, whose father was McDonaldite elder John Compton, was accompanied by his wife, Flora Grace (née Munn), their two-year-old son, Hector D., the future secretary-treasurer of the Comptons' utopian community, and an infant daughter. John Henry's cousin George Compton from Bangor (infamous to a later generation for his extramarital relations within the kin circle) was accompanied by his first wife, Mary, their son Daniel, and Mary's sister. No record survives of the two families' long journey from PEI; like most migrants and immigrants at the time, they probably travelled west on American trains. One strand of family lore incorporates a memory of a covered wagon for the last part of the trip, but that may have reflected later journeying within Manitoba, since in 1881 it became possible to reach Brandon from Winnipeg on the new Canadian Pacific Railway (CPR).[5]

In old age Hector gave two different explanations for his family's momentous move to western Canada, one related to religious tensions among post-McDonald McDonaldites, which I discuss later in this chapter, the other economic. In the latter explanation, Hector maintained that his father, a furniture maker, had been responding to the prevailing cry: "Go West, young man."[6] The slogan Hector cited was not in fact Canadian – it came out of a particular and earlier American context and was associated with the journalist Horace Greeley – but by the late nineteenth century, it was widely interpreted as a call to take advantage of agricultural opportunities in the Canadian West, and it resonated with tens of thousands of eastern Canadians. The Dominion Lands Act of 1872 had created the opportunity to obtain homesteads of 160 acres in the newly available lands of western Canada in exchange for a fee of ten dollars and the completion of a three-year residency requirement. It would perhaps have sounded particularly wonderful to Prince Edward Islanders like Hector's father in the contrast it provided to the Island's historically oppressive proprietorial landholding system. Homesteading and the opening of the West to agricultural settlement would later come to be associated in the popular mind with the arrival of waves of British and European immigrants and a period of sustained prosperity. But initial settlement was undertaken mainly by eastern Canadians in the new province of Manitoba (created in 1870), and it would not be until near the end of the century that the promise of prosperity would start to be realized. Meanwhile, the promise of "the Last Best West" outshone the reality, particularly for would-be settlers with little or no capital to invest. Many who tried to homestead failed to establish viable farms and ultimately abandoned the region, "impoverished and disillusioned."[7]

This proved to be the experience of the two young Compton families. They would have heard of a brief pre-1882 "boom" in Manitoba from other Islanders who had previously made the move. One of them was John A. McDougall, described by his Manitoba neighbour and fellow Scot William Wallace as "an old highlandman from Prince Edward Island." Wallace was a twenty-two-year-old bachelor when he arrived in the province from Scotland in 1881 with his widowed father and teenaged brother. His surviving letters provide us with a good deal of information about the Shell River and Russell districts northwest of Brandon where he and, later, the transplanted Islanders attempted to homestead. With its overwhelmingly Anglo-Protestant makeup, the region was culturally comfortable for immigrants like Wallace and the Island migrants, however challenging environmentally.[8] Like Wallace, McDougall was already homesteading in the district when the Comptons arrived. They had first spent time in Brandon. It was there that John Henry and Flora Grace had buried Mary, their first-born daughter, who died in October 1882, just short of her first birthday. After taking jobs in the Brandon area, including construction work on the CPR, the two family heads had taken up quarter sections around Asessippi. Several promising wheat crops were ruined by early frosts, according to Hector's reminiscences. The families then moved on to Russell.[9]

Writing in February 1883, the young William Wallace anticipated the newcomers' arrival with enthusiasm. Like many other homesteaders, the Wallaces had undertaken the hardships of Prairie homesteading unaccompanied by any female relatives. Like many another young bachelor, too, William looked forward to the arrival of women settlers who might become helpmates and companions. Writing to his sister, Maggie, in anticipation of the arrival of what he evidently assumed would be just one Compton homesteader, William observed that "Compton" would be arriving "with his wife and family, and better, a young lady, his niece. So you better hurry out quickly else I might be smitten."[10] This "Compton" would have been George. Alas for William's hopes for a possible marriage partner, the "niece" would have been George's unmarried sister-in-law, who became the mother of George's out-of-wedlock daughter, born later that year. Wallace makes no reference to the presence in the area of Hector's family, but in his own reminiscences Hector recalled that his first formal schooling began in Russell.[11]

Fortune continued to elude the two Compton families in Russell, as it had earlier in Asessippi. But they were not alone in their misfortune. Writing to his sister in April 1884 with an account of how he and his father and brother had fared in the preceding three years, William Wallace stated, "We are the only ones of all our neighbours who have made any money from our farming operations."[12] Like thousands of other failed homesteaders, both Compton families moved on to the US. They went first to St. Paul, Minnesota, and then to four different places in Illinois, always chasing building booms, according to Hector. The last four years "abroad," as Hector called life anywhere beyond the Island, were spent in Chicago, where the families experienced the effects of an economy that collapsed after the end of the Chicago World's Fair. By the time they were summoned back to PEI in 1894 following the serious illness of John Henry's father, the sojourning couple's household had increased to include seven children. Like George's family, they were too poor to return without the financial assistance scraped together by Island kin.[13]

Hector's sister Libby, born near Brandon in 1883, also reminisced in old age about their years in the West. Interviewed for a local history project that drew on the memories of elderly Belfast community members, she recalled her father's friendship with "the Indians" in the area and her own fears when they visited, his lack of aptitude for farming ("he was more of a carpenter than a farmer"), and their subsequent move to the US. Her school days in Chicago stood out as "the happiest days I ever knew." Libby particularly cherished the memory of a wonderful day when her father took time off work to accompany her to the World's Fair, her reward from her school for coming first in a spelling match. Less cherished were memories of the family's return to the Island after getting word of Grandfather John's stroke: "You leave a great big stone school with a couple of hundred pupils in it … to come home to a little two-room schoolhouse in Belle River. I felt lost for a while."[14] For the adults in eleven-year-old Libby's family, the hardship of returning to PEI would have been far more serious. Not only were they returning in the humiliating circumstances of their dire poverty, but also some immediate kin, including Grandfather John, had been exiled from the McDonaldite community that had been the Comptons' spiritual home for half a century. The next section steps back in time to discuss their place in that spiritual home and the circumstances that preceded their exile from it.

After McDonald: From Unity to Rupture

McDonald's following did not melt away after his death in February 1867. Nor was there immediate disunity. A history of Prince Edward Island written a few years after McDonald died described a community of mourners numbering in the thousands and united in grief. On the day of his funeral, the author wrote, a cortege of more than 350 sleighs moved through the countryside to the new cemetery at Orwell Head where McDonald was to be buried and where, later, a monument would be erected bearing inscriptions in Greek, Latin, Gaelic, and English. Despite the winter cold, weeping families stood in their doorways to watch the cortege as it passed. The historian compared their devotion to that of clansmen to their Highland chief.[15] Such a comparison missed the fact that, notwithstanding their otherness as non-Scots, Comptons were a recognized part of the mourning community, as were many families, English and Scottish, with whom they had intermarried, including Bears, Grants, Humes, Martins, Munns, and Sanders. Upon hearing about McDonald's passing, Lydia Compton, the oldest daughter of elder John, wrote a lengthy and subsequently much published memorial poem that seemed to speak for all the bereaved, irrespective of their locality or ethnic background.[16]

The disunity that subsequently developed among the McDonaldites arose initially over the mixed messages that the old minister had left about what they should do after he died. At meetings in DeSable and then Orwell Head, the relevant portions of McDonald's will and some of his oral remarks were carefully parsed for guidance by elders delegated to attend from his various congregations. A majority of the elders concluded that they should seek a "duly qualified" minister from the established Church of Scotland as his successor. A minority, however, echoing views of a sort expressed by numerous evangelicals going back at least to the time of the Great Awakening, chose to recall McDonald's warnings to his elders against accepting a minister who was an "unconverted" man – in practice, someone who did not adhere to McDonald's teachings. They quoted passages of Scripture "in proof of the authority of elders to labour in the word and doctrine."[17] The minority was also keen to avoid what McDonald himself had steadfastly resisted: control by a larger ecclesiastical body. Meeting in December 1867, elders of the Belle River and Brooklyn congregations – mostly Comptons and connections by marriage – were in the forefront in urging their fellow McDonaldites to maintain their historic autonomy and "stand fast in the liberty wherewith Christ hath made us free and be not entangled again with the yoke of bondage." To accomplish and perpetuate this liberty, they must stand together as "a visible body into which we may initiate our children by baptism." Resisting the view of the McDonaldite majority that a duly qualified Church of Scotland minister should be called to replace their revered minister, they declared: "We believe there are men among us who are as well qualified to administer the ordinances ... as any that can be sent us, for our qualification is not of men, neither by man, but by Jesus Christ."[18] In taking the position that no special training was necessary for effective, spirit-filled religious leadership, they were manifesting a scepticism about higher education generally that would persist well into the twentieth century.[19]

Two months later, armed with passages from the New Testament and assisted in their deliberations by elders from two other congregations, and having determined that there was nothing in the civil law to prevent their doing so, another meeting of elders of the Belle River and Brooklyn congregations appointed one of their own, George Bears, brother-in-law of elder John Compton, to "administer the holy ordinance of baptism in this section of the church and wheresoever [else] it may please the Lord to call him." Later meetings made it explicit that Bears was constitutionally appointed "to the full office of the ministry" and as such also entitled (as were two elders for other, like-minded, congregations) to preach and administer communion. Although there was evidently no precedent for it in Presbyterian polity, the term they adopted for this fuller role was "ministering elder."[20]

Despite ongoing splits between, and within, the majority and minority McDonaldite remnants, the movement did more than just survive. The first minister to serve the majority faction, the Reverend James McColl, soon decamped, briefly to Nova Scotia and then back to his native Scotland. But his successor, the Reverend John Goodwill, began a long-lasting Island ministry in 1875 after several years as a missionary in the New Hebrides, even touching off a revival in the early 1890s that no less a critic than elder Ewen Lamont pronounced worthy of comparison with McDonald's revivals. The majority did suffer a major loss in 1886 at Orwell Head, the very place where McDonald was buried, when after several years of strife over the question of whether or not to join the pan-national Presbyterian Church in

Canada, most of those present at an April meeting voted in favour of doing so. Even then, however, there were enough diehard McDonaldites at Orwell, Ewen Lamont among them, to resist the union and contrive to continue their separate existence.[21]

The Reverend George Monro Grant was able to experience firsthand and from an outsider perspective the size, distinctiveness, and vibrancy of the late McDonald's followers when he came from St. Matthew's Church, Halifax, in 1871 as a young Church of Scotland minister to preach for a week in several churches belonging to the majority remnant of McDonaldites. Grant was already a strong advocate of church unions and, for his time, a holder of liberal views; he would go on to become a nationally known figure for his ecumenism, nationalism, and imperialism. Yet he did not write in a denigrating way about the parochialism and peculiarities of the McDonaldite remnant. There was, certainly, condescension in his comments. But he was also moved and astonished by the size of the audiences that came to hear him preach – more than one thousand people inside the church at DeSable on a communion Sunday, he estimated, and another five hundred outside – and by their hunger for religious services. He had dreaded encountering the McDonaldites' infamous performative religious outbursts, regarding them as "physical and nervous entirely" rather than "signs of the Spirit." But he was reassured by the fact that only a small minority actually engaged in such outbursts, "chiefly women, and those of a sensitive or hysterical religious temperament," and he did not regard the phenomena as spurious. The congregants, "most of them Highland, but with a sprinkling of Lowlanders," were, Grant judged, a "primitive" people but "very kindly" and not unintelligent. As he neared the end of his Island stay, Grant was grateful for the time he had spent among them: "It is a pleasure indeed to preach unto people whose only grief is that you are drawing to a close, and who will walk miles or drive tens of miles to hear the Word of God. I wish that Halifax, – St. Matthew's – people had the same spirit."[22]

The religious zeal that Grant observed also expressed itself in the establishment of new places of worship in the post-McDonald era. In the 1870s new buildings were begun at Caledonia, where the use of Gaelic was still a practice when the parents of future Island premier Angus MacLean worshipped there in the early twentieth century, and in the much different community of Belle River. A surviving record book shows that the building of a small and unadorned church at Bangor in 1893 benefited from contributions from fellow worshippers elsewhere on the Island as well as from McDonaldites in other parts of Canada and the US. The Reverend John Goodwill was among the donors and one of the church's occasional preachers. In the same decade, a church was built at Coleman, northwest of Summerside in Prince County. Finally, in 1895, following up on the enthusiasm and early initiatives of expatriate McDonaldites in Cambridge, Massachusetts, the indefatigable Goodwill helped organize a congregation there. It remained in existence, albeit precariously, for much of the first half of the twentieth century.[23]

It is unlikely that either McColl or Goodwill or the briefly visiting George Grant would have been invited, or wanted, to preach to the congregations of the minority faction at Brooklyn and Belle River. The elders there, along with like-minded elders from several other communities, had opted at an April 1871 meeting to identify their people for purposes of the upcoming census as members of "Mr. McDonald's *Unattached* Church." It was at that same meeting that they had unanimously appointed George Bears as their first ministering elder,[24] a position he retained until his death in 1879. Like the Comptons, the Bears were of Loyalist background. Prior to settling at Belle River and coming under McDonald's influence, they had lived in mainland Nova Scotia and been practising Methodists. George had somehow acquired reading and writing skills that went well beyond basic literacy, becoming something of a poet and a prolific writer of hymns.[25] Under his leadership, a constitution was prepared to which elders representing several other minority McDonaldite communities assented. He was also authorized to prepare a brief statement of "what we believe to be the true meaning of what the Scriptures teach." This was not with a view to superseding the standard Presbyterian doctrines of belief – he cited, for instance, the Shorter Catechism – but rather to provide a shared understanding of McDonald's distinctive teachings and to delineate the scriptural authority for the role of ministering elder. The 1876 statement was clearly meant, too, to assert and justify George's personal authority and the appropriateness of his being entrusted with the deed to the partly constructed Belle River church, for, despite the earlier unanimity in selecting him, there were already some challenges to his leadership.[26]

Challenges to George Bears's authority and doctrinal teachings came from McDonaldites from other parts of the province, but also from relatives connected to him by birth and marriage.[27] Writing in old age, Hector Compton claimed that his father, John Henry, was one of those shunned – even denied baptism for the infant Hector – for "'holding false views,'" viz., salvation for all and not just the elect. If Hector's account is accurate, John Henry's "false views" would at the time have put him at odds with his own father as well as his Uncle George Bears, for it was elder John Compton who had seconded the resolution approving Bears's statement of their faith with its adherence to the strict Calvinist doctrine of election. In the same reminiscence – this time making no mention of economic motives – Hector claimed that this theological dispute was the reason for his father's decision to leave the Island and move west with his family.[28]

Shortly before he died in April 1879, Bears wrote a document as guidance and instruction for those he had served as ministering elder. Referring to the document as his last will and testament and asking that it be read at his funeral, he enjoined his fellow believers to follow the golden rule in their dealings with one another, called for younger elders to oversee the completion of the still unfinished church at Belle River, and urged that "one of the aged elders" be put in charge of "the last and most delicate part of all ... the administration of the ordinances." Mindful that other Island Presbyterians had written disapprovingly about disorderly behaviour at their communion services in the years just after McDonald's death,[29] and of the potential for greater disorder following his own passing, Bears called for "everything [to] be done decently and according to order as you have been taught." And if someone "duly qualified" should emerge – presumably someone ordained *and* evangelical like the Reverend Donald McDonald himself – then "let all the offices of the ministry centre on him." Not surprisingly, no such someone emerged. After initially appointing elder John Compton to conduct baptisms and communion on an interim basis, the Belle River and Brooklyn congregations unanimously agreed in July of that year (though only after "considerable discussion") to retain him on an ongoing basis as Bears's successor as ministering elder.[30]

Like George Bears before him, John Compton performed numerous baptisms, beginning in July 1879 and continuing into January 1891. Like George, too, he performed the ordinance in other minority McDonaldite communities in addition to Brooklyn and Belle River, in Murray River, for instance, and across country in Morell. Early on in John's ministering eldership, a committee was appointed to arrange for publication of the hymns Bears had written. And, prior to the 1881 census, the decision was again taken to adopt the single word "McDonaldite" as their denominational identifier. In the heading for occupation, the same census listed John as "ministering elder." The use of this designation as his occupation signified the importance that John, and perhaps the enumerator, attached to the holding of this office. It would be used again in the 1891 census.[31]

And yet, just a short time after the 1891 census was conducted, a rupture occurred that severed John and a small group of close kin from their cherished McDonaldite community, leaving them in permanent religious isolation. The surviving minutes of the Brooklyn-Belle River congregations, kept in rich and careful detail from the end of 1867 (generally by George Bears's son Thomas), contain no account of the rupture. Indeed, the minutes largely cease in mid-1885, not to be resumed for eighteen years. An account of what happened comes instead from elder Ewen Lamont in an appendix to his brief memoir of minister Donald McDonald, published in 1892. Though he does not name any of the participants in the event, which had taken place in Brooklyn the previous July while the elders were preparing for the group's communion Sunday, it was almost certainly Lamont himself who orchestrated the purge of "some intending communicants."[32]

Ewen Lamont's association with the Brooklyn-Belle River congregations had come about as a result of the split among his fellow worshippers at Orwell Head in the early 1880s over the question of union with the national Presbyterian Church in Canada. Lamont's family had been fervent McDonaldites from the time they had experienced the Reverend Donald McDonald's first revival following their arrival from Skye at the end of the 1820s. The Lamont family, it was said, had chosen to settle in the Orwell area in order to be close to minister McDonald, who, when not travelling, found a home there with his brother Findlay. Ewen, a successful long-time schoolteacher and a farmer as well as a McDonaldite elder, was remembered in the Island's main newspaper at his death in 1905 and long afterwards for his own abilities and those of his accomplished sons. But he was also remembered in family lore for his strong will and dogmatism. One account told of his having defied McDonald himself by voting in a colonial election contrary to the minister's position. Another story has him tearing up a pamphlet that some of his fellow elders in Orwell, including William Macphail, proposed to use in Sabbath-school teaching: in Ewen's view, only the Bible should be used.[33] Given this temperament and his confidence in his own strongly held views, it was perhaps inevitable that some members of the Brooklyn-Belle River congregations would eventually fall afoul of Ewen's judgment after 1883, when he and a fellow Orwell elder sought to join the elders of those congregations for purposes of being part of their self-styled presbytery. He was initially authorized by that body to act as ministering elder to the Gaelic-speaking McDonaldite remnant in Orwell; later, the presbytery decided that Ewen Lamont and John Compton should act jointly as church convenors and together call general church meetings "when they consider it requisite."[34]

Writing about the rupture at Brooklyn about a year after it happened, Ewen Lamont prefaced his account of what had transpired by dismissing the claims of some that it had been "a shameful proceeding" and "a disgraceful row." Rather, he wrote, "grave charges" had been brought before the assembled elders "by men of unquestioned veracity." Those "arraigned" had

> maintained and taught that no portion of the human race was to be consigned to endless misery, let them be ever so wicked in this world. That no person need fear hell as a place of endless torment. That even Judas Iscariot is not lost ... As the arraigned denied none of the charges preferred, and as they would not acknowledge their views to be wrong, they were suspended from Church fellowship, until they would publicly renounce their heresy.
>
> May the example set by the Brooklyn Session cease not to be followed wherever it is needed until heresy be no more![35]

Whether or not elder John Compton had personally come to hold these "heretical" views or was simply tainted and affected by extension because some close family members held them, the 1891 dispute evidently marked the end of his years as a McDonaldite elder. It may even have played a part in bringing on the stroke that left him paralysed. That the dispute revealed conflicting theological positions is clear: Lamont was defending a strict (though by then widely lapsed) Calvinist orthodoxy, while "some intending communicants" were accused of holding views at the far extreme of Arminianism. Variations of such differences had, of course, been playing out in the Anglo-Protestant evangelical world for more than a century, so whether or not they were conscious of it (and Ewen, at least, probably was), the men gathered in Brooklyn on that particular Saturday were actors in a much larger religious drama.[36]

But it is likely that local factors, particularly personal and ethnic factors, as well as theological issues had also been at play. John's relationship with Ewen as a fellow ministering elder – both of them were by now old men – had probably been a somewhat uncomfortable one even before the falling out of 1891. Though he was the duly appointed successor to George Bears from 1879 and proud of that fact, John seems not to have been regarded by some in their tiny religious community as his equal in spiritual gifts.[37] His status would have suffered a further decline when he had to share leadership with Ewen, who outshone him in terms of recognized secular and spiritual accomplishments. In terms of hymn writing, only George Bears among the elders had contributed more to the McDonaldite corpus than Ewen Lamont, and, like McDonald himself, Lamont composed in Gaelic as well as English. John, for his part, wrote just one hymn and may well have been assisted by his poet daughter Lydia. The importance of the hymns for McDonaldites went well beyond their musical appeal. They were, wrote Ewen's son Murdock, "mostly sermons in verse, very much in demand where there is no weekly sermons [sic] and as they dwell much on the vital experience of religion they are prized by those whose experiences correspond with them."[38] Facility in hymn writing was one of the ways in which ethnic differences continued to matter within the community, just as they had when the Comptons – "the English" – had first arrived on the Island and been regarded by some of McDonald's Gaelic-speaking followers as outsiders.[39] As noted, many of these Comptons, including John, had nonetheless intermarried early on with Scottish immigrant families. It was an English rather than a Gaelic identity that came to predominate in the Brooklyn-Belle River congregations.

Finally, there was the matter of morality. To the ultra-respectable Ewen Lamont, it probably seemed that some of elder John Compton's people were not only Arminians but also adherents of another view that strict Calvinists like himself found heretical: the antinomian idea that saved Christians were above the moral law. Had not John baptized his illegitimate six-year-old grandson, born to his unmarried daughter Louisa and fathered by their kinsman George Compton before George's departure for the West?[40] Were there other moral irregularities that John had sanctioned or to which he had turned a blind eye? Was John perhaps one of the drinking Comptons with whom fellow McDonaldite elder William Macphail had imbibed before determining to become wholly temperate, perhaps even the "famous elder" referred to by William's author son as having a periodic "infirmity for drink"?[41]

John Compton lived on for another ten years after the 1891 rupture that put an end to his and his family's intense involvement with the Brooklyn-Belle River congregations. His grandson Hector was profoundly affected by the rupture, even though he had not personally experienced it and did not refer to it directly in his extensive writing about the Comptons' faith lives. When Hector's impoverished family returned from the West in November 1894, they lived for four years with his grandfather John, now an invalid widower, and his spinster daughter Catherine, who cared for him. It seems likely that it was from his grandfather and perhaps even more from his Aunt Catherine that the teenaged Hector came to believe that it was solely his people's resistance to the harsh doctrine of election that had led to their expulsion from their faith community. It also seems likely that in Hector's old age his father John Henry's early experience of having been shunned for his expansive view about who could be saved, and the rupture at Brooklyn in 1891, merged in his mind, becoming essentially the same event.[42] The attention to detail and care with chronology that would be characteristic of his correspondence and record keeping about business matters is sometimes absent in Hector's writing about the end of his family's participation in the McDonaldite faith community and those within it who opposed their Arminianism.

Notwithstanding the exodus that took thousands of people from Prince Edward Island in the post-Confederation decades, Comptons among them, most descendants of William and Mary were still living in the province at the end of the 1800s, spread out in pockets of settlement across Queen's and King's counties. There had also been some religious wandering. Over the years, some descendants had found their way into mainstream Presbyterianism, a few perhaps into other Protestant denominations. Most, though, remained within the McDonaldite fold. The two families who returned from the West in 1894 became part of the smallest and most isolated fragment of what had once been a large and tight-knit faith community, a fragment that was now without even a church. They were also returning, as Hector later wrote, not just in poverty but "into poverty": Grandfather John was a bed-ridden old man, and there were no males in his household to provide a livelihood. For the next few years the returnees would share their close relatives' material hardship as well as their religious isolation.[43] Then, towards the end of the first decade of the twentieth century, they became part of a robust millenarian communitarian enterprise spearheaded by another and more successful sojourner, kinsman Ben Compton (1854–1921). A distinctive version of McDonald's teaching would be central to the faith aspect of that enterprise, later incorporated as B. Compton Limited. Chapter 4 touches briefly on the historiography of utopias and locates B. Compton Limited within the history of earlier North American utopian experiments before focusing on its economic development.

PART II

Prince Edward Island's Unique "Brotherly Love" Community

4

The Founding and Growth of
an Island Utopia

Descendants of two of the seven sons of William and Mary Compton were involved in the establishment of the Compton utopian community.[1] Founded in 1909, the community functioned informally for more than two decades before its incorporation in 1933 as B. Compton Limited. Hector Compton, thirty years old when the community began, was its secretary from the outset and secretary-treasurer from 1921. Writing in old age, he recalled for relatives how it had come about. He began by acknowledging Benjamin Compton's leadership:

> He made a start and helped us start lobster fishing. It was hard going at the outset but we kept at it and learned a difficult business. Other cousins were invited from abroad, always coming penniless and we added more boats, ran a Cannery and besides this began to build up land or soil and Buildings. For years we each took our Shares and spent it as we pleased. A Crisis arose in 1909 and Benjamin suggested that we leave all our funds in the Bank add to it as we could and live from it, thus supporting some dependent relatives jointly etc. We all of us about ten young single men, cheerfully assented. We were standing outside a kitchen door where we chanced to meet. There was never a paper signed or a By law made.[2]

In another piece of correspondence, this time official and written by Hector a few months after the company had ceased to exist, he described the essentials of its communal functioning:

> The shares in our Community carried with them the obligation that each Member and his Household contribute their labours and

talents to the welfare of the Community as a whole, without Salary or wage or Dividend. In return they received a full reasonable living and beyond that, the Company stood behind each and every individual in case of illness, accident, Fire loss, old age or death, to pay all costs without any charge whatever to the Member or his Family.[3]

Hector's surviving correspondence – he began keeping copies of his typed correspondence in 1923 – is the single most important source on the business and spiritual aspects of the community.[4] Neither in the two passages just quoted nor elsewhere in what has survived did Hector refer explicitly to B. Compton Limited as an instance of a utopian endeavour. But journalists and scholars who wrote about the Compton community during the thirty-eight years of its existence had no hesitation in likening it to other North American utopian communities.[5] Moreover, Hector, and almost certainly founder Ben before him, had owned and read Edward Bellamy's 1888 novel, *Looking Backward: 2000–1887*, the book that came to be the best-known American work to envision a functioning utopia. Indeed, in a 1945 letter to one of his brothers, Hector claimed – though this was something of a stretch – that Bellamy had described a system just like the one their people established.[6]

Looking Backward was, as its title suggests, a futuristic novel. Though the ideal world it envisions is sweeping in scope, the utopia it depicts is an urban, industrialized society – its characters live in Boston – served by an array of technological conveniences. Despite his unease with urban life, Hector would have found the book's broad vision congenial, particularly with its condemnation of unbridled individualism and poverty in the midst of plenty and its emphasis on the establishment of a harmonious, orderly, and cooperative way of living. Furthermore, while Bellamy, the son of a Baptist clergyman, had become disillusioned with many aspects of traditional Christianity, his book was informed by a "profoundly religious sensibility" and by a millennial vision that, one scholar argues, helped to catalyse the early social gospel movement.[7] Within a decade of its publication, *Looking Backward* had sold close to half a million copies in the United States alone, and its audience extended to all social classes. In his introduction to the 2007 edition of the book for Oxford University Press, Matthew Beaumont explained that it "quickly acquired cult status. Almost everyone who was interested in the so-called 'social question' debated the book, 'down to the bootblacks as they s[a]t by the curbstones.'"[8] *Looking Backward* influenced the founders of utopian communities in western Canada as well as the founders of the Social

Credit Movement and the CCF and numerous individual socialists. "Right down to the 1940s," Ian McKay writes, "many socialists would include Bellamy along with [Herbert] Spencer in the narratives they constructed on the theme, 'why I became a socialist.'"[9] Given its setting and broad concerns, then, and its early and wide-reaching impact, it is likely that founder Ben Compton (1854–1921) had acquired the book while employed in Boston as a carpenter and, returning to Island relatives in economic distress, was interested in applying some of its broad principles.

"Utopianism" as "a bright vision of a world where things will be better than they are now" existed, of course, long before Bellamy wrote *Looking Backward*. It also predates Sir Thomas More's 1516 invention of the word as the name for his fictional and highly regimented cooperative commonwealth on an imaginary New World island. The Hebraic Garden of Eden and Plato's *Republic* have both been viewed as expressions of utopian dreams, as have millenarians' expectation of a transformed world following Christ's second coming.[10] Given its long and varied history, utopianism has been a concept of sufficient interest to scholars to merit its own international journal, *Utopian Studies*, published in the United States since 1988. The establishment of the journal in the late twentieth century reflected the intellectual curiosity then being shown in such nineteenth-century utopian communities as Robert Owen's secular experiment at New Harmony, Indiana, and John Humphrey Noyes's Perfectionist commune at Oneida, New York, as well as in better-known endeavours such as those undertaken by the Shakers, Hutterites, and Mormons. American scholars' penchant for "looking backward" at these earlier utopias arose in the wake of a remarkable if short-lived contemporary phenomenon: the establishment across North America in the late 1960s and early 1970s of numerous hippie or counter-cultural communities.[11]

Canada had its share of such movements during the long 1960s, particularly in British Columbia, though they were also salient in the Maritimes.[12] They did not, though, result in the kind of scholarly interest in earlier utopian experiments that occurred in the US. There have, certainly, been popular and scholarly accounts of individual Canadian utopian communities such as Sointula, a short-lived Finnish socialist endeavour in early twentieth-century British Columbia, and the religious utopias of the Prairie West.[13] Historian Colin Coates provided a brief overview of these and other Canadian utopias some years ago at a meeting of the Canadian Historical Association. And in their Canadian Utopias Project, which draws on their backgrounds in, respectively, urban planning and human geography, scholars Beth Moore

Milroy and Brian S. Osborne have been building on the unfinished work of a deceased colleague to compile a list and briefly describe "Built Utopian Settlements to 1945."[14] To date, however, there have been no scholarly book-length studies of historic Canadian utopias. Although John Cousins's *New London: The Lost Dream/The Quaker Settlement on P.E.I.'s North Shore 1773–1795* stands as something of an exception to this statement, Cousins has not explicitly conceptualized this remarkable late eighteenth-century Quaker initiative as a type of utopian community.[15] Likewise, while Mennonites are sometimes mentioned in broad surveys of utopian or quasi-utopian communities, scholarly studies of Canadian Mennonite communities typically focus on their ethnic and religious dimensions, largely eschewing any discussion of utopian aspirations or characteristics.[16] Nor have Canadian utopias found a noteworthy place in Canadian works of fiction, as has been the case with US utopias in, for instance, Nathaniel Hawthorne's 1852 *The Blithedale Romance* (the Transcendentalists' Brook Farm) and, as recently as 2018, Barbara Kingsolver's *Unsheltered* (Vineland).[17]

Like other would-be explorers of utopian communities, I have learned that attempts at definitions of such communities are fraught with difficulties – excessively broad at one extreme and too narrowly restrictive at the other. The notion of a "bright vision ..." quoted in the preceding paragraph illustrates the expansive approach, as does Ruth Levitas's 1990 observation that the constant in all utopias is a "desire for a better way of living and being."[18] More recently, the authors of *The Historical Dictionary of Utopianism* identified what they saw as some defining characteristics:

> Utopianism, ancient or modern, has almost always been marked by the following: group-based isolation from contemporary worldly corruption ... equality of goods and a rejection of luxury; regimentation of the lives of the participants ... to assure the perceived common good; and direction of the new model society being placed in the hands of leaders ... endowed with a vision ... that will bring peace and justice to all adherents within time.[19]

But isn't this *too* restrictive? There are some well-known and long-existing communities that are commonly considered utopian, the Old Order Amish, for example, in which one or more of the characteristics mentioned in the *Dictionary* is weak or absent.[20] Given the problematic range of meanings and approaches illustrated in the works just cited, the more limited concept of "communal utopias" seems more helpful for locating the Compton community within the broad utopian tradition.

Introducing the concept in a collection of essays entitled *America's Communal Utopias*, Donald E. Pitzer writes: "In this type of close-knit community much or all property is shared communally. Members join voluntarily and live in rural settlements or urban housing partly isolated and insulated from the general society. They share an ideology and lifestyle while attempting to implement the group's ideals."[21] Communalism was an essential element in the life of the Compton community. It was founded more than half a century after what scholars of American utopias have viewed as their "golden age." (The 1840s is often highlighted and, in terms of location, the "Burned-Over" district of New York state.)[22] Yet like many communal utopias of that earlier efflorescent period, the Compton community had a deep concern with religion and, in particular – and here one sees the ongoing vitality of their nineteenth-century McDonaldite heritage – a sense of urgency about the coming of the millennium and the importance of waiting as a unified body of believers. At the same time, B. Compton Limited was also an attempt to respond practically to the immediate material needs and social challenges facing a small kin group in a quite different time and place. A consideration of its approach to gaining a livelihood for its members makes it clear that, in this case, commonplace understandings of "utopian" as a synonym for "visionary" and "impractical" are exceedingly wide of the mark.

Starting Out and Gaining Ground

As shown, Hector readily acknowledged his cousin Ben's leadership in the founding of the community. A generation older than Hector, Ben was a brother of George, the man who had accompanied Hector's father on the two families' ill-fated western sojourn. Unlike George and John Henry, though, Ben had returned from his time "abroad" with a few hundred dollars in his pocket. No information is available about when he went to Boston or how long he stayed. He was living in PEI at the time of the 1891 and 1901 censuses. Most likely he made the move after the death of his first wife, who died childless in 1897. In any case, in making the journey, Ben was following in the footsteps of the many other Island men and (to an even greater extent) women who had been drawn to that city by its abundant and easily accessible employment opportunities.[23]

In the last half of the nineteenth century, Boston was experiencing dynamic growth. By 1900 it was primarily an industrial rather than a merchant city. It had a population of more than one million people, and it had sprawled beyond the old city core to such new suburbs as Cambridge, Watertown, and Everett, places that had become easily reachable by a network of street railways. Men from the Maritimes like Ben were very much in evidence in the building trades, including those involved in constructing the new suburban housing.[24] Without a family to support and perhaps living cheaply with kin or other Maritimers in a lodging house of the sort operated by wealthy Island-born widow Mrs. Annie Tennyson,[25] Ben would have been in a position to save money in a way that would not have been possible for the two kinsmen who had gone west as heads of households, even had they stayed in one place and experienced steady employment and not been responsible for numerous offspring.

Hector's recollection was that Ben was "a great leader of men, a leader in spiritual as well as material matters," and that, under his direction, the community "went ahead financially or in the acquisition of property in miraculous speed the first dozen years."[26] Yet despite Ben's evident success as a founding figure, he remains an enigma. Unlike many founders of utopian communities, he left no body of writing behind. Nor can much in the way of specifics be discerned from Hector's occasional written references to him. Even details about the nature of the "Crisis" that arose in 1909 and influences additional to *Looking Backward* that might have turned Ben's mind towards a communal approach as a means of dealing with the crisis are absent from Hector's reminiscences. Hector's sister Libby (1883–1986), who became Ben's second and much younger wife in 1908, had even less to say about her late husband and his role as the community's founder than Hector when she was interviewed in old age for a local history project, though she was clearly happy to reminisce about other matters.[27]

Ben died in 1921, the victim of an accident in the company sawmill. Describing the event in grisly detail on its front page, the *Charlottetown Guardian* spoke of the mill as one of the most successful in the province and, in the formulaic language still used in local obituaries, described the late Mr. Compton as "a splendid type of citizen" mourned by "a large circle of friends."[28] No long period of disarray or uncertainty was allowed to take place in regard to the company's future following Ben's death. At a meeting of company men held just four days later, his nephew Daniel G. Compton, who lived in the company's satellite settlement of Bangor, was appointed president. William Jardine, Hector's brother-in-law, became vice-president, and Hector was officially confirmed in his role as secretary-treasurer. Dan and Hector were to have joint signing authority on company cheques and other documents. In 1923, however, Dan himself died unexpectedly. Some sixteen months later, at another company meeting, Hector was entrusted with all signing authority and overall management of the company in consultation with "an attorney or attorneys" acting on the company's behalf.[29] Ben's role as founder of the Compton community was permanently acknowledged when in May 1933 it became a limited joint-stock company incorporated as B. Compton Limited. Its net worth at the time of incorporation was $103,000.00, including the assets of its settlement in Bangor.[30] The incorporation process was initiated, Hector explained years later, because of repeated warnings from the community's attorney and its banker about the legal risks of continuing to operate in an informal fashion.[31]

As overall manager of the company from 1923 onward, Hector executed all aspects of its business, including the incorporation arrangements. He was no doubt the person best placed to succeed Ben by virtue of his ability, his education, and his early and substantial involvement in the community. Although his schooling had ended at age fifteen, in 1894, when his family returned to PEI following the years in the West, he had evidently received a solid training in the basics during the period when they lived in Chicago,[32] and was something of an autodidact. As for his initial contribution to the communal set-up, writing in 1948 in the wake of the company's dissolution, when there was briefly some tension about allocation of assets, he stated: "At the time we Pooled all earnings in 1909, I had a boat & Fleet and a Share in Cannery to throw in, Bought 12 ½ acres of land and threw that in, had a Trade [carpenter] and kit of tools as against others who had none, had saved $3200.00 [sic; perhaps $320.00?] which later was also thrown into the common pool."[33]

Hector periodically consulted in person or by letter with "Big John" Compton, Dan's younger brother and his successor as leader in Bangor.[34] Bangor was exclusively a farming settlement, located a few miles from the nearest post office and railway station in the village of Morell. As shown in Chapter 2, Comptons had been living along the straggling dirt road that was Bangor since the 1870s. Not all of them, however, became part of the Compton community. Indeed, Hector's only paternal uncle is said to have opted out at the behest of his second wife, who feared losing her own inherited property to the communal arrangement.[35] On the other hand, there were families bearing different surnames who came to be linked to the community by virtue of marriages to Compton women in the nineteenth century. The Jardines were one such family. A daughter of McDonaldite elder John Compton had married into a branch of this family, whose immediate ancestors had immigrated from the Scottish Lowlands to the Morell area in the early 1800s, in some cases becoming prominent local citizens. Through such marital connections, other "outsiders" also became part of the Compton community, but generally they seem not to have been given much voice or credit for their contributions in matters of business or religion.[36]

The more populous Belle River segment of the community was more compact than Bangor, set apart from the rest of the Belle River settlement on an ever so slight rise of land known locally as "the Hill." In addition to farm buildings and the sawmill, there was a cluster of houses grouped around the company's general store and machine shop in a kind of oval formation, with large stacks of logs and lumber nearby. The two community settlements were about thirty miles distant across country by road. The cross-country route was largely unpaved until the 1950s (only 6 per cent of Island roads were paved in 1943),[37] and the company may not have had its own automobiles before the 1930s. Still, it was a feasible trip by wagon in summer, and doable even in winter if snow conditions made for good sleigh travel, with one or more stops en route, including, for the Bangor travellers, the hospitality of kin in Brooklyn.[38] A more circuitous trip was involved if undertaken by train, since it meant travelling by way of Charlottetown. A spur railway line had opened for regular traffic from Charlottetown to Murray Harbour in 1905, with a station stop at Belle River. Served at first by a simple shelter, the Belle River stop later had a proper booking station with freight shed. Despite the longer distance involved in travelling by train, the railway was an important factor in linking the two settlements. Train service was even more important in transporting products from, and bringing supplies to, the community businesses at Belle River, particularly before they had automobiles.[39]

Movement between the two settlements would most often have involved men. For some years, though, it also included a few young women who came to Belle River from Bangor for seasonal work in the Compton lobster factory, the existence of which predated the communal setup of 1909: it is said to have been the first such factory in the Belle River area.[40] Catching and canning lobsters was an important business for the nascent Compton community, as it was in the late nineteenth and early twentieth centuries for Prince Edward Island overall. Barely in existence in the province in the early 1870s, lobster canneries multiplied over the next decade. The value of packed lobsters peaked in 1881, exceeding the combined pack value of Nova Scotia and New Brunswick. Not surprisingly, many Islanders became involved in the industry, often on a part-time basis. Canneries of varying sizes and degrees of technical competence "sprang up along the shore like beads on a necklace," peaking in number in 1900 at 246 factories.[41] Nor was it surprising that Hector himself was attracted by the great lobster boom and had his own fleet and a share in the cannery for some years before both became part of the communal enterprise.

Nevertheless, the lobster business did not give Hector much personal satisfaction, and as a company industry it was short-lived. Although government regulations had been established following periodic investigations of problems in the lobster fishery, beginning in the 1880s, the industry continued to suffer from overfishing and poor quality control of the canned product.[42] Writing in 1948 in connection with the dissolution of B. Compton Limited, Hector stated that returns to the company from its lobster business had been poor in its last years; it was sold in 1927. The last of its own fishing vessels had been "beached" four years earlier.[43] The company's exit from the industry – well before the sale of live lobster became a significant part of it – was an early instance of what would become a larger Island pattern: In 1926 there were still 146 lobster canneries in the province; two decades later there were just 68.[44]

The Compton community had not been unusual in employing some of its young women members in its lobster cannery. During the boom years, Island lobster canneries had provided seasonal employment for a significant number of Island women.[45] Before the birth of her children, Libby Compton worked seasonally in the cannery. Unlike Hector, she had good memories of that period in the company's business life. Interviewed in her old age, she remembered the enjoyment of being down at the shore and recalled packing as "an easy job." Perhaps remembering the many stories of spoiled lobster meat that had spurred investigation and regulation of the canning industry, she was eager for her young interviewer to understand that "We had a good name for our lobsters" and no problem in marketing them. The end of the company's involvement in the lobster industry in Libby's remembering was related not to turbulence in the industry or anything to do with the company's product but rather to the increasing demands of its woodworking operation.[46]

As well as a pragmatic decision to focus increased attention on a more profitable line of work, the shift away from lobstering would have been in keeping with a family tradition of involvement in some form of woodworking that went back to Loyalist William Compton. The furniture workshop shown on the property of elder John Compton in the 1880 *Illustrated Historical Atlas of Prince Edward Island* was probably operated by his son John Henry, who, as his daughter Libby had observed in connection with his failed attempt at Prairie home-steading, was more of a carpenter than a farmer. A few years after his return from Chicago, the inventive John Henry had built a two-wheeled windmill. It provided the power to saw fencing and other materials, including the lumber for his own and several other sub-stantial family homes. The windmill was torn down in 1915, and over the years the woodworking shop was replaced by larger mill facili-ties. More reliable sources of energy were established to provide the power for producing a variety of products for communal use and for the market. In addition to hardwood flooring and other sawn lum-ber for construction, the mill produced custom box materials called shooks, used in various kinds of commercial operations. A business ledger from the 1930s records specifications for making shooks for butter boxes, poultry, fruits and vegetables, smelts, and lobster crates. It also records the costs involved in the components for custom-made caskets.[47]

The Belle River branch of B. Compton Limited also operated a machine shop and had a large farm and woodlots. In addition to the products it supplied to Island purchasers, it shipped agricultural produce to Cape Breton and eastern mainland Nova Scotia, mainly Pictou County, on one of a succession of its own schooners, often returning with coal and gravel. Its general store was the business endeavour that gave outsiders their best opportunity to observe – and sometimes misunderstand – communalism in action, and as such it aroused great interest. The store provided members of the Compton community with groceries, clothing items, and other supplies on a needs-based arrangement, while also, like other general stores in the province, serving as a retail store and a site of produce exchange for nearby settlements.[48]

The company's fortunes during the interwar years provide inter-esting sidelights into the Maritime region's economic circumstances during the two decades. Historians of the region have shown that, despite the popular stereotype of the 1920s as a decade of national and international prosperity, there was no "Roaring Twenties" for most Maritimers. Indeed, the regional out-migration that had been a fact of life for decades reached a peak in the 1920s, with Nova Scotia and PEI experiencing an absolute decline in population.[49] The Compton com-munity's abandonment of its lobster business appears to accord with the decline narrative. But as shown, the community had other irons in the fire. The sawmill became a commercial success, notwithstand-ing the hazardous working conditions – common at the time to all such mills – that, in the 1920s, took the lives of founder Ben and one hired worker.[50] The company's assets were also significantly boosted by mortgage loans and by its investments in Victory Bonds during the First World War.[51] During the 1920s, Hector continued to invest on behalf of the company. Writing in 1948 when the process of dividing the company's assets was still underway and he was seeking to respond to a suggestion that he had been responsible for "a large money loss in the slump of 1929," he declared, "I find that our Net worth in 1921 when Ben died was $65,138.00 and that by 1929 it had been raised to $142,044.00 or an increase of $76,906.00 ... [The increase] was largely made up from Turnover Profits every time we exchanged a security in those years."[52]

While Hector's response spoke to gains made during the 1920s, it did not really address the concern about investment losses resulting from the crash of 1929, for which there was validity.[53] The community's net worth at the time of incorporation in 1933 was, as noted, just $103,000, down some $39,000 from what it had been three years earlier. Some of the decline would also have reflected disappointing sales and low prices for farm and mill products. In 1932 and again in 1933 there were concerns about lagging sales in agricultural produce shipped to Nova Scotia. And in November 1932 hired workers in the lumber mill were alerted to the possibility that the mill might have to close in the face of falling prices.[54]

Overall, however, the community's assorted economic activities seem to have fared comparatively well during the Depression years, as they had in the 1920s. In 1935, following poor market conditions the previous year, the community reportedly decided to grow only enough potatoes for its own needs and opted not to participate in a nascent movement seeking government support in the form of a "tuber bonus." But it appears that in most years, in spite of sometimes slow markets, the company continued to ship produce from its farms in Belle River and Bangor to markets in eastern Nova Scotia.[55] Far from closing, the sawmill coped effectively with fluctuations in demand. Production of butter boxes for use by creameries was an important component of the mill business. Demand evidently fell off for a time in 1932 or early 1933, when the creameries bought cheaper boxes shipped by train from the Mainland. Hector responded by travelling to nine Island creameries "to see if we could get our trade in butter shooks back again." His two-day trip proved successful. He was assured that the shooks supplied by B. Compton Limited were a superior product and would again be ordered, and he guaranteed delivery direct to the creameries.[56] At the end of 1936 there was said to be more business for the mill than could comfortably be handled, with several "good orders" being redirected to other mills. In 1938 Hector reported more logs coming into the mill than ever before, eighteen hired men in the summer season, and, again, more orders than they could handle. A brief closure in November was perhaps a strategy for labour discipline on the part of the pragmatic Hector as well as a difficulty over management: "The shake up did a lot of good by getting as foreman the one who should have been there since a long time [Hector's brother Jack], and the men have a new viewpoint as to production."[57]

By 1935 a generator installed in the machine shop provided electricity for the operation of the shop and mill and other company businesses on the Hill as well as for its families' houses. Two years later, following "active petitioning" by the company, Maritime Electric Limited was evidently persuaded to run a branch line to the Hill from a power line extended earlier from Charlottetown to nearby Wood Islands. Its innovations and lobbying meant that B. Compton Limited had access to electrical power for its businesses and for its Belle River members' homes more than a decade before rural electrification became official provincial policy. Indeed, in 1941 only 27 per cent of Island homes had electrical service.[58] As for the general store, it began operating out of a new building in 1937. Hector presided over the company's business affairs from his new upstairs corner office in the building. From his office window, he wrote, he could survey the mill and other work sites while being "more out of the way of casual callers who only want to waste time chatting," although, he went on to add, "there were three Comm.[ercial] Travellers up here since this letter was started."[59]

What is striking from the records available on the business life of B. Compton Limited is the degree to which it was operating in an economy in which interventions from outside the province, whether in the form of competition, unionization, or state regulation, were still minimal. Striking, too, is Hector's patriarchal approach to his role as head of a strong business/family endeavour rooted in that economy. Fair dealing and generosity were unquestionably important in his value system, but these qualities were expressed in a spirit of *noblesse oblige* that arguably had more in common with the outlook of a nineteenth-century small businessman than with conventional notions of utopian relationships. A hard worker himself, he could be a demanding employer even with company members, and he expected gratitude and compliance in return for assistance given to neighbourhood employees and their families, as was strikingly evident in his hard dealings with the widow of the worker killed in the mill accident in 1925.[60] But if stressful circumstances such as these brought out a certain mean-spiritedness, the obverse was a readiness to respond generously (perhaps even naively) to would-be employees who expressed a cooperative attitude and a willingness to work hard for whatever they received.[61]

By the mid-1930s, B. Compton Limited was said to be supporting about one hundred members, though the journalist who reported this figure did not clearly indicate that it included the settlement in Bangor as well as Belle River.[62] Some members, of course, were too young to be full working contributors, though as soon as they were able, they were expected to do their part by taking on chores appropriate to their age and gender, as was the norm in the province. The contributions of women in the Compton community were mostly made within their homes. To an even greater extent than was common in Island families, what community women did as homemakers was vitally important for the image the community sought to project of immaculate, well-run households. As seen, some young, typically unmarried, community women had also worked seasonally in the company lobster cannery, where they generally received a small payment in cash or in kind. Nineteen-year-old Louisa Jardine of Bangor, for instance, had been paid in cash and corsets for her labour in the spring and summer of 1912.[63] But there could be inequities in regard to reimbursement for women's labour. A fascinating acknowledgment of one such inequity had occurred in April 1923 when Hector had made an addendum to an earlier list of adult male community members so as to include the names of two community women. The names were added, he explained, "by approval of six members" and "so as to correctly represent the labors of these women not otherwise paid for services accorded equally with male members from the founding of [the] company to the present." Whether Hector's statement meant that they were to be paid in future for their work is unclear; perhaps it was simply being recognized. Nor can it be assumed from this incident that women's place in the community figured importantly in male members' considerations. Indeed, women's roles seem largely to have been taken for granted.[64]

As well as surviving the Depression and keeping its own adult members employed, B. Compton Limited was, as shown, an important source of local employment for outside paid labourers. Looking back in 1948 a few months after the company had officially been wound up, Hector was proud to recall that the company had been able not only to lift its own members out of "abject poverty" but also to become "an acknowledged benefit to the country around us through the operation of Mills, Cannery and vessels."[65] In a context in which there were few opportunities to find paid work and in which leaving for the Boston states had ceased to be a viable option – during the Depression, out-of-work young people were instead returning to the family farm for shelter and subsistence[66] – the company's contribution to the neighbourhood economy was not insignificant. M., a non-member kinsman, would not have been unusual in being grateful to get his mill job back after having been let go, in his case for another of his bouts of periodic drinking.[67]

Like M., most workers were local men. Yet remarkably, in a province characterized by extreme ethnic homogeneity and where the vast majority of residents had origins in the British Isles, a small number of Danish sojourners also became part of the community's labour force. Danish immigration to Canada had increased substantially during the 1920s, rising to 3,835 in 1927/8 and then decreasing to under 1,000 as the Depression took hold. New Denmark, in New Brunswick, was the oldest Danish settlement in Canada. Its existence may have been a factor in bringing more Danes to the Maritime region than would otherwise have been the case. Near the end of the 1920s, a small number of Danish farm labourers had found work on PEI as a result of arrangements orchestrated by the Canadian National Railway and the Ministry of Agriculture. But they were evidently not free to leave the province to seek work elsewhere if they disliked their initial job placement. This may have been the pool from which the Compton community's Danish workers came during the 1930s, and, given Denmark's own experience with cooperative organizations, they would not have found its communal set-up entirely alien. Though some of these workers eventually returned to Denmark or moved on to Ontario, several others remained on the Island and continued to be connected to the Compton community.[68]

From Hector's perspective, providing hard-up people with the chance to earn an income was the best form of social assistance. During the Depression, however, the Compton community also practised small-scale ad hoc philanthropy. Over the years, as a community it had generously supported such civic and charitable causes as the Protestant Prince Edward Island Hospital and a much-needed sanatorium (tuberculosis was "the number one killer of Islanders").[69] In a province whose citizens were notoriously tax averse, governments had always been happy to leave the financing of hospitals, sanatoria, and orphanages largely or wholly to private religious or secular efforts. In 1929, for instance, the premier had singled out the wonderfully civic-minded Women's Institute (WI) for praise in the provincial legislature, observing that, because of its efforts in promoting charitable giving, the government didn't much need to trouble itself about financing such institutions.[70] Unfortunately, this small-government mentality persisted even when the Depression brought an unprecedented level of economic challenges to the island province, especially to people already living at or near the margins. As the Depression began, there was still little in the way of state relief from any level of government. Direct relief payments from the provincial government were set at such low levels that even families who qualified to receive them remained in hardship, and in 1937 Premier Thane Campbell's Liberal government threatened to discontinue even this aid.[71] In this context it fell to religious organizations such as the Sisters of St. Martha, founded on the Island in 1916, and to comparatively prosperous groups such as the Compton community, to try, in however small a way, to address individual and family needs.[72]

The help provided by the Compton community to non-members took a variety of forms, but it seems most often to have been in-kind assistance. One of Hector's sons remembered that meals were provided to indigent individuals who showed up at his family's door; it is the kind of unremarkable Depression-era anecdote familiar to students of Canadian history. He also remembered – and this would have been more important for local families' self-respect – that the company agreed to accept logs for the mill, perhaps as payment for groceries, even when it had more on hand than it could process.[73] Hector's correspondence provides further instances of the types of help given: to kin facing hardship in 1935 who were not community members but considered to be deserving, new clothing sent direct from a Charlottetown store for one family; and, for another, a cheque to help cover a bank note, since the people involved seemed "square and honest." In 1938, another letter mentions providing a casket "gratis" to a widow whose husband had just died and who was so poor that her home was to be closed up and her seven children "distributed."[74] These examples bear out the observations of scholars Enid Charles and Sylvia Anthony, who came to know about the Compton community in the course of their close-grained comparative study of Belle River and another Island settlement: beyond its own members, they wrote, the utopian community's "ideals of social obligation" extended "first to relatives who have not accepted the group *mores*, and secondly to all neighbours." Overall, they believed, its social ideals "more than come up to standard."[75]

In the last part of the 1930s, a new and inventive form of help for the working poor was introduced on Prince Edward Island. A cooperative movement modelled on the Antigonish Movement at St. Francis

Xavier University undertook efforts to assist impoverished Island farmers and fishers, not through acts of charity but through strategies of
self-help. The Island movement initiated cooperative purchasing, pro-
cessing, and marketing schemes and the establishment of credit unions
and adult education. Led by an American-born educator, J.T. Croteau,
it introduced the principles and methods of cooperative self-help at the
local and provincial level and supplemented its outreach through radio
broadcasts. Like the Antigonish Movement, the Island cooperative
movement attracted international attention, albeit on a smaller scale.[76]
    It might have been expected that, at least in its broad aims, the
movement would have been considered a worthwhile endeavour by
a utopian group such as B. Compton Limited as a means of combat-
ing the Depression. Yet no mention of it can be found in Hector's surviving correspondence. It is hardly likely that Hector harboured the
view held by some Islanders that the cooperative movement was the
work of Communists. And, given its coverage in Island media, he can
hardly have failed to be aware of it. Most likely the absence of reference to it, much less friendly commendation, reflected the fact that,
like the Antigonish Movement, the Island cooperative movement was
led by Catholic social activists. In a province where Catholics and Protestants still lived in many ways as two solitudes, social assistance in
whatever form it took reflected that reality. Hospitals, orphanages,
homes for the indigent elderly, assistance to impoverished families –
these were all organized on religiously distinct lines. This did not mean
that Catholics in the Island cooperative movement shunned Protestant
involvement, or that the Compton community refused to help individual Catholic families in need. But the two entities were located in a
province where religion, and religious differences, still mattered a great
deal, so that in practice their constituencies usually remained distinct.[77]

In a 1935 article on B. Compton Limited, a Charlottetown journalist referred to the company as "Prince Edward Island's unique 'brotherly love' community."[78] Unique on the Island it may have been, but
B. Compton Limited was nevertheless a utopian community whose
people had deep roots and extensive kin ties in the province. In this
respect it stands as a contrast to many utopian communities in nineteenth-century America and to the hippie communes of the late 1960s
and early 1970s, whose founders, arriving from elsewhere and living
unconventionally, aroused curiosity and sometimes hostility. As this
chapter has shown, the Compton community's several businesses and

its sense of social obligation necessarily involved it in interaction with the larger Island society. Indeed, Charles and Anthony, the two visiting scholars mentioned earlier, observed that "their leader [Hector] is also regarded as a leader in the Belle River neighbourhood and is consulted on all points of communal action." The two would have heard, for instance, about Hector's involvement in the late 1930s on a matter of considerable local concern: the question of establishing a car ferry service from nearby Wood Islands to eastern Nova Scotia. At the same time, neighbours were aware, as were Charles and Anthony, that in terms of other types of social interactions, the community tended to keep itself to itself.[79] What tensions arose from the Compton community's attempt to exist as both a public and a private entity, and to what extent was its private life and apartness *imposed* by the community's leaders? Histories of communal utopias directed by powerful and charismatic individuals such as Oneida Community founder John Humphrey Noyes provide us with some insight into such questions.[80] Yet the challenge of maintaining a utopian community's integrity and enforcing its boundaries was obviously different and in some respects more difficult when it was as rooted in place as the Compton community. What sacrifices of members' individuality and personal freedoms were required for the community to function organically, and how much of its interior life was known to the outside world? The first part of Chapter 5 considers aspects of the Compton community's life that were at least somewhat private and, in some cases, deeply problematic. The second part turns to public perceptions of its communal and entrepreneurial life that brought the community favourable international attention in the context of the Depression.

5

Living in Community:
Family, Faith, and Fame

People living in Belle River and nearby settlements would have been aware of the economic enterprises of B. Compton Limited and often affected by them. They could work in and sell lumber to the company mill, get equipment repaired at the company machine shop, buy tea, boots, tobacco, and other basic items from its general store. In times of emergency they could use the telephone in the store or borrow a company vehicle if they did not have these things themselves.[1] There would have been less chance for them to have a close knowledge of the inner life of the community. Still, some aspects of that life would have been both public and private. Bereavements, for instance. The deaths themselves would have been known and, as shown in the *Charlottetown Guardian*'s account of the death of founder Ben Compton, cited earlier, sometimes publicly and respectfully acknowledged. But what such losses meant within the group as sources of grief or disruption, or perhaps relief, would have been less clear to outsiders, especially if funerals were conducted, as seems often to have been the case, mainly as private, intra-community events.[2] Secretary-treasurer Hector D. Compton's surviving correspondence shows a strong, albeit highly selective, preoccupation with community bereavements. It comes across as a preoccupation arising not so much out of grief over family tragedies as a concern for the stability and future of the community. Though it might seem more obviously a way to conclude, I have chosen to begin this chapter with a focus on the theme of bereavement, since it speaks to the reality that long-surviving utopian communities like this one needed to be pragmatic rather than sentimental and "utopian."

Losses

Writing in 1944 to a US-based cousin about various deaths in the years since founder Ben's fatal mill accident more than twenty years earlier, Hector noted that there had been "about forty deaths, mostly ahead of time."[3] The figure seems high and perhaps included kin who were not part of the company. In any case, the bereavements that occasioned the most comment from Hector were not those that seem the most tragic or moving from a twenty-first-century perspective but rather those of men – almost always men – who had been important in community labour or leadership roles and whose deaths created gaps that were difficult to fill.

The death by suicide in February 1932 of a younger, Chicago-born cousin of Hector's, George Emerson Compton, a Great War veteran, was not one of these. George Emerson, wounded near Lens, France, in 1917, shot himself in the company barn in Belle River after a period of heavy drinking and a failed attempt to get either medical help at the veterans' hospital in Halifax or a pension increase to compensate for his inability to work. The inquest that followed reported his earlier, poignant remark that all war-damaged vets like himself should be gathered in a field and gassed. It also recounted instances of other behaviours, some of them predating the war, that pointed to periodic bouts of mental instability.[4] With the exception of two brief letters to pension officials, I have found no evidence that Hector wrote about this tragic event, even though George was his brother-in-law as well as his cousin – their wives were sisters – and had ultimately succumbed to his self-inflicted wound in Hector's house after being moved there from the barn. The troubled veteran was not a significant figure in the company's work force, much less in its decision-making structure. He had lived variously in Bangor and Brooklyn, Prince Edward Island, and Boston before signing up as a married man, lived again in Brooklyn and Boston after the war, and then, in his last months, in Bangor and Belle River. As well as being an ineffective economic contributor to the community, he would have incurred Hector's disapproval by choosing to end his own life – the kind of act that Hector generalized about later that year as the product of "weaker minds" – and thereby bringing unwelcome attention to the community.[5]

By contrast with his apparent near-silence about this most poignant of deaths, Hector wrote to several correspondents in 1936 and later about three losses that, from his perspective, made that particular year an *annus horribilis* for his community. In November his brother Oliver disappeared, apparently washed overboard when the company's forty-ton schooner *Hatavan*, which he was piloting, ran aground on a sandbar off Nova Scotia en route back to PEI with a load of coal.[6] Although the *Hatavan* sustained minimal damage and was pulled free of the sandbar the next day, a decision was quickly made to sell the vessel "to have it off our minds." Less than two months earlier, two other active "partners" (Hector's term) had died of pneumonia.[7] Hector was especially hard hit by the second of these losses: the death of Will Jardine. Will was both his cousin and brother-in-law and the mild-mannered and able work companion of his younger days. As unmarried men, "Heck and Will" had worked out as a team of carpenters for several summers before the needs of the community absorbed them fully.[8] In the 1930s Will ran the machine shop and, thanks to his self-taught mechanical ability, was invaluable at keeping the company's machinery in working order. In the 1944 letter to his US cousin mentioned above, Hector was still remarking on the loss of the man he called his teammate: "He could not be replaced."[9] By contrast, the accidental drowning of Will's teenage daughter just months after his death was not recalled in this epistolary retrospective of family losses, even though it was the subject of a *Guardian* news story.[10] Quite simply, in terms of the company's productivity and stability, young Mary's death mattered less.

"Delusive Alcohol"

Although it seems not to have figured in Will's death, excessive alcohol consumption was a factor in a number of other losses and a fact of life among some male members of the Compton community as well as among its hired workers. Periodic overindulgence had been reported among some men in the Compton line dating back to the nineteenth century. Was it an inherited trait, as some family members believed?[11] One expert suggests that "genetics appears to play a role in about half the total risk for being alcohol addicted," but acknowledges the complexity of the question.[12] In any case, one does not need a genetic legacy to explain community men's drinking; getting drunk was very much a part of the province's contemporary masculine culture, despite, or perhaps partly because of, the long-lasting prohibition regime on Prince Edward Island. In 1900 it had become the first province to enact a prohibition statute. And it remained prohibition's "last outpost," enacting new liquor legislation only in 1948. Acquiring liquor remained easy under prohibition, whether direct from a bootlegger or through a note from a doctor, or by purchasing alcohol-laced cooking extracts at a general store or bringing drink in from outside the province. From the 1920s, rum runners brought large quantities of liquor to the province, anchoring offshore outside the three-mile limit, where they transferred their cargo to fishermen willing to supplement their meagre incomes by smuggling the liquor ashore. A popular book-length account of the illicit trade suggests that it was viewed with amused tolerance rather than disapproval by many Islanders.[13]

It is unlikely that the Compton community men who manned the *Hatavan* participated in commercial-scale rum running. But business trips to the Mainland made it a simple matter for them to acquire gin, wine, and especially rum for private consumption. This probably explains Hector's concern after hearing about a planned visit to the schooner by the RCMP in 1932.[14] Although the mature Hector did not absolutely abstain from alcohol use, he was temperate in this and other habits and lamented the transgressions in speech and conduct that resulted from excessive alcohol consumption among some of the men in the Compton community. Writing in 1933 following a meeting in Charlottetown at which he had shared some wine with "Big John" Compton, the cousin who was then the Compton community's Bangor head and, at the time, newly returned from a business trip to Nova Scotia, Hector was glad to report that their meeting had not been marred by intoxication. In the curious phrasing that sometimes characterized his writing, he declared, "[I]t was one of the times when I did not feel like allowing any liquor discount off the value of our communication. Sometimes that discount has been so large that the value of an intercourse had almost to be thrown away."[15]

The episodes of intoxication within the community that so disturbed Hector in the interwar years are best understood as a continuation of a pattern that had existed in the extended family for decades, or as manifestations of the larger Island culture of masculinity and drink, rather than as peculiar to their communitarian religious beliefs. Clearly, the Compton community did not forbid alcohol consumption, as did some utopian communities, most famously the millenarian Mormons but also much smaller and more ephemeral groups such as the Finnish socialists at Sointula, British Columbia.[16] But neither did they make it an intrinsic part of their worship services, as numerous non-Christian and Christian groups have done over time with alcohol or other drugs, most characteristically, of course, in the case of Christians, with the use of wine in communion services. And yet, there does seem to have been a link of a sort between patterns of drinking and religious observances within the Compton community, particularly among some of its leaders. Writing in 1964 in a one-page note on "Compton Genealogy" and evidently in response to a relative's inquiry, Hector observed that the general character of their ancestors had included a deep reverence for "the True Spirit," but that "oft when it seemed to abate, they tried to substitute it with delusive alcohol."[17] A brief outline of the community's religious practices as gleaned from Hector's writing and from the memories of now elderly family members provides some basis for understanding a felt need for alcohol as an aid to spiritual performance.

A Faith Apart

The small group of Comptons who found themselves outside the McDonaldite fold because of theological differences from the early 1890s onward probably worshipped on their own even before the formation of the Compton community in 1909. As a separated remnant of the McDonaldite movement, they were effectively cut off from the society and practices of the vibrant faith group that had been their spiritual home for half a century. Lacking ordained clergy or even ministering elders, they had no leader to conduct marriage ceremonies or funerals or to perform the sacraments of baptism and communion. Their marriages were properly solemnized by a clergyman, but they conducted their own funerals and their children went unbaptized. As for the lengthy Sabbath communion services and the preparatory meetings that had preceded them – the most significant events in the nineteenth-century McDonaldites' calendar year – Compton community members were deprived not only of that religious rite but also of the opportunity it provided for visits and fellowship with fellow believers, some of whom would have travelled long distances to attend the services.[18]

They were, of course, by no means unique as Christians in being without clerical leadership and the sacrament of communion as it developed over time in the Christian tradition. The early Christian church had itself been an informal community of believers without established leaders. As one recent scholar/reviewer reminded his readers, even the Catholic Mass "originated in a leaderless communal meal taken by the earliest followers of the Jewish Messiah, Jesus."[19] Long after the Compton community had ended, Hector would still seek to make a virtue out of its distinctive religious practices and the absence of an institutionalized church life by observing that, like the early Christians, his people had turned exclusively to the Bible and to their own resources for inspiration.[20] Much closer in time than the early Christian church as usable precedents for the Compton community's way of worship were groups such as the Quakers, Mennonites, and Amish, who had come from England and Europe to North America and who had made the rejection of professionally trained spiritual leaders and of particular rituals associated with mainstream Christianity a defining part of their religious identity.

Groups such as these were not, however, part of Prince Edward Island's denominational landscape and thus not available as a source for useful comparisons at a time when religion was still central to Islanders' individual and family identity, and to respectability. PEI's religious landscape was dominated at the turn of the twentieth century by just a few Protestant denominations – the numerically dominant Presbyterians and smaller numbers of Methodists, Baptists, and Anglicans – and by Irish, Scottish, and French Catholics. All of these groups practised such faith rites as baptism and communion, and they worshipped in church buildings whose design, whether simple or elaborate, added to the beauty of the Island countryside as well as to the pride of congregants.[21]

Compton community religious services, by contrast, typically took place in the largest of the homes in Belle River and Bangor. As with their McDonaldite forebears, women and men sat apart. Services featured the reading of scripture, usually by one of the leading men, and the singing of psalms and McDonaldite hymns. As noted, dozens of the latter had been written by McDonald and his elders, many of them dealing with millennial themes. Often they continued through multiple stanzas, contrasting the darkness and gloom of the present world with the promised glory awaiting the redeemed. As to whether there were actual sermons, memories about this among the few descendants still old enough to recall the community in its last years are divided. Writing in the 1960s, Hector described Big John Compton as, before his stroke-induced decline in the 1940s, "a teacher of doctrine and behaviour," not only in Bangor, where he lived, but also in Belle River during his visits there.[22] There were certainly precedents for lay preaching in the McDonaldite tradition. In his biography of McDonald, Murdock Lamont wrote that during the minister's lifetime his elders had been "debared [sic] from preaching" but that, in the course of leading in prayer, some of them had rendered their prayers "objectionably long and sermon-like" in an effort to work in words of "warning and instruction" to the congregants.[23] In the post-McDonald era, as seen earlier, ministering elders in some McDonaldite congregations were authorized to preach and to perform the sacraments of baptism and communion in the absence of duly qualified and acceptable clergy. It seems probable that, reminiscent of those earlier practices, a few of the senior men who read the Bible aloud during the Sunday evening meetings of Compton community members might have followed Big John's example and added some interpretive commentary or injunctions, especially if they had arrived primed with alcohol to give them courage for their leadership task.

What seems not to have been carried over from the larger McDonaldite tradition to these in-home Compton community services was the tendency of some of McDonald's followers to display the extravagant physical manifestations of religious transport that had made them an object of mockery among more orthodox Island Christians and a challenge, as noted, to professionally trained clergy like the young George Monro Grant. It was not that this performative aspect of McDonaldite tradition had died out altogether. Indeed, it still occurred in the early twentieth century in the larger McDonaldite remnant on the Island and in its Boston-area offshoot. But in family memory, "taking the works" came to be recalled as something that Compton community members regarded with disdain, a kind of religious showing off.

Had Ben actively discouraged the practice of "taking the works" in his role as company founder and leader? Or did members themselves recognize that such behaviour was simply too over the top to be indulged in, in the context of the gathering for Sunday worship of a few kin in a family parlour or kitchen? And had Ben needed alcohol to give himself the confidence to lead the community's worship services? Regrettably, there are only brief references in Hector's correspondence to provide clues to the nature of Ben's faith, beyond the fact of its ardent millenarianism, or insights into the style of his religious leadership.[24] As for Ben's Bangor-based nephew Dan, who served as company president for just two years before his untimely death in 1923, he was remembered fondly within and beyond the Compton community for his leadership abilities and for un-showy practical Christianity rather than religiosity.[25] Big John, Dan's younger brother and his successor in Bangor, emerges from the paper trail and from relatives' memories as an erratic leader, something of a loose cannon, especially in later years when his drinking became a problem. Nevertheless, Hector wrote respectfully of John's spirituality and was inclined to make allowances for instances of unpredictable and unbecoming behaviour, mindful that he was often "under stress." Hector would continue to defend John's memory even in later years when some younger members of the former community recalled with resentment his flaws as a spiritual mentor. There is, unfortunately, no surviving record from John's own pen to provide evidence of the religious leadership qualities that Hector claimed for him. They perhaps included such quixotic initiatives as their shared action in the 1930s in sending national Conservative leader R.B. Bennett a copy of one of the Reverend Donald McDonald's books, *The Subjects of the Millennium*.[26]

Although he was officially just the secretary-treasurer of B. Compton Limited, and John "the recognized spiritual leader" after the deaths of Ben and Dan Compton,[27] it is clear that Hector bore a great sense of personal responsibility for the community's religious welfare as well as for its business enterprises. Although he had been born more than a decade after the Reverend Donald McDonald's death, he undoubtedly had more familiarity with McDonald's religious views than any other community member, having at one time, he said, owned all of his books. He felt a powerful attachment to the late minister's teachings, taking issue only with what he understood to be McDonald's full-throated support for the Calvinist doctrine of salvation only for the elect.[28] While Hector could not help but be aware of his group's anomalous religious status on Prince Edward Island, his contention was that his people's separation from institutionalized observances was a higher and purer form of faithfulness to Bible-based Christianity and to the millenarian teachings of McDonald than that carried forward in any church, including the still existing McDonaldite churches. As for remembered taunts directed against children like himself who had not been baptized, taunts that perhaps came from relatives who were part of the still churchgoing McDonaldite remnant, Hector approvingly recalled an elderly aunt's response that such children were perhaps being saved for something higher than mere water baptism.[29]

More distressing for Hector than any sense that his community's religious practices were regarded by outsiders with disdain was his concern that such practices might be falling into desuetude. Writing to distant kin in old age about the baptism issue and other aspects of the former community's religious practices, he reminisced that their worship services, held "on Sundays or oftener," were frequently reverent and moving. Yet while weekly home-based religious gatherings may have been the norm in the years when his people were first separated from their former McDonaldite congregations, that seems not to have been unfailingly the case in the 1930s. Writing in 1933 to Big John, then away on business on their schooner *Hatavan*, Hector spoke of the challenge of bringing community members together for a religious service on a recent Sunday evening in Belle River and the difficulty of moving them beyond "the usual ordinary talk." It took "a daring effort," he wrote, to steer them towards spiritual matters. But music served as the vehicle:

[T]he old Hymns are still the great medium they were intended to be to elevate the minds and to help them to even [ever?] look "towards Jerusalem." Their language has not yet been paralleled in any modern writing. The chapter opened was the first of Lamentations. It was sweet because we can feel its conditions fulfilled upon the people and the fulfillment of its desolations also implies the assurance of restoration more abundant, because it is the Father's pleasure to bless rather than to chastise.[30]

Even in old age, Hector would continue to love and find comfort in the McDonaldite hymns. But what was crucial for him on that Sunday evening when the group eventually came together was that the hymns functioned as a segue into an attentive response to Bible reading and a focus on millennial themes. Decades later, some of his younger relatives whose memories reached back to the last years of home-based worship would have good memories of the Sunday evening music even if they remembered little else about the services – or remembered them with a shudder. One relative, writing to his Uncle Hector in 1962 as an expatriate, recalled the Sunday gatherings with fondness even as he made it clear that the particulars of Hector's religious views had not been his: "Sometimes as I drive among the hills and lakes of Maine, my mind flashes back to the days when we worked together at Belle River, when on Sunday evenings while Aunt Bessie [Hector's wife] played the organ, we sang the Psalms and the Hymn tunes. I remember the respectful way you read the Bible, and the feeling of unity and strength which was shared." It was a letter that Hector cherished, for it provided a rarely stated positive reminiscence about the community's mode of worship. In a note he added at the bottom of the letter, Hector wrote that the fact that its author "did not quite see eye-to-eye with me ... only enhances his kind testimony."[31]

What *were* the particulars of Hector's religious beliefs? Although he wrote a great deal about religion both during and after the community years, his statements of belief are difficult to parse. Rejection of the harsh Calvinist doctrine of election seems to have been an ongoing theme, with an accompanying emphasis on "Universal Salvation" by a loving and endlessly forgiving rather than a harsh and vengeful God.[32] And yet Hector's loving God seemed to have a special blessing in mind for the Anglo-Saxon peoples, who were presumed by British-Israelite aficionados like himself to be the true descendants of the ten lost tribes of ancient Israel.[33] Moreover, there was a suggestion – though it was conveyed infrequently and indirectly, rather than explicitly, in his writings – that his very own people and community might have a special part to play in the Second Coming.[34] While it may be tempting to dismiss Hector's strand of millenarian thinking as the outdated and eccentric theology of a self-taught and isolated rural believer, it is important not to do so, for the twentieth century provided many instances of diverse and eccentric millenarian thinkers.[35] Indeed, after the Second World War, as historian Paul Boyer observes, "popular interest in Biblical prophecy burgeoned under the impetus of the atomic bomb, the founding of Israel, and other factors."[36] As a result of such influences, Hector's interest in prophetic matters would likewise flourish, especially during his long retirement years when there were no longer Compton community business affairs to preoccupy him. His writing in retirement and during the community era gives us little reason to believe that ordinary community members were as preoccupied as he with spiritual matters. Nevertheless, the community's Sunday observances seem to have survived more or less intact into the early 1940s.

Congested Blood

If the Compton community's private religious observances were anomalous in early twentieth-century Prince Edward Island, so also were its marital practices. Cousin intermarriage was so common that the term "cousinage" seems altogether apt.[37] Degrees of consanguinity between marital partners, sometimes close degrees, had, of course, been a fact of life in many cultures at least from biblical times: sanctioned, for instance, for purposes of state continuity or purity of lineage, most famously among the pharaohs and, later, the Hapsburgs and British monarchs; or for purposes of social and entrepreneurial cohesion, as among industrializing England's rising bourgeoisie.[38] In New World colonies, intermarriage was practised frequently for lack of other options in isolated or thinly populated communities. Close blood relationships, including incestuous relationships, were sometimes outcomes of illicit sexual encounters, including those in such malign circumstances as the sexual exploitation of enslaved women.[39]

Given its tiny population and isolation, and cultural values that prioritized marrying someone with whom one shared ethnicity, denominational identity, and social standing, nineteenth-century Prince Edward Island perhaps had more than its share of marriages among kin. Before she became a celebrated novelist, Lucy Maud Montgomery (1874–1942), for instance, was briefly engaged to her cousin Ed Simpson, both of whose parents were Simpsons and whose Scots Presbyterian ancestors had, like Maud's, settled in the Cavendish area more than a century earlier. Born more than a generation later than Maud, Conservative MP and Island premier Angus MacLean (1914–2000) was the son of cousins whose shared Highland background and McDonaldite/Presbyterian identity made them suitable life partners for each other, albeit socially "lesser" in the eyes of Islanders like Maud's people, who were proudly conscious of their superior Lowland Scots background.[40]

As for the Island descendants of William Compton and Mary Vaughan Compton, the first generation necessarily had to marry out. As shown in Chapter 2, there was frequent intermarriage with nearby Scots and other immigrants as they settled in Prince Edward Island. Henry, one of the sons of William and Mary, went back to his native New Brunswick after the death of his first wife, returning to PEI a few years later with a new partner, a widow with Loyalist links. However, Henry's son and namesake illustrated a different pattern by marrying his first cousin in 1869. Common surnames of brides and grooms, as in this case, bear testimony to an increase in cousin marriage from this time onward (though it was not unknown before that). The practice appears to have become more common after the splits among McDonaldites following the Reverend Donald McDonald's death in 1867. Marriages among Comptons, and with other kin bearing different surnames (chiefly Bears, Grants, Humes, Martins, Munns, and Sanders), would have been a logical outcome of the felt need to unite with a partner within the same faith community, particularly in the Brooklyn and Belle River congregations. The practice intensified and the marriage pool shrank from the 1890s for those Comptons who became part of the most isolated fragment of McDonald's disciples following the theological disputes of that decade. Having been driven from their former congregations and effectively become an unchurched people, they were likely undesirable partners on the local marriage market. Finally, with the formation of the utopian Compton community in 1909, there was a powerful new incentive for intermarrying.

Historically, utopian communities have had particular, if varied, motives for forming endogamous relationships and varied strategies for maintaining them. American Quakers, for instance, sought to prevent declension in the mid-eighteenth century by forbidding marriages to non-Quakers and participation in non-Quaker marriage ceremonies ("marrying out of meeting"). Old Order Amish in the American Midwest retained their opposition to exogamy for religious reasons even in the late twentieth century.[41] Historically, too, many utopian communities, whether only marginally Christian, like the Transcendentalists of Brook Farm, or, as was more typical, excessively religious in character, became targets of societal disapproval for defying traditional gender roles and for engaging in sexual, marital,

1 This marker, erected in Brooklyn, PEI, in 2006 by descendants of William Compton and Mary Vaughan Compton, attributes the family's move from Cape Breton to PEI to their desire to follow the Reverend Donald McDonald, who had relocated to the smaller island in 1826. Author's photo.

2 Emily Compton Martin, born in St. Martins, NB, in 1817, a daughter of William Compton and Mary Vaughan Compton, married on PEI in 1836, becoming part of an early family pattern of intermarrying with Scottish settlers in the colony. The Martins were among some eight hundred Scottish settlers brought to the Island by Thomas Douglas, Fifth Earl of Selkirk. The spinning wheel is said to have come from Scotland aboard the *Polly*, one of the three ships that carried the Selkirk settlers. Photo courtesy of Robert Martin.

3 John Henry Compton and Flora Grace Munn Compton and children outside their Illinois home in 1889. This sojourning family would return impoverished to PEI in 1894, where their eldest son, Hector, shown here at left, would eventually become the secretary-treasurer of B. Compton Limited. Hector D. Compton Family Collection.

4 Studio photograph of John Henry and Flora Grace in old age,
probably taken in Charlottetown. Hector D. Compton
Family Collection.

5 This church, built in Bangor, PEI, by McDonaldites in 1893, more than a quarter-century after the Reverend Donald McDonald's death, reflects the ongoing influence of the sectarian religious movement that began under his leadership.
Photo courtesy of Mark MacLaren.

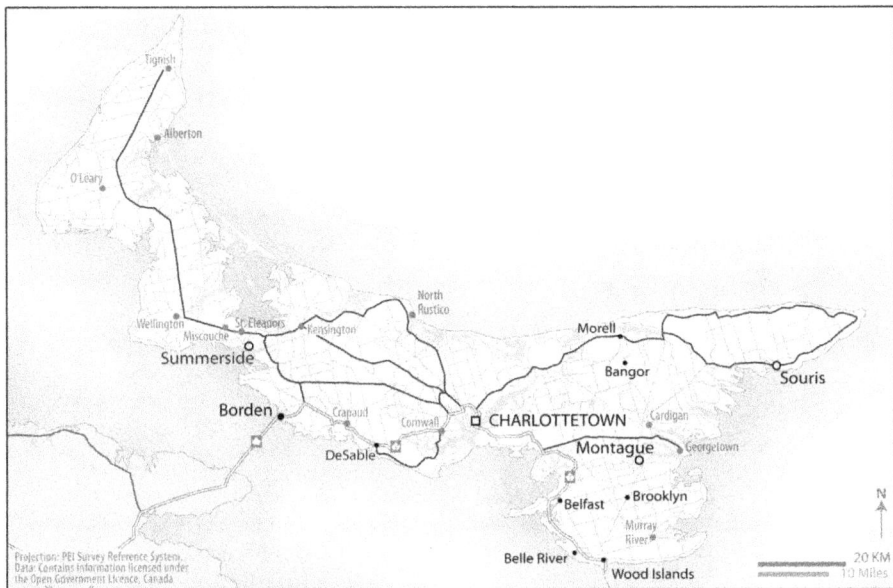

6 Map of PEI showing settlements of various sizes, including Bangor and Belle River, where families belonging to B. Compton Limited lived. Map courtesy of Will Flanagan, Department of Geography, Saint Mary's University.

7 Entrance to Belle River, PEI, about 1910, showing fishing vessels belonging to Compton men who became part of B. Compton Limited. This image, probably a postcard, was found in Hector D. Compton Family Collection.

8 Delivery of logs to rear entrance of sawmill, Belle River. The mill produced a wide variety of products and became the most important source of income for B. Compton Limited. During the Depression, local farmers sometimes brought in more logs than the company could process, in exchange for cash or goods from the company store. Hector D. Compton Family Collection.

9 Undated photo of Captain Oliver Compton (right) and Wallace Jardine aboard the *Hatavan*. When the vessel ran aground in 1936 while returning from Nova Scotia, Oliver disappeared and was assumed to have fallen overboard. Hector D. Compton Family Collection.

10 The B. Compton Limited company store in Belle River. A new store replaced this building in the 1930s. Hector's oldest son stands in the foreground. Hector D. Compton Family Collection.

11 Some Compton community members in Belle River joined by visiting relatives from Bangor, probably late 1930s. Hector D. Compton Family Collection.

12 Group photo, probably taken at the home of "Big John" Compton in Bangor about 1940. "Big John" is at left; Hector is third from left. Their community leadership status is signified by the fact that, like the visiting US relative standing between them, they are more formally dressed than others in the photo.
Hector D. Compton Family Collection.

13 Two Marys: Like numerous other Islanders, some members of the Compton community moved to the "Boston States" as sojourners or permanent exiles. Mary Jardine from Bangor (b. 1882), shown here in white blouse, returned to the Island, later marrying Bangor community leader Daniel Compton. Mary Compton (b. 1902), also of Bangor, fled from the home of her imperious father, George, in the early 1920s. She remained in the US, marrying fellow Islander William Gerrard. Photos courtesy of Isabel Dingwell (Mary Jardine) and Keith Gerrard (Mary Compton Gerrard).

14 Sara Elizabeth – "Libby" – Compton (1883–1986), the much younger wife of B. Compton Limited founder Ben Compton, was born in Brandon, Manitoba, during her parents' sojourning years. Interviewed in old age, she reminisced readily about topics as different as the second Riel uprising and her informal medical work in the Belle River area. But when it came to questions about her late husband, she largely evaded her interviewer's questions. Photo by Lionel Stevenson, probably taken in 1985 for *Elders of the Island*, reproduced by permission of Terry Stevenson, Camera Art, Charlottetown.

15 Hector D. Compton (1879–1970), studio photograph taken some months after his eightieth birthday. He sent copies to a wide range of his non-Island correspondents as well as to his own family. Hector D. Compton Family Collection.

and family practices that departed from generally held norms.[42] The best-known such example in nineteenth-century North America was the Church of Jesus Christ of Latter-Day Saints, the Mormons, whose prophet, Joseph Smith, drew on the marital examples of the Hebrew patriarchs and erected "an elaborate theological edifice" in the 1840s to institute the practice of polygamy. (The Mormons' own term was plural marriage.) Under Smith's successor, Brigham Young, the practice flourished (he personally fathered fifty-seven children), and brides' ages became younger to facilitate the birth of more children. Mormons officially abandoned polygamous practice in 1890 in the face of anti-polygamy legislation.[43]

More useful than the Mormons' history for comparing the communitarian Comptons with other religiously based utopian practitioners of atypical marriage arrangements is the nineteenth-century Oneida Community founded by John Humphrey Noyes. Trained in Congregationalist ministry at Yale, Noyes was banned from its premises after he began preaching Perfectionism and his own sinlessness. In 1848 he relocated his community to Oneida, New York, from Putney, Vermont, in the face of legal threats and societal outrage about his community's unconventional sexual practices. Drawing on his idiosyncratic interpretation of holy scripture, Noyes instituted what he called "Complex Marriage," and, briefly, in later years, "Stirpiculture." Scholar Louis Kern explains complex marriage at Oneida as an "arrangement whereby all the members of the community were considered united by marriage ties." Notwithstanding the use of the term "free love" in her book *Oneida: From Free Love Utopia to the Well-Set Table*, Ellen Wayland-Smith makes it clear that complex marriage was not so much a sexual free-for-all as non-monogamous relationships that Noyes sought to direct by mating young members with older, "spiritually accomplished" members like himself. Among its benefits, complex marriage would, in theory, prevent couples from forming exclusive love relationships and raising children with the "selfish" (what the Oneidans called "sticky") attachments typical in a nuclear family. As for stirpiculture, it involved what was, in effect, small-scale "scientific breeding" through closely orchestrated conjugal relationships. Incestuous pairings, including Noyes's sexual relations with a niece, were part of these orchestrated relationships, though some of them, like this one, predated the stirpiculture experiment.[44]

No close parallel to these Oneida practices or to Mormon polygamy was sanctioned within the Compton community. Properly solemnized marriages were the norm, as were nuclear families, though at intervals many of these households had unmarried, widowed, or aged relatives as residents. Non-monogamous behaviour and out-of-wedlock births seem to have existed to a greater degree than in society at large, typically occurring within the kin circle. The most egregious instance of sexual excess passed along in private intergenerational family story-telling predates the formation of the community. It is that of western sojourner George Compton. George is remembered in family stories as the father of children born to two of his first wife's spinster sisters as well as to other female relatives. Three family women were said at one point to have been pregnant with his children at the same time, probably while the two families who had gone west together were sharing a crowded home.[45] All but one of George's acknowledged children are shown in a genealogy chart as the children of his two marriages. But the closeness of some of the births listed there, taken together with the variety and reliability of other sources on his family life, make it impossible to dismiss the stories of his sexual excesses as just familial tall tales.[46]

What is one to make of George's sexual conduct? As in the case of the Mormon leaders and Oneida's John Humphrey Noyes, precedents set by Old Testament patriarchs with their concern for fecundity and lineage may have served as a licence or rationale for what will strike many twenty-first-century readers as straightforward cases of lustful behaviour and abuse of vulnerable women. There may also have been an echo of the antinomianism that had loosened the sexual and moral constraints of some New Light Baptists in the 1790s in the part of New Brunswick where the Loyalist Compton and Planter Vaughan families were then living. There, a subset of New Lights called the New Dispensationalists had believed themselves set free of the usual norms of proper Christian conduct and of institutionalized religious observance. Writing of PEI's nineteenth-century McDonaldite community, of which his austere father was an important member, Sir Andrew Macphail observed (albeit with tongue in cheek) that "the Antinomian heresy … flourished in that community."[47]

While George's transgressions against contemporary sexual and familial norms, whatever their "causes," live on as the most notorious such cases in intergenerational story-telling, another, vaguer, rumour, less frequently shared and by now beyond the reach of anything like confirmation, related to his brother Ben. It suggests that before he became the founder of the Compton community and while he was still a widower, Ben may have fathered two children as a result of relations with the married woman who later became his mother-in-law: the same woman who, earlier, during her family's sojourn in the West, almost certainly bore two children fathered by George.[48] If this complicated sexual entanglement was in fact part of Ben's history, it helps to account for later reticence about elaborating on his achievements as company founder by those who knew him best.

Children conceived outside the marriage bed, whether or not they were subsequently identified as "illegitimate," were by no means uncommon across western societies either before or after the time period I have been discussing. So it may seem unnecessary, even prurient, to include family stories about two men born in the 1850s as part of a discussion of a utopian community formed after those transgressions took place. There are, however, interlinked aspects that make the transgressive conduct relevant. It was, as noted, taking place *within* the kin circle. Whether in spite of that fact or, most likely, because of it, these instances of sexual misconduct seem not to have been a subject of openly expressed conflict or moral outrage within that circle. Indeed, Hector, who could be exceedingly judgmental about what he perceived as the sexualized appearance or demeanour of young women of the Compton community (the use of lipstick, or a tight sweater, for instance) and whose own marriage was by all accounts a loving and faithful union, sounded almost proud, certainly not disapproving, when in his old age he wrote about the fecundity of an older generation of male kin ("as Israel of old, they did their share in populating the earth"). It was an attitude consistent with concerns he had expressed decades earlier about the importance of continual childbearing by community women "mated" with community men.[49]

Tragically, though not surprisingly given the Comptons' practice of close endogamy, there were two instances of half-sibling unions as a result of George's transgressive sexual conduct during his years in the West. The sadder of these unions resulted when two "cousins" had sexual relations, seemingly without knowing about their common paternity. Though a daughter was born, they were forbidden to marry by the community's leaders. It was only in 1923 when their daughter was about eight years old and another child was expected that they and the other half-sibling couple were given permission to marry. While no physical or mental handicaps were ever confirmed as negative outcomes of either of the half-sibling unions, the young girl born "illegitimately" would live with a permanent sense of shame about a situation over which she had had no control.

How great *were* the genetic risks created by the transgressive sexual conduct just described? Did the half-siblings who married simply dodge a bullet? And what of the many first-cousin marriages that took place over some two generations? Scientific thinking about the risks of close intermarriage, including cousin marriage, had changed significantly over the course of the nineteenth century. When Charles Darwin married his first cousin Emma in 1839 (a year before Queen Victoria married *her* first cousin Albert), the two were carrying on a long and valued family tradition: their common grandfather, potter Josiah Wedgwood, had been married to his cousin, and the same was true for many of their other relatives. Their contemporaries, Adam Kuper writes, would not have regarded cousin marriage "as abnormal or verging on the incestuous." But by the middle decades of the nineteenth century, concerns were emerging in England about worrisome outcomes from "inbreeding," and by the 1920s, even cousin marriages were "routinely condemned" by eugenicists.[50] In the US, by the mid-1800s, every state had laws against incest, and by the later part of the century some states included first cousins among those prohibited from having sexual intercourse or marrying. These legal interventions reflected contemporary American concerns about reproductive risks and hereditary degeneracy as expressed by such presumed experts as physiologists and phrenologists. By the late nineteenth and early twentieth century, the work of anthropologists was adding to the concern: famed American ethnographer Lewis Henry Morgan, who had married his first cousin in 1851, came to believe that consanguine marriages should be avoided.[51] Concerns such as Morgan's in the US did not translate into similar legal prohibitions against cousin marriage in Europe or Canada, and most US states no longer criminalize it. Nonetheless, such concerns could easily cross borders. Some Maritimers working in the Boston states, for instance, came to see cousin marriage in their place of birth as yet another aspect of the region's backwardness. By the early to mid-twentieth century, the practice came to be widely regarded as distasteful even in the "backward" Maritime provinces and, when there was the possibility of passing along a hereditary disease, unacceptably risky.[52] Writing in 2016, Adam Rutherford brought the perspective of a twenty-first-century geneticist – and a degree of caution – to the assessment of risk: "There is an increased risk of the emergence of recessive genetic diseases when new genes fail to make their way into the genomes of children. But it's easy to overstate them, and easier to allow cultural practices to foster and foment prejudices." That said, "if you keep on doing it generation after generation, it's not good news."[53]

As the best-read member of his community, Hector was certainly familiar with prevailing views about the dangers of cousin marriage as they filtered down into popular culture in the early to mid-twentieth century. Set against his awareness of perceived risks in close consanguine unions, however,[54] was a greater concern about whether outsiders marrying into the Compton community could accept its religious beliefs and communitarian practices and enter fully into its value system.[55] Referring to the Compton community in their 1943 article for *Rural Sociology*, Enid Charles and Sylvia Anthony noted that "members do not marry outside the group." They were probably citing Hector when they wrote that its members "felt that their pattern of life depended on keeping themselves 'unspotted from the world.'"[56]

By the time their article was published, community marital patterns had, in fact, already begun to change, with the first important breach having taken place a decade earlier. It should not have been surprising that young men and women growing up in the small community would have looked beyond the pool of cousins in Belle River and Bangor for romantic partners when opportunities arose. But with schooling ending by about age fourteen and with no participation in a church congregation or local recreational activities, such opportunities did not often occur. The exception came in the case of outside workers employed by B. Compton Limited. Several Danish immigrant labourers married into the community, beginning in the early 1930s when the eldest daughter of the community's founder effectively challenged its practice of close endogamy.

Hector's approval of all community members' marriages was evidently regarded as necessary, at least in Belle River; Big John Compton seems to have played the same gatekeeper role in Bangor. The marital choice of Ben's daughter presented Hector with a dilemma: the moral character and work ethic of her intended were exemplary, but he was unwilling, in marrying her, to become part of the community:

> He is bound to be independent in earning for his family and to have all goods etc. Charged and Credited. Very commendable in one way but he has declined the free offer of being a brother with us in all things. Now we are up against the strange proposition of using cold Figures against the daughter of the man who first opened his home for this system and Founded us. It is no use to force him. We do not want slave minds. He is one of the most useful men we have ever had here but how long will he stand in the way to resist all powerful love or what strains will there be between them before he yields to freedom?[57]

No challenge precisely like this one would confront Hector for the next several years, but the marriage of this couple did set a precedent. In the 1940s, marrying out by community members would become a new norm and a factor in the community's unravelling.

Hector and the Boston Diaspora

In December 1936 Hector made a visit to relatives and acquaintances in the Boston area, accompanied by Bessie, his wife, and their youngest daughter. In doing so, he said, he was yielding to long-standing invitations and to the urgings of Island kin concerned about the heavy load of responsibilities he had been carrying during a particularly trying time (the loss of the three male community members still in their prime had occurred just a short while earlier). Although the Depression had put the brakes on the migration of Maritimers to the Boston states, Hector could still look forward to finding a large circle of relatives among the many expatriate Islanders living in the Boston area. Many of them were well known to him, since, even if they had been long away, with permanent homes and good jobs in the US, they returned to the Island for holidays and corresponded between visits. Others were sojourners, working in the US seasonally or year-round for several years before returning to settle down on the Island. Hector's wife, Bessie, had been one of them, working as a seamstress and housekeeper until she returned to PEI to marry Hector in 1919. Likewise, Bessie's sister Janie and Janie's husband, the tragic George Emerson Compton, as well as female cousins from Bangor, shuttled between the two places. These ways of being an expatriate Islander in Boston were part of a larger Maritime pattern, as historians such as Gary Burrill and Betsy Beattie have shown.[58] For Hector, the 1936 visit seems to have been his first trip outside the Maritime Provinces and his first return to the US since his impoverished family had come back to the Island from Chicago when he was a teenager. To prepare for the trip, prior to his departure he wrote to various people with whom he hoped to have brief meetings en route as well as to relatives and acquaintances in and around Boston.

His correspondence during and after the Boston visit indicates that he experienced the trip as a personal triumph on several levels. In what was, in effect, a report back to community members in Belle River and Bangor, he explained that, at a large gathering in the Cambridge home of one of the US kin on 25 December (an "event ... not spoiled with liquor"), he had unfurled the Union Jack and reminded them of the ties that bound them to their British background. He had then transitioned to his British-Israelite beliefs and spoken about the providential wisdom that "had caused a Seed, the seed of the House of Israel to be placed on a wonderful little out of the way island, Prince Edward Isld." Far from opposing or mocking his views, he reported to those back home, his audience had listened with warmth and respect.

It was a response he found all the more gratifying in that it included some relatives in the Boston area who had not previously had contact with one another. Moreover, "there were no party prejudices at all in evidence and no principles sacrificed. In fact it was the other way about, because some people came together and met on common ground, who had been apart for years around here."[59] Hector's odd terms, "party prejudices" and "principles," seem to refer to religious differences among the expatriate kin that went back to their Island roots and to long-ago splits among McDonaldites. While some at the gathering had been raised in or otherwise connected to the Compton community, others were at least occasional worshippers at the local (Cambridge) McDonaldite church. Still others would have found their way into a mainstream Protestant denomination if they attended church at all. In giving him a warm hearing, it is unlikely that these diverse kin and their marriage partners were concurring with the specifics and eccentricities of his religious views but rather showing affection and respect for their able and dignified Island relative.

One of the men at the Christmas night gathering was probably responsible for the invitation Hector received to address a Rotary Club meeting in Watertown during his visit. In later years he was still recalling this travel experience and the themes of his Watertown address with obvious pride. His Rotary audience, he recalled, had included "all the big shots of the city." And in addressing them he had evidently again dwelt on the themes of Anglo-American amity and the two great people's shared destiny and duty as descendants of the House of Israel.[60] Overall, the trip to Boston and environs made it clear that Hector regarded his own Christian duty as extending across geographic and cultural boundaries and as involving more than just the small rural world of B. Compton Limited and his role there as secretary-treasurer.

A "Rise in Valuation"

It is likely that Hector's visit to the Boston area contributed to a remarkable development in the last half of the 1930s: a flurry of media interest and personal inquiries about B. Compton Limited, its communitarian nature, and its apparent success in negotiating the shoals of the Depression. Journalistic attention within Prince Edward Island had evidently begun in 1933 with two very similar articles in the *Charlottetown Guardian*. Both focused exclusively on Bangor and both were riddled with errors of fact or interpretation.[61] The two pieces were anonymous, as was another *Guardian* article, published in January 1935, this time based on facts as well as fancies about both settlements. For the unidentified authors of the latter, a particularly fascinating aspect of "this apparent Utopia" was the company store at Belle River: "For the Compton 'customers' no cash register rings. No entries are made in the ledger for the bags of flour, barrels of sugar, canned goods and farm equipment that are delivered. 'We ask for the things we need, no more, and these are given to us freely. We do not abuse the system,' one of the colony explained."[62]

Later that year, a more substantive and reliable article, written by Charlottetown journalist and broadcaster Flora S. Rogers, was published in the *Halifax Chronicle*. Rogers's "Brotherly Love Rules This Community" explicitly related the Compton community's cooperative practices to historic utopian ideals. Like the author of the January article in the *Guardian* and other, later, writers, she was struck by the size, tidiness, and modernity of the community's houses, barns, and sawmill and fascinated by the role of the community store. The community's material success, she wrote, was an outcome of its idealism as well as its practical business ventures: "Fundamental spiritual values hold a high place ... and a distinct religious philosophy based on prophecy and revealed truth has been evolved. It is a continuation of the McDonaldite religion which in turn sprang out of the old church of Scotland." Rogers's respectful treatment and her familiarity with the background of the community's religious beliefs probably reflected the fact that early on in the broadcasting life of CFCY, the Charlottetown radio station started by her husband, its programming had featured devotional talks by his neighbour the Reverend Ewen MacDougall. A Bangor-born McDonaldite minister whose weekly broadcasts brought mail to the station from as far away as the New England states and the Gaspé coast,[63] MacDougall had connections of several sorts with the Compton community, including as a marriage officiant.

The articles in Maritime newspapers – some of them picked up by the then relatively new Canadian Press wire service[64] – led to inquiries about the functioning and philosophy of B. Compton Limited from writers in other parts of Canada and in the US. By the beginning of the summer of 1935, the letters of inquiry had increased substantially. One early letter was from the director of the National Sociological Survey in Cincinnati, Ohio. Having heard about the success of the Compton "colony," the director wrote, he was eager "to inject the virus of co-operation into the body economic of the United States." Might he quote some of his statements, the writer asked Hector, as a source of inspiration, especially in view of the dreadful state of the world? About a year later the staff correspondent for the *Packer*, the Maine

and Maritime Provinces branches of a US agricultural trade publication, wrote to Big John Compton to inquire in detail about the community, having just read an article about the Bangor "colony" in the
Prince Edward Island Agriculturalist. The *Agriculturalist* article was
similar to the two *Guardian* pieces published in 1933, but even more
unreliable, riddled with errors of fact and wild exaggerations about
the size and achievements of the settlement. The common source was
evidently John himself, whose accounts no journalist seems to have
questioned before putting pen to paper. Such pieces should immedi-
ately have set off alarm bells. But like earlier inquirers, the correspondent for the *Packer* showed no scepticism about what he had read.[65]
Such responses spoke to the widespread North American desire for
hopeful stories about how to cope with the challenges of the Depression. Perhaps, too, the stories were all the more convincing to distant
inquirers in being about hard-working, God-fearing people in a tiny
and remote rural utopia. As seen earlier, international interest in rural
self-help was likewise created during this decade by the Antigonish
Movement and the PEI cooperative movement, albeit on a larger scale.

In August 1937 there came the most astonishing inquiry of all: Hector was contacted by Phillips H. Lord Radio Productions, New York,
producers of a radio program called "We the People," and invited to
take part in the program that autumn. Lord, the letter writer explained,
was none other than the creator of the nationally famous radio character "Seth Parker." Clearly, Hector was meant to be impressed by this
piece of information. As for "We the People," it was designed to bring
individuals from all over the continent "to tell their unusual story" to
a national audience (*Time* magazine is said to have called the program
"anybody's and everybody's soap box"). The committee that selected
presenters, the writer told Hector, believed that "in a world where there
is so much misunderstanding and where disputes are commonplace,
the story of your community with its model behaviour would serve
as a powerful example to the people of America."[66] It is possible that
this particular invitation came about through Hector's acquaintance
with John Hays Hammond Jr., a wealthy, well-connected, and eccentric American inventor who founded the Hammond Radio Research
Laboratory and who served on the Board of Directors of RCA. Hector
had become acquainted with Hammond when the latter visited Prince
Edward Island on his yacht in the summer of 1936. Later that year,
Hector had written to him to try to arrange a meeting during his visit
to the Boston area.[67]

There is no indication that Hector took up the invitation to appear
on Lord's program. Writing to Big John Compton in 1935 just after

inquiries about the Compton community had begun to arrive, Hector expressed concern that two local male journalists with whom he had discussed their community and who had "promise[d] to publish nothing without our permission" had broken their word. In fact, having given the interview that had led to their rosy and factually flawed account of the community in the *Guardian* in early January, he seemed at a loss about how to respond to the subsequent flurry of interest in the community's way of life. He was at once chuffed and apprehensive:

> What to write and what not, is a problem. Would it be out of place to leave it open to the Ohio man to come and see us next summer if he wished? Cannot write what he asks for. We used to liken our prospects to stocks on the market in no demand. It begins to look like a rise in valuation and if our labors are acclaimed by the greater powers, where will the local neighbours fit who had refused and opposed all their lives[?][68]

The last remark in this gnomic passage seems to be at odds with the position Hector characteristically adopted vis-à-vis outsiders: that the Compton community could best maintain its way of life and its religious values if its people kept themselves to themselves and, both as a spiritual community and as a business, remained a family affair. It may be, though, that the "local neighbours" to whom he referred were relatives from whom they had been separated in religious practice since the 1890s and who had opted not to join the community when an opportunity to do so had been presented in its start-up days.

Years later Hector would claim that during this period there had been some forty letters of inquiry about the community, so many that he had not had time to reply to them. Among the inquirers were journalists proposing to do features on the community for the Montreal-based weekly *Family Herald* and the CBC, as well as numerous individuals, some of them writing from faraway places and wanting to join the community or invest in it.[69] What to do? Hector's retrospective claim that he had simply not had the time to respond to all inquiries is not wholly convincing, especially given his lifelong propensity for engaging in letter writing that went well beyond business requirements and the immediate family circle. More likely he had quickly come to realize that granting interviews was a fraught exercise and that publicity came with risks. Journalism more rigorous than that practised on Prince Edward Island might mean that stories about "peaceful, happy and contented people" would give way to more nuanced and critical portrayals if the more unconventional details of the community's religious beliefs, its problems with alcohol, and its close-kin relationships were closely investigated and publicized. Or inquirers, having read positive stories about the community and wanting to join it, would inevitably include people wholly unable to accept its way of life, as well as "jobless youths" desperate for work.[70] Finally, there was the risk that runaway publicity would turn the heads of younger community members and ultimately lead to restlessness.

Some publicity, though, could not be checked. At the end of the decade, the Compton community became grist for inclusion in a travel book. In *Over on the Island*, author Helen Jean Champion included segments about the "Communist" settlements at Belle River and Bangor. Champion was a native Islander, the daughter of a Prince County physician. She was also a historian who in 1936 had won a scholarship to do doctoral studies in London. But in her well-received book – it was reprinted in 1946 – she made no reference to her own Island ties and altogether eschewed a scholarly pose, instead writing as a chatty and fascinated outsider absorbed in the history and life of the province as she cycled its red roads with a friend.[71]

She knew they had reached "the Communist settlement at Belle River," she explained, when she saw the impressive barns, "barns – par excellence," and the fine-looking homes:

On the verandah of a near-by house a woman was shaking rugs. To reassure ourselves, we went over and asked:
"Is this where the Communists live?"
"Communists!" snorted the woman. "I get sick and tired of people coming around here and asking about Communists. Communists indeed!" And she gave the mat another angry flip. Our bicycles slid away towards the store … We resolved to be more diplomatic in future. The store was next. We bought chocolate bars and tried again.
"Is this the district where people do things together?"
Apparently that was better.[72]

Her condescension notwithstanding, Champion was somewhat better informed about the details of, and differences between, the two communitarian settlements than earlier writers had been, perhaps because of her own Island background. She also moved beyond chattiness to express some misgivings. Thus, following her brief account of the community's Bangor settlement, its "contented"-looking people, and their fine farms, she declared that intermarriage was "still too prevalent," education devalued, and higher education still entirely outside the range of the community's experience.[73]

In her remarks on education, Champion had touched on a significant absence in the life of both Compton-community settlements.
But were the community's members only marginally worse off in this
respect than their non-communal neighbours? After all, educational
opportunities in the province would remain dismal until the 1960s.[74]
Or, were the community's youth deliberately discouraged from pursu-
ing education beyond the local school, despite the fact that B. Compton Limited clearly had the means to afford it? Champion believed
it was the latter, as did demographer Enid Charles, whose research
on Island communities was conducted at roughly the same time. Yet
neither Champion nor Charles was portraying the community's members as benighted yokels. Having seen its material accomplishments,
Champion observed that the community benefited from the talents
of some gifted and inventive self-taught individuals. Meanwhile,
Charles, aware of members' access to radios, newspapers, and other
media, considered that "their level of culture and of comfort is higher
than that of their neighbours."[75] Deprived of access to high school and
university, then, but not altogether without opportunities to expand
their mental horizons.

Utopian organizations face challenges from the moment of their
founding, both those generated by the community's policies and
internal dynamics and those impinging on it from the outside world.
Among the challenges facing the Compton community in terms of its
long-term stability was the reality that the same abilities and interests
that could be harnessed and deployed for the well-being and prosperity of the community could, in particular circumstances, express
themselves in restiveness. This kind of restiveness, especially in conjunction with the wartime social changes that penetrated its always
porous boundaries, ultimately led to its dissolution. The next chapter
deals with that subject.

6

Restiveness Within,
Pressures from Without:
The Road to Dissolution

B. Compton Limited was, comparatively, a long-lasting utopian community. Longevity has been regarded by some scholars of such communities as an important criterion for determining their success. Writing in the 1970s, Rosabeth Moss Kanter considered utopias to have been successful if they continued for at least twenty-five years.[1] By this standard, the Compton community more than measured up, lasting almost forty years. Not quite as long as the Oneida community, but far longer than the Transcendentalists' Brook Farm, established, like Oneida, in the 1840s in the northeastern United States, or, on this side of the border, Sointula, planted on a tiny island in British Columbia just a few years before B. Compton Limited was established. Like many other utopias, especially those without strong religious beliefs to provide cohesion, Brook Farm and Sointula ended in the same decade they began.[2]

The Compton community was, then, no flash in the pan. Nor was it destabilized by early financial struggles such as those that derailed Brook Farm, much less by anything like the irreligious freethinking at Sointula. Nevertheless, there were features of the community's life, economic, social, and ideological, that were sources of actual or potential trouble from early on. These were exacerbated and new challenges introduced in the 1940s, particularly under the impact of the Second World War. During the war years, events occurring in the outside world impinged on the tiny province of Prince Edward Island to an unprecedented degree and ultimately ushered in a new way of life. So far as war-related economic development is concerned, it is likely, as historian Ernest Forbes argued, that, to an even greater extent than the other Maritime provinces, PEI missed out on the kinds of benefits that came in abundance to some other parts of Canada. Yet when one turns from Forbes's article-length, development-focused overview to Edward MacDonald's more detailed and anecdotally inflected history of the province, one finds plenty of evidence of the war as "a tangible presence on Prince Edward Island." Not only did the province experience significant if belated economic stimulus, there was also a markedly higher level of military enlistment than occurred during the First World War and an unprecedented degree of government intervention.[3] All of these aspects made themselves felt within the Compton community, providing both the backdrop and important contributing elements to its unravelling.

"All Things in Common"?
Scriptural Ideals and Material Realities

In one of the many letters in which, in retirement, he reminisced about the days when his people had lived as a community, Hector Compton recounted for distant American relatives its interwoven religious and business aspects. "[I]n material matters," he wrote, we "'held all things in common,' using the word 'ours' instead of 'mine' as a rule." Drawing on wording from the Acts of the Apostles, he directly linked the community's practices to early Christianity: "And all that believed were together, and had all things common" (Acts 2:44); "And the multitude of them that believed were of one heart and of one soul: neither said any *of them* that ought of the things which he possessed was his own; but they had all things common" (Acts 4:32).[4] Favourable portrayals of the community in the print media in the last half of the 1930s had conveyed the impression that these apostolic goals were indeed being realized and not merely aspirational. In its January 1935 article on the community, the *Guardian*, for instance, lent support to this impression when it attributed to Hector the proud claim that "As head of the colony, I receive no more for my labor than does the youngest farm boy."[5]

In a certain monetary sense this was perhaps true: community members were meant to receive what they needed rather than fixed salaries based on marketplace values. Certainly, there was more in the way of economic equality within B. Compton Limited than typically existed in capitalist enterprises, and perhaps more even than in many comparable utopian endeavours. Nevertheless, reports of egalitarianism and equality of condition were wide of the mark, as Hector himself would acknowledge in official correspondence in 1948 when the process of dissolution was being wrapped up.[6] There were differences in the degree of material comforts existing in the community's two settlements and even among households within them. None of the homes in Bangor had electricity, for instance. The most impressive of the Bangor homes, that of "Big John" Compton, was the only one with indoor plumbing and the only one with a piano. Even children couldn't help but notice material differences. One now elderly daughter of a Bangor community family remembers that, on her girlhood summer visits to Belle River cousins, there were more things to play with, including a pony. As for Hector, his role as business leader necessarily involved a different and better style of clothing, as well as opportunities for a wider range of experiences than were available to most community members, men as well as women. John, for his part, certainly lived larger than the other household heads in Bangor. Did the differences matter? Since members of B. Compton Limited were somewhat better off materially than many of their non-communal neighbours, particularly during the Depression years, and since, except for the founding generation, they had grown up knowing nothing different, perhaps none of these material and experiential inequalities on its own was considered remarkable, or reason for resentment. But when coupled with restrictions on individual freedoms, and especially as conditions changed in the larger world, they could become more significant and weaken the bonds of community.

Boundaries and Resistance

There was some resistance, even early on, to restrictions on individual freedoms and to the narrow confines of the community's religious and social life. One of the resisters was Mary, the youngest daughter of the infamous George Compton and his second wife. At the time of the 1921 census, Mary, age nineteen, was still living in Bangor with her now twice widowed seventy-year-old father and her half-brother William. She experienced her life as the only female in their dreary household as that of family drudge. At one point when Mary dared to attend the local McDonaldite church, her father arrived, threw open the door, and ordered her to leave. (As teenagers, three of her siblings also defied the religious practice of the Compton community by seeking baptism in a McDonaldite church.) Finally, denied the opportunity to train as a nurse, Mary fled to Boston without saying goodbye. There she met and married a fellow Islander, possibly through the Cambridge McDonaldite church. Later, as a hard-working widow, she took great pride in the fact that both her sons had graduated from elite universities and become successful lawyers.[7]

For a young woman like Mary with no source of income it would have been difficult, if not impossible, to break away to a different kind of life had there not been some form of outside assistance, in this case money sent to her by a sister who had gone to Boston some years earlier. But even men of the community who wanted something different could not easily move on to a new way of living. While there were fewer limits on men's access to experiences in the outside world, there were role expectations and strong bonds of familial and communal affection to hold them. One community man may have made a particularly dramatic escape in 1936 as he approached his fortieth year. Was Captain Oliver Compton – Hector's younger, bachelor, brother – really swept overboard and lost to the sea when the *Hatavan* ran aground on a sandbar en route back from Nova Scotia in November of that year? Or did he stage his own disappearance in order to pursue a romantic interest at odds with community norms, as some of his relatives later speculated? The accounts of his death by drowning written at the time may well be true,[8] but the fact that an alternative explanation for the disappearance of the kindly and highly experienced seaman persisted in family memories even decades later – and seemed plausible – is significant.[9]

Speculation about Oliver's possible defection notwithstanding, constraints on the lives of Compton community women were unquestionably greater, and more isolating, than they were for its men. In this respect, B. Compton Limited appears to have been something of an anomaly among utopian communities, including even some religiously based communities. Many writers on American utopias deal with groups that claimed to provide, and in some cases actually delivered, greater opportunities for gender equality than existed in the society around them. Histories of communities such as Brook Farm and Oneida provide solid evidence of comparatively expansive occupational and intellectual horizons for nineteenth-century women.[10] Even in early Mormonism, Laurel Thatcher Ulrich contends, there were strong women – active agents in work, religion, and political matters – whose lived experience contradicted the larger society's view that Mormonism's polygamous system made wives mere pawns of their husbands' desires and political machinations.[11]

In contrast to these earlier American utopias, the Compton community appears to have maintained and even extended the norms and practices of patriarchy. As noted, its Sunday religious gatherings continued the nineteenth-century practice in McDonaldite services of having women seated apart from men, and they had no leadership role in worship. In terms of work roles, adult women in B. Compton

Limited were, and were expected to be, exemplary homemakers. The young women who worked at the community lobster factory in the early days probably enjoyed the chance it brought to socialize with others, including some non-community employees. But they were there because the men in charge determined that they were needed. That was certainly the case when, during the Second World War, Hector summoned a niece, a teenager from the Bangor settlement, first to do housework in his family home and then, when she proved capable, to fill in as clerk in the company store, replacing the young male cousin who had gone into military service. At the time, neither the girl nor her parents considered that refusal was an option.[12]

For unmarried women to work outside the community seems not to have been considered acceptable. Few jobs would have been available locally in any case. Even when there were "redundant" spinster daughters, they would not have been permitted to become domestics in the homes of non-family members. What became of them? It is not an idle question. Permanent spinsterhood was a common phenomenon in late nineteenth-century Prince Edward Island,[13] and a reality for at least three women in McDonaldite elder John Compton's family. Daughter Catherine cared for her widowed and handicapped father in the family home until his death in 1901, while two of his other unmarried daughters were evidently transferred from the Belle River household to one of the Bangor family homes early in the twentieth century as they approached what would have been considered old age.[14] Whatever their age, the limited education of these three women and of other unmarried Compton community women would not have qualified them even for the most obvious respectable local job possibility: rural school teaching.

For much of the first half of the twentieth century, Prince Edward Island overall remained a society dominated by traditional rural values and traditional gender roles. The Compton community was in some respects simply a more pronounced version of the province's ethos. What stands out, though, as a great difference in the case of Compton community women was the extent to which they were isolated from the society around them, even from activities that were widely regarded as an acceptable part of "women's sphere." Perhaps they were not actually forbidden to do so, but it seemed to be taken for granted that they would not join outside organizations such as the Women's Institute (WI), an important force for civic improvement across the Island, with lively branches in Belle River and nearby Wood Islands. There were also two Protestant churches in the district,[15] but, since Compton community women were not congregants, there would have been no possibility of their participating in women's missionary society meetings, helping to organize church suppers, or teaching Sunday School. Even outings for shopping seem seldom to have occurred, perhaps even for personal garments such as corsets, a purchase that shows up several times in a company ledger for 1920 and 1921.[16] Significantly, the woman who had been brought from Bangor to Belle River as a teenager to work during the war years would later attribute her lifelong foot problems to ill-fitting shoes purchased on her behalf at that time.

There were some exceptions to the pattern of isolation among community women. Founder Ben's widow, Libby, the eldest of Hector's sisters, had somewhat broader horizons as a result of her ability to help out in the larger Belle River neighbourhood through her practical nursing skills: in old age she reminisced about being called to numerous confinements and cases of injuries prior to the arrival of a doctor or to fill in in his absence. An independent-minded, proud, and intelligent woman, Libby reportedly staged occasional quiet acts of resistance to Hector's dominance of the Belle River group's religious lives by making time for the teachings of visiting Jehovah's Witnesses, or sometimes absenting herself from the Sunday worship at his house.[17] Mostly, though, the world of Compton community women, though characterized by material security, was a world of narrow social experience and extremely limited demographic horizons. In these circumstances it was not surprising that some of them broke with community practice by marrying out.

Just a few years after the eldest daughter of Libby and founder Ben married a Danish labourer employed by B. Compton Limited in the early 1930s, her sister and another young community woman did likewise. Hector remained opposed to the practice of marrying out, but since in the second of these cases the would-be bride was already pregnant, forbidding their wedding was not a practical option. In the next decade, marrying out would become a new norm, one of many changes that would contribute to the fraying of community bonds.

Change and Declension: The 1940s

In the Abstract preceding their 1943 article "The Community and the Family in Prince Edward Island," published in *Rural Sociology*, authors Enid Charles and Sylvia Anthony noted that "The pattern of life described already shows signs of disintegration and is unlikely to endure."[18] Although their article did not concern itself with the causes of this disintegration, the Second World War was unquestionably a significant factor. This was the case for B. Compton Limited, as it was for the province overall. In terms of business-related changes brought about by the war, Hector was most concerned about manpower problems and an unprecedented degree of government regulation. In regard to the first of these, Prince Edward Island, as noted, experienced a markedly higher level of military enlistment than it had in the First World War. For B. Compton Limited, the manpower drain involved both hired labourers and young community members. Prior to the war, the company is said to have employed a total of thirty-six persons. In 1941 the woodworking mill, the single biggest employer of outside labourers and the biggest source of company income, was down to a crew of about ten and thus unable to handle the unprecedented volume of product orders even with occasional overtime shifts. Hector's personal workload increased when the only son of founder Ben signed up; he had been Hector's right-hand man in the store and in the overall management of the company's business.[19]

His absence added to the problems Hector was encountering as a result of increased government intervention in business affairs. Already in September 1941 Hector had complained about – and perhaps exaggerated – this burden in a letter to another young kinsman in military service:

> We are this year, since May 1st under Sales Tax regulations, accounting each month for 8% on all taxable sales, then we now have Unemp. Insurance with a separate book for each hired man and the buying of Stamps and accounting for every days work with stamps for 4 [cents] out of his wages and 5 [cents] out of our own pocket per day per man. Then we still have to "induce" them to continue contrib. to War Savings and mail a lot of reports to Ottawa.[20]

As both a big and small "c" conservative, Hector was predisposed to blame Mackenzie King's Liberal government for burdensome bureaucratic requirements. When disaster struck the company the following summer in the form of a nighttime fire that rapidly destroyed the woodworking mill, Hector wrote bitterly about the event as a release from government officialdom and other management burdens: "This marks ... Liberation from all the Gov't forms, from pleading with hired help, striving with log sellers on one hand and shook customers on the other and forever solving some mechanical difficulty, in order to keep the thing going." The fire, for which there was no insurance coverage, occurred at a time when Hector was already feeling unappreciated by community members for the burden he had been carrying on their behalf, and in these circumstances he gave no thought to rebuilding the mill. Nor, though the fire might have been deliberately set, did he seem much exercised by rumours that "a foreign looking man" who had come into the area on the nearby and recently established Wood Islands ferry service might have been involved.[21]

These challenges coincided with a time when Hector was increasingly absorbed by what he took to be clear signs that the millennium was imminent. It was a perspective shared by many contemporary American prophecy writers,[22] whose work he was then in the process of discovering. In these years he spoke particularly and repeatedly of the US periodical *Destiny*, which had, he believed, been sent to him providentially to provide a richer understanding of biblical teachings on end times. He followed war news from an eschatological perspective. Once Germany was defeated, he believed, Russia would emerge clearly as the Antichrist.[23] As for the dropping of the atom bomb in 1945, it was "just a natural symbol of the greater Force in the Spiritual Realm" and clear evidence that "Babylon's time ... can be terminated just as quickly as was the power of the great threatening 'Empire of Japan.'"[24]

What concerned Hector most particularly during these years was his own community's lack of readiness for the coming cataclysm. In both settlements, but particularly in Belle River, he despaired over what he took to be moral and spiritual declension, especially among the younger generation. Thus, in 1944 he wrote that he was

> gravely concerned for the welfare of this small lot of people. We were once a body, united by a living prospect, and now that this prospect is unfolding, we should still be a unit, be watching and waiting the outcome, but it is far from being the case ... The Greatest World Crisis is just ahead of us when the present Babylonian systems are due to fall. [But] our children have somehow lost ear for these subjects and do not fear to move out and drink of the world's cheap pleasures. They are as lambs among wolves, far worse off than worldlings who were always inured to their lot.[25]

In at least one respect, Hector's concern reflected a kind of reality: it was, in fact, becoming easier for his community's young adults to access "the world's cheap pleasures." Writing in 1943, scholars Charles and Anthony observed that, thanks to the availability of automobiles, young people in the Belle River area now had "access to frequent movies and dances within a radius of about 20 miles." Even within the Compton community, they believed, the longstanding prohibition on participation in "outside social functions" was "being disregarded by the younger members."[26]

To the extent that this was so, it would have contributed to the breakdown in unity of purpose and religious belief that was occurring on the Hill. Writing at the beginning of 1946 to his Nova Scotia-based brother, Hector spoke of "disagreement of minds, disorganization of purpose[,] confusion in work and operation, losses and blights, of drink stealthily brought in almost daily." And he despaired over the failure of the younger generation "to stand as a Unit to await and to hail His Coming."[27] In writing as he did in letters like this one, Hector was probably exaggerating both the degree to which younger community members had ever been absorbed by millennial expectations and the extent and rapidity of their fall from grace.[28] But his assessment of disorganization and disagreement in the business and material aspects of the Belle River settlement was undoubtedly accurate.

Ironically, compromise measures taken by B. Compton Limited at the end of 1943 to fend off calls for dissolution from some members had only made things worse. A formal meeting had been held on the last day of the year "to consider ways and means of better distributing responsibility, and for giving the younger membership a more direct and lively interest in their work and in the welfare of the Community as a whole." Especially given how tightly Hector had held the reins of management of B. Company Limited in the years since 1924, the new set-up agreed upon was a recipe for chaos and friction: "certain men or persons" were to be put in charge of each line of company work and given responsibility for finances and record keeping for their own unit over the course of the year. They were then to submit to "a general accounting and comparison," to be carried out by "the Directors and officials of the Company in session." In addition, "a friendly rivalry between the various units" was to be encouraged in order to "create a keener interest in the progress of each section" and to "benefit the people as a whole." Only some of the changes agreed upon at the 31 December meeting had been fully implemented thereafter, and only some of those named on paper as "Directors" had the capacity or the opportunity to direct.[29] Yet to the extent that expectations had been raised about new roles and opportunities, there was fertile ground for the growth of tensions and resentments.

Notwithstanding the partial devolution in the business structure of B. Compton Limited following the 1943 meeting and the election at that time of Hector's Bangor-based brother James Munn Compton as company president, Hector did not cease to regard himself, or to be regarded, as the company's real leader. He remained in charge of the company store, and he evidently sought to micromanage other lines of company business in Belle River. Not surprisingly, stress created by changes in the business affairs of B. Compton Limited during these years, in conjunction with his concerns about spiritual matters and his ongoing reluctance to accept marriages out, created health problems for Hector.[30] They also made him a more impatient and judgmental leader. Inevitably, his laments and reproaches exacerbated the decline in community cohesion. It was in these circumstances and in this frame of mind that he dealt with further, and this time insistent, calls for dissolution. They included a call from members of the community's satellite settlement in Bangor wanting to be "'cut loose.'"[31]

Bangor and the Road to Dissolution

Compton community households in Bangor had had more potential and capacity for everyday autonomy than those in Belle River, even before the changes initiated in company management at the beginning of 1944 and before Big John Compton's death later that year. A stroke had damaged John's physical and mental faculties some three years earlier, but, even before that, he had been a somewhat unpredictable leader and, as a result of business activities, frequently absent from Bangor. Geography also made a difference to the way that the two community settlements functioned: the distances that separated the five Bangor households meant that they were freer of oversight than those in Belle River, where, as noted, residences and work buildings were clustered in a rough oval formation on the Hill, all within Hector's line of vision from his home or his office in the store. There was also potential in Bangor for more social engagement with, and influence from, the surrounding district. An example, probably from the late 1930s, is illustrative. Several schoolgirls whose parents were community members were able to participate in the school's Christmas concert after John withdrew his initial veto. One of them could still recall in her late eighties the crepe-paper costumes made by an aunt and grandmother for the girls' role in a concert skit and her own pleasure in being able to take part. A few years later, John allowed her and his eldest daughter to visit a Bangor cousin whose marriage out to the son of resident English immigrants he had initially opposed: their visit was John's version of an olive branch.

John's gregariousness and the drinking that, especially in his later years, lubricated his personality and sometimes prompted acts of showy generosity to outsiders no doubt made him a more approachable figure outside the community than the dour Hector, from whom capable local leadership on such matters as hospital fundraising and the establishment of a ferry service at nearby Wood Islands was routinely expected, rather than acts of sociability.[32] But within the Compton community, on the matter of religious services, John was evidently unbending. The Sunday services held at his home were remembered as a command performance – attendance was expected even for children and nursing mothers – rather than a time of spiritual nourishment. When his illness put an end to the gatherings, it was experienced by the young as a deliverance, except perhaps within his own immediate family. Evidently no thought was given to appointing a successor to conduct Sunday services following his death.

Meanwhile, in 1942, with the burning of the mill in Belle River, the two settlements had lost their single most important source of shared cash income. Along with the fraying of the spiritual bond resulting from John's death, the economic loss raised serious questions about the rationale for and the viability of their communitarian structure. Although there is no hard evidence that it made any difference in their decision making, the Bangor members were able at this time to observe that another and less restrictive kind of economic cooperation was possible: the cooperative movement that had begun on Prince Edward Island in the 1930s flourished in the nearby village of Morell, where the Bangor leaders purchased such supplies as were not obtained directly through B. Compton Limited. The cooperative in Morell was more multi-faceted in its services and more active than any other in the province.[33]

Hector had personally opposed the compromise measures agreed upon at the end of 1943 to fend off calls for dissolution. And he remained opposed to full dissolution for their communitarian company over the next several years. Writing in 1946, he seemed resigned to separation and independence for the Bangor group. But breaking up the communal operation at Belle River was a different matter. It was "mad or impossible," even shameful, particularly at a time when provincial civil servants were said to be looking at B. Compton Limited's communal structure as a possible model for veterans returning from military service to farm but unable to purchase the expensive equipment necessary for successful modern agriculture except on some sort of cooperative basis.[34] The truth was, though, that the Belle River set-up was no longer the model utopia that it had seemed to be a decade earlier when journalists and visitors had waxed enthusiastic over its evident prosperity and communitarian spirit. Hector's own correspondence had chronicled the decline: the wartime drain on manpower had meant neglect in the upkeep of once well maintained buildings and an inability to take advantage of business opportunities. The financial blow resulting from the burning of the mill had been followed by further losses in what should have been a still profitable machine shop. The selling off of securities had become necessary, and then, in 1947, another catastrophic fire destroyed the company's dairy barn, one of the most modern in the province, according to Hector.[35]

External factors such as manpower shortages, and the two fires, had contributed significantly to the community's economic problems. But those problems had been exacerbated by the changes in management and operations introduced in 1944, and by the increasing demoralization, friction, and restiveness that Hector had chronicled in his correspondence. In dwelling on the community's material and spiritual decline, Hector's focus had been mainly on the younger generation. In reality, though, dissatisfaction was not confined to the young people living on the Hill, nor to the Bangor contingent with its understandable practical concerns. One of Hector's American-born brothers, whose yard adjoined Hector's, wrote to him movingly in 1945 about wanting out of the community structure. His wording suggested that his unhappiness was not a recent phenomenon, though the death of his wife in 1941 and tensions with Hector may have added to it:

> I am now over 50 years old and have spent the best part of my life in this firm. I, like a lot of others, have spent years working hard and drawing nothing more than board, clothes and tobacco, until most of the time, one felt of little more consequence than the horse he was driving; the result was individualism gone, personality dwarfed, and a most glorious dose of inferiority complex.

Any real sense of community, he believed, had long since become "bondage," and the result was a gradual declension in the spiritual life of their people.[36]

The company limped on for another two years after this poignant letter was written, but it was a clear indication that an end point had been reached. In August 1947, the male shareholders of B. Compton Limited held a formal meeting, their first since the one held at the end of 1943, in order to consider "ways and means for fairly dividing the real estate and other assets of this firm between the shareholders and then terminating the Company by surrendering our Charter."[37] For more than a quarter-century, through good times and bad, Hector had helmed the community. Now he was tasked with being the architect of its dissolution.

As he undertook the job of unravelling the affairs of B. Compton Limited, Hector was understandably hurt by and defensive about real and perceived criticisms of his decades-long management of the company and his own family's share in the division of its assets.[38] And yet, faced with the unavoidable, he dealt with the complex legal requirements and personal negotiations involved in the dissolution process with what appears to have been remarkable fairness and flexibility and with no undue benefit to his own children. In a twice-drafted 1948 letter to provincial officials detailing aspects of the dissolution process, he explained that circumstances connected with the community's incorporation as a limited joint-stock company in 1933 were now creating difficulties: when asked, unexpectedly, to name their shareholders, spokesmen for the community (perhaps just Hector on his own) had provided the names of "Twenty-Two 'Active Senior Members.'" "To us, this was mere formality and the whole thing belonged still to the whole People." But some of those named in 1933 had since died; other still living and hard-working contributors had not been listed as members. In these circumstances, Hector believed, adhering to the usual regulations about transferring the assets of a limited joint-stock company only to named shareholders would "work great injustices." Furthermore, there were problems that went beyond that legal difficulty:

> No two of the homes is conditioned quite alike. We have persons of all ages and of varying degrees of responsibility. Some young men can take a farm and run it. Other workers are dependent to live in and to work with one of the established Homes. Since our Paper Securities are gone and our money almost used up, we must do the balancing with Real Property which is less easily distributed.

Easing the problem of the division of assets, however, was the fact that in Bangor, "where there is less money value per Person," members had agreed "to settle with what they now have there." In fact, overall, "so great a degree of self-sacrifice and consideration" had been shown that the challenges of working out a settlement had been simplified.[39]

By the time Hector wrote this account of the dissolution process, the winding-up notice had already been publicly advertised, and the company's debts had largely been paid. It remained only to collect monies owed and to deed company property to various former members as already arranged. As of 31 December 1947, B. Compton Limited had officially ceased to exist:[40] Prince Edward Island's "unique 'brotherly love' community" was history.

Given their exclusive focus on farming, there was less economic dislocation for the households in Bangor as a result of the unravelling of B. Compton Limited than for those in Belle River. With a higher proportion of young children, the Bangor families would also have benefited more from the cushion provided by the implementation of a national family allowance plan in 1945.[41] In Belle River, the loss by fire of the mill and the dairy barn had meant the disappearance of former places of work as well as of substantial community income.[42] As for what had been the company store, it became the sole property of founder Ben's son after a brief period when he co-owned it with an uncle. The machine shop where the mechanical skills of the late William Jardine had once drawn visitors' admiration became the business of his youngest living son. Other former members took over the farmlands and sharecropped the woodlands.[43] But these former community resources did not provide sufficient employment for all working-age ex-members. Even before the dissolution was finalized, some of the younger men in Belle River were emulating other young Maritimers and leaving the province in search of jobs, now typically sought in Ontario and western Canada rather than the Boston states.[44] For Hector, the threatened depopulation of Belle River was more than just a variant of a region-wide phenomenon; it spoke to the extent of the Compton community's material decline and loss of spiritual unity – and to the cause. As a community they had ceased to seek first the kingdom of heaven, and for that, he believed, they had deservedly suffered. "While we as a society sought that Kingdom we prospered miraculously; when that ceased to be the main objective we went down materially as well as spiritually. His will is being done."[45]

Members old enough to remember their people's way of life before B. Compton Limited came into existence would not necessarily have endorsed all aspects of Hector's explanation of what had gone wrong with their utopia. But they would have shared some of his memories of olden-days economic hardships and perhaps some of his millennial expectancy. By the time the community was dissolved, however, many members of the founding generation had died. In contrast, members born in the first three decades of the twentieth century knew no life outside the community's material and religious framework. Their comparative basis for evaluating their circumstances was not an earlier era of impoverishment but the way of life they saw around them in the larger Island society and what they heard about life elsewhere in North America. As for children born into community families in the 1940s, they had few or no memories of life in community, and the next generation none at all. Nevertheless, for good and ill, these two generations would also grow up with its legacies.

7

Life beyond Community:
Diverse Paths in an Era of Change

Studies of utopian communities often conclude with the end of the community. Ellen Wayland-Smith's account of Oneida shows how useful it can be if, instead of concluding a study of a utopian community with its dissolution, one follows its alumni beyond that point to see how they fared in the outside world. In the case of Oneida, one branch of the Noyes founding family, of which Wayland-Smith herself is a descendant, turned one of its former product lines into what became a hugely successful cutlery business. In post-Second World War North America, Oneida Community silver plate was effectively, if ironically, marketed to young engaged women as an elegant symbol of marital bliss and respectable middle-class homemaking. Oneida's business-minded descendants were understandably anxious to hide the former utopia's unorthodox sexual and family practices and to thwart the interest in those practices shown by researchers like Alfred Kinsey. Hence the wartime destruction of a trove of relevant historical documents described in a chapter Wayland-Smith calls "The Burning."[1] There were parallels to these and other facets of Oneida's post-utopian existence in the afterlife of the Compton community. But as one would expect, they occurred on a much smaller and less dramatic scale: minor success stories, on the one hand, quiet evasions on the other, and, as among Oneida descendants, an ongoing sense of the importance of kin ties.

In the case of B. Compton Limited, any consideration of life beyond community must return to a point made earlier in this work: unlike many utopian communities, it had never fully kept itself to itself. To borrow a term used by Albert Schrauwers in reference to the Children of Peace, a breakaway Quaker sect in nineteenth-century Ontario,

B. Compton Limited was always a "part culture," "at once contained by a larger society, yet dissenting from it." Indeed, as Enid Charles and Sylvia Anthony had observed in their 1943 study for *Rural Sociology*, its people were "in no sense alien" in the larger society of Prince Edward Island; an "eccentric group," to be sure, but by no means exotic.[2] Their faith was a variant of the province's strong Presbyterian tradition, and their charity, while it began with a concern for their own elderly and dependent members, had never ended there. Moreover, community children had attended local schools. Community men had worked alongside hired employees, particularly in Belle River, and routinely had dealings with local farmers and businesses. The company store was also a general store for the larger Belle River neighbourhood. The community's leaders had interacted with the larger world as business heads and, in Hector Compton's case, as a respected civic leader. Crucially, though, the leaders had always sought to restrict and control their members' interactions with the larger society. When that gate-keeper role ended with the winding up of the community, they all – Hector included – entered a challenging new era, albeit in a familiar setting.

Hector

In the immediate aftermath of the burning of the mill in 1942, a despondent Hector had written that he would take no lead in rebuilding what his community – and the larger neighbourhood – had collectively lost through the conflagration, and that he looked forward to "be[ing] engaged in a pursuit nearer to my heart than Shooks."[3] Ultimately, he got what he wanted. He had struggled mightily to maintain B. Compton Limited, but when that had proved futile and the winding-up tasks had been completed, that painful phase was succeeded by a sense of relief that business responsibilities were at last behind him and that he could pursue interests nearer to his heart.

To be sure, it was not clear sailing. He began the 1950s with financial worries, for in the dividing up of company assets there was very little to provide him with personal income, and since by the standards of the time he was already an old man, looking elsewhere for work was not a realistic option. In these circumstances, the newly established federal old age pension, universally available from 1951 to Canadians over seventy, was a great – if ironic – boon. Over the years, Hector's opposition to state intervention had become well established. Yet when the new pension plan began he was not slow to apply, providing the regional director in Charlottetown with assorted materials to establish his age, since he had no baptismal or government record as proof that he qualified.[4] The death of his wife in 1957 was a deep personal loss – as well as a pension lost. But it was followed by a beneficial transition in his living arrangements: his only Island-based son and his young family moved in to share the large and comfortable home that Hector had helped his own father to build at the end of the 1800s. The arrangement provided financial security, the housekeeping talents of a much-appreciated (if long-suffering) daughter-in-law, and the loving distractions of grandchildren. Fortuitously, despite his age he had himself shingled and otherwise renovated the house just a few years earlier. He would continue into his eighty-sixth year to earn occasional income doing custom repair work in a small workshop. These and other physical and monetary contributions allowed him to maintain a sense of independence and dignity. Meanwhile, with the "erstwhile parlour" now converted to a study, he had ample space within the shared household in which to pursue the interests that would see him well into the last of his ninety-one years.[5]

"Since Bessie departed over three years ago," he told his US-based cousin Marion in 1960, "my chief interest in life is found in Living Scripture, in correspondence with relatives and with eminent Friends abroad."[6] In addition to close family members, the correspondence with relatives included distant expatriate kin like Marion, some of whom he had seldom or never met, but with whom he had overlapping interests. With Marion, the link was Compton genealogy, but in many cases the shared interest was religious questions. By the late 1950s he estimated the number of his correspondents at almost fifty. He used much of his old age pension to buy books from conservative religious publishers and to subscribe to their periodicals on behalf of others as well as himself. A record-book entry written a few years before he died noted that "In an earnest endeavour to spread the Gospel of the Coming Kingdom of God on earth I have devoted much time and I think about $2000.00 in cash in literature & postage over the last thirty years."[7] His "eminent Friends abroad" were chiefly authors and editors of the publications he received and heads of associated organizations, many of them propounding the claims of Anglo- or British-Israelism, flattering him with their brotherly salutations (they "address me as 'Dear Brother' or 'My Dear Brother'"), and soliciting subscriptions and donations.[8]

Although Anglo-Israelism had attracted an eclectic range of followers in the English-speaking world in the nineteenth and early twentieth centuries, it lacked any grounding in respectable scholarship and by the 1950s was very much a fringe movement, largely ignored by mainstream theologians and baffling in its paradoxical – and, increasingly, hostile – attitudes towards contemporary Jews. Even on the religious Right, there were writers who found it far-fetched and regarded it as harmful to the evangelical cause, not least because of its overt racism.[9] As shown in earlier chapters, Hector had been attracted by Anglo-Israelism even as a much younger man, notwithstanding its seeming lack of fit with other more expansive and generous elements in his theological outlook. Not only was it part of McDonaldite religious tradition but it also meshed with Hector's ongoing belief in the virtues of the British Empire/Commonwealth and his pride in British identity.[10] His encounters in retirement with Anglo-Israelite publications took him well beyond his earlier and comparatively anodyne interest in the subject and built on his wartime discovery of the US periodical *Destiny*. He regarded the American and British authors whose views he read in this and other publications as learned men who had developed a unique understanding of scriptures and of world events. Persuaded by these "great Minds" and flattered by their correspondence, he himself wrote letters that echoed their obsessions.[11] Thus, writing in 1954 to Angus MacLean, his Conservative member of Parliament and a future provincial premier, to express opposition to any attempt to eliminate the Union Jack from Canada's flag, he identified what he saw as analogous evils on the international scene. They included the United Nations and other expressions of One Worldism, the papacy, and the "'Zionist-Communist' monster with the funds of the International Bankers at their disposal."[12] To be sure, many other individuals and organizations with a conservative Christian worldview also denounced organizations like the United Nations, and, in the US, sought mightily to influence foreign policy. But Anglo-Israelites seem to have been particularly given to outright racism and made themselves increasingly marginal even on the religious Right.[13]

How successful was Hector in persuading others to accept his views and prejudices? Angus MacLean, replying to his letter, claimed to agree with him "almost completely." But he went on to clarify that he was particularly in accord on the flag issue. An outright repudiation of Hector's more troubling views was hardly to be expected, for MacLean would have known Hector and his people personally and been mindful of the fact that they were long-time Conservative voters.[14] Some other correspondents, though, both distant relatives and immediate family members, took him politely but firmly to task. An American cousin with whom he corresponded regularly on religious matters wrote in 1960, "In your letters and reading material, I find no love for peoples other than Israelites" (she did not, of course, mean contemporary

Jews). Hector's long and defensive reply would certainly not have led her to change her mind.[15] Hector's eldest son, writing to him three years later from Alberta and commenting on the most recent tract sent by his father, took issue both with repeated claims for the imminent coming of the Kingdom of Heaven (hadn't preachers been saying that since ancient times?) and with purported hierarchies of race and religion. Though not a skilled letter writer, he made his points with forcefulness and sincerity:

> You will think I am an unbeliever but I am not and I too have a right to think things out for myself and I like many others have to live and work with this world and one sees many things to open his eyes and think about[.] [W]hether it be from Catholic, Jew or whatever a person can learn something from any of them and I don't want to spend the rest of my days hating any part of the world just because they are not supposed to be Israelites. If that is religion I don't want any part of it. It seems to me the main theme of all those writers is to condemn certain classes of humanity. Well as I understand [it] that is Gods work not ours. And I don't feel one bit above another race and some of them haven't corrupted this earth nearly as much as the white man with his greed and money.[16]

There is no correspondence between Hector and nearby kin to cast light on how his views were being received locally. But letters he wrote to out-of-province recipients indicate that he saw himself as something of a martyr to his chosen cause. Thus in 1954 he spoke of being "ostracised, ridiculed" for his end-times expectations, and in 1960 of being "silently but tenaciously hated" because of "my Israel beliefs."[17] It is unlikely that the prejudice and racism in his "Israel beliefs" and in the literature he wanted them to read caused much discomfort to his Prince Edward Island kin, for in this most ethnically homogeneous of Canadian provinces[18] there would still in the 1950s and early 1960s have been little awareness of, much less sensitivity about, the identities and claims of "the Other." Indeed, such now odious phrases as "heathen hordes" – used by Hector in reference to anticolonial agitation in Africa and Asia – would still have been in the vocabulary of numerous Canadians and unexceptionable in much of the media. Moreover, the events being referenced were far away, remote from Canadians' everyday concerns, and not generally understood in apocalyptic terms.[19] More likely his blood relatives, and some of those who had married into his family, were discomfited by the elderly Hector's repeated exhortations about end times and frustrated by his continuing opposition to the longing of a younger generation to lead normal lives by doing such things as attending church, if they so desired, and celebrating Christmas. For Hector, these were acts of apostasy and rebellion. Organized religion was an evil akin to "International Finance." Churches "coddled" their members and offered only "Churchianity." Meanwhile, he made clear, he himself had a uniquely large collection of Bibles and other sources of sound doctrine with which to provide spiritual guidance.[20] As for celebrating Christmas, much like seventeenth-century Puritans, he regarded doing so as a form of idolatry.[21] Feeling himself to be judged and unappreciated for his religious views and contrarian stances, he found solace in the company and unconditional love of young grandchildren, with whom he was a gentle and tender-hearted presence.[22]

In truth, Hector probably exaggerated the opposition to his personal brand of religiosity. I have seen no evidence that he was "tenaciously hated." But he was undoubtedly regarded as excessively preachy by some relatives in Bangor and Belle River, especially the younger ones. Still, they were taught to respect him as the elder statesman in the extended family, an accomplished, dignified, and intelligent old man. As long as he lived, he formed something of a bond between the two former community settlements.[23] When he died in July 1970, relatives from Bangor left off their work and made the cross-country trip to attend the funeral. Two ministers presided at the service,[24] a concession to changed times and one Hector himself had reluctantly made when his wife died in 1957.[25] But, honouring his opposition to "Churchianity," the funeral service took place in his home rather than in a church. Neighbours joined his children and extended family, so many that they spilled out of the house and onto its neat lawns to participate in the service as best they could. Though the utopian community over which he had presided had ceased to exist more than twenty years earlier, he had remained a living link with that past. His death marked the end of an era.

A Changing Province

The changes that took place in the lives of former community members after B. Compton Limited was wound up coincided with a period when their province was being transformed. A multi-faceted process of modernization was altering the face of Prince Edward Island in the mid-century decades. It would reach a climax in the 1970s, historian Edward MacDonald writes, but "it was in the 1950s that modernization became manifest." Significant new federal funds and services came into the province. A great increase in paved roads and rural electrification, school and farm consolidation, the redundancy of horses, the advent of television – all were part of the changing scene. Despite these and other changes, the province's overall standard of living remained well below the national average. The provincial and federal governments sought to address the gap at the end of the 1960s by making modernization official policy with a costly and controversial Comprehensive Development Plan.[26] Island residents knew and cared that theirs was a have-not province. Arguably, though, what mattered most on an everyday basis was not national standards of living or the opportunities for fulfilling lifestyles in the country's largest cities but rather the material and cultural way of life they observed around them.

Varieties of Religious Experience

One aspect of Island culture that did not change appreciably in this period of modernization was the role of organized religion: in practice, Christianity. Even after church involvement began to falter nationally in the 1960s, beginning with the mainstream Protestant denominations that had flourished and expanded in the preceding decade, churchgoing remained part of the Island way of life. It was, quite simply, an important component of identity and respectability – and sociability. As well, even after national leaders of the mainstream denominations began moving away from traditional beliefs and orthodoxies in the 1960s, starting with the United Church of Canada's controversial "New Evangelism," Islanders, like other Maritimers, remained more comfortable with the faith of their forebears. Religious observance, irrespective of denomination, would remain salient in the province even late in the century.[27]

And yet, the older generation of former Compton community members did not rush to associate themselves with organized religion. This was neither because they continued to gather on their own for devotional purposes nor because they had adopted a wholly secular outlook.[28] Probably they felt some uneasiness about the prospect of partaking in what was for them an unfamiliar cultural practice as well as concern about how they would be received. But so long as Hector lived, awareness of his hostility towards institutional worship was perhaps an even stronger deterrent. The unmarried and still resident children of that older generation likewise seem not to have become regular churchgoers in the 1950s and early 1960s. Some of the Bangor children in these years did sporadically partake of a vacation Bible school conducted by itinerant evangelists in the settlement's former but now otherwise unused McDonaldite church. But they somehow sensed their parents' discomfort with this.

Not surprisingly, marriage to a religiously observant partner became, for some, a segue into regular churchgoing. For others it came after the Reverend Ted MacDougall, a gifted and charismatic young minister of the Free Church of Scotland on Prince Edward Island, returned from studying outside the province and was inducted into that church's Eastern Charge in 1964. The Free Church, a tiny denomination affiliated from mid-century with a like-minded body in Scotland, had deep roots in the province's McDonaldite tradition and remained more conservative in doctrine and on social issues than the mainstream Presbyterian Church in Canada, despite a shared background in the Reformed church heritage. Ted MacDougall was himself a product of that tradition. His father was the McDonaldite minister who had preached weekly radio sermons during the early days of CFCY and, in the same period, conducted the marriages of several Compton community members. Ted MacDougall was, nonetheless, something of an anomaly among local religious conservatives with his strong academic background in science and his openness to young people struggling with faith issues in the turbulent religious climate of the late 1960s and early 1970s. His engaging personality and the fact that he was a kind of kinsman as a result of much earlier marriages between Comptons and MacDougalls would also have facilitated an effective outreach to a people long estranged from churchgoing. It was he who in 1970 was asked to take the lead in conducting Hector's funeral service. He also reached out to Bangor Comptons and other Islanders whose people had been part of the McDonaldite tradition. Among those who began attending his services on a regular basis in the 1970s was Hector's youngest, Bangor-based, brother as well as some members of the next two generations, that is, men and women who had been young adults when the community ended, and their children.[29]

For those next generations, whether they remained on the Island or left it, or were born and raised "away," there were varied patterns of religious involvement. For the son and daughter-in-law with whom the elderly Hector had lived, it took the form of decades-long participation in the local Presbyterian church, as it did for at least one of his daughters.[30] Meanwhile, a grandson of founder Ben Compton became a minister in the increasingly liberal United Church of Canada, while a grandson of "Big John" Compton trained in Scotland for ministry in the Free Church of Scotland on Prince Edward Island and became pastor in a historic McDonaldite church. Neither man linked his career choice to his ancestor's role as a religious leader in the Compton community. Evidently, neither at the time knew much about that aspect of his family background. Rather, both spoke of Ted MacDougall as a positive influence on their vocational choice.[31]

In the last half of the twentieth century, newer evangelical denominations such as the Church of the Nazarene and the Pentecostal Assembly joined older denominations with an evangelical orientation on Prince Edward Island. Groups such as these attracted some descendants of former Compton community members from the same generational cohort as the two ordained ministers, among them some musically gifted granddaughters of founder Ben. They became well known in the eastern part of the province for a gospel-singing repertoire that, even in the twenty-first century, continued to include at least one McDonaldite hymn.[32] The McDonaldite musical legacy had been passed along by those with living memories of Compton community worship. In the last half of the twentieth century, a few extended family members still gathered occasionally with others to sing and record the most familiar of the old hymns. More commonly, snatches of half-remembered hymn tunes were sung privately and perhaps unconsciously by some former communitarians in the course of their working day.

The foregoing paragraphs may suggest that a kind of "gene" for religion, especially of the evangelical Protestant variety, lived on in families whose people had been Compton community members. Contributing to this impression is the fact that, even among Compton community descendants who had been born and raised away and whose community-raised parents had never become religiously observant, there were some who as teenagers or young adults had found a sense of stability and direction for their lives following a vital religious experience of the sort commonly described and shared in evangelical Christian circles. One American professional woman with this background wrote, "The decision to follow Christ was mine alone, however it was definitely influenced by the faith of others in my family and the changes I witnessed in their lives as they came to know Christ themselves."[33]

Nevertheless, on matters of faith, the trajectories of former community members and their descendants were more varied and complex than the foregoing would suggest. In addition to those for whom religious belief and practice played a central, even dominant, role in their lives, there were two other broad patterns. Some became members or adherents of mainstream Protestant denominations. They typically did so without becoming consistently active in their church's Sunday services or fully subscribing to its creeds. Rather, they were involved in such things as its social outreach, its fundraising events, and such elements of worship as lay reading. How and why they became involved and what they did varied according to where they lived, the marital and social relationships they established, and their degree of comfort with leadership roles. They identified with a particular denomination, but that identity was neither the most salient aspect of their private and public lives nor the source of their closest personal associations and friendships. Meanwhile, another, perhaps larger, group of descendants lived religiously non-observant lives and raised children who typically weren't baptized and had little or no exposure to such practices as Sunday School attendance. To the extent that clergy played a role in the lives of this secular sub-set, it was simply to preside over their marriages and, eventually, their funerals. This was, of course, a pattern reflective of the increasing movement in the 1960s towards secularization in Canada and the western world generally.[34]

In their study of Christianity in Canada since 1945, historians Brian Clarke and Stuart Macdonald document national patterns of secularization and highlight the importance of the 1960s as the decade when such patterns clearly emerged. Before the 1960s, they write, "Christian rituals and world views were part and parcel of Canadian culture; after the 1960s that was no longer the case, and as a result, many Canadians fell out of the habit of joining a congregation and sending their children to Sunday School."[35] People whose parents had never formed the church habit – indeed, had been raised to reject it, as in the case of Compton community alumni – were arguably more likely than others to drift into the culture of secularization that was becoming normative and to raise children who, as adults themselves, showed little or no interest in any form of religious observance. The norms of a culture of secularization would have been strongest if their upbringing took place off-Island in urban Canada.

Changes and Continuities in Work and Education

The Belle River settlement that had been the birthplace and centre of B. Compton Limited struggled with the transition to a post-community way of life for several decades after the dissolution of the company in 1947. The departure of young men that had already been a concern for Hector in the late 1940s continued. It both resulted from and contributed to the economic decline in the once thriving community. With the burning of the sawmill and the large dairy barn, there had remained no substantial means of employing young adults. A few, such as the son with whom the elderly Hector lived, created their own small businesses, but Hector's four other sons moved away. Over the next few decades, many of the young of both sexes, and even a few of the not so young, also left the settlement, through marriage in the case of some young women but mostly in search of job opportunities elsewhere in the province or, more usually, beyond. Most eventually succeeded in creating viable new lives and livelihoods. A few were unable to do so.

In a conversation with Hector in the early 1960s, his sister Libby identified excessive drinking and the bad example in that regard set by some leading men during the community era as the reason for the "present floundering" of the young. Their difficulties, Hector conceded, were undeniable.[36] Yet the pattern of excessive drinking that troubled Hector and his sister was more than just the result of bad examples in the past. It was an attempt to cope with a problem that, as shown in the previous chapter, one of Hector's brothers had diagnosed in 1945. He interpreted it as a by-product of their restricted and regimented communal life with its consequent dwarfing of individual personality and "a most glorious dose of inferiority complex." That sense of inferiority, he had written in his anguished letter to Hector, was something that "you can see growing on the younger generation steadily, and which one feels every time you come in contact with the rest of His Creation [the outside world]."[37] Such problems would lessen only in later years and with the passage of time. In regard to alcohol abuse, the positive example set by Libby's son may also have helped. A Second World War veteran and merchant, and later a provincial politician, Dan Compton, like many other North Americans, achieved a lasting sobriety by joining Alcoholics Anonymous (AA), an organization that helped to sustain his own faith and will power. Through AA, he assisted other Islanders within and beyond his kin circle, a contribution for which he was formally recognized in the larger Belfast neighbourhood.[38]

Not surprisingly, over the years many of the buildings on the Hill that had once so impressed visitors deteriorated or passed into new hands. The former company store, operated for several decades by Dan, was sold by the early 1980s. After his death in 1990, his lifelong home also passed out of family hands. When the century-old house in which Hector had lived was sold in 2005, the last physical tie to the community era was gone. Only a short road on the Hill named for Dan Compton provided a link to the cluster of closely connected families who had once lived and prospered there.

Overall, the families that had been part of the Bangor branch of B. Compton Limited had a less fraught transition to the new era. Struggles with alcohol and instances of out-migration occurred as they did in Belle River, and in the province overall, but to a lesser extent. All five Bangor households had been farming households, and, as explained in Chapter 6, they had operated with a greater degree of autonomy even before the community era had ended. Quite simply, there was more continuity to see them through the period of change. Though the five families now owned outright the land that they had formerly farmed communally, they continued to share farm machinery and woodland by the terms of the winding-up agreement. For some years, therefore, they did a good many things cooperatively during the annual planting and harvesting cycle. Then, in the 1960s and early 1970s, several sons in the family headed by Hector's youngest brother made a transition to larger-scale farming on their own, first as an informal partnership of father and sons and then as an incorporated business. Their practice of assembling large acreages through purchase or rental agreements and engaging in monoculture, with potatoes as their cash crop, was in keeping with transitions in Prince Edward Island agriculture in this period. The transitions included the virtual end of subsistence farming, fewer but larger holdings, increased mechanization, and significantly increased production of a single cash crop.[39] Meanwhile, in the other Bangor households that had once been part of the Compton community, those who did not leave the settlement to live and work elsewhere eventually combined off-farm jobs with small-scale farming and eventually sold or rented much of their land. In contrast to Belle River, the family name did not disappear from the settlement's mailboxes. Indeed, whether because of a family tradition of working cooperatively or simple good fortune, the incorporated family agriculture business was able to carry on into the twenty-first century and into a second generation.

What happened in Belle River after the community era ended was an extreme example of depopulation and infrastructural decline on Prince Edward Island, but otherwise the socio-economic transitions that occurred in the Compton households in both settlements in the mid-century decades were in keeping with larger Island patterns. This is evident, as just shown, in regard to changed agricultural patterns. But it was also the case in the matter of education. Like their nineteenth-century ancestors, leaders of the Compton community had not encouraged higher learning for their children. And yet, children born to community members in the 1940s, and certainly the next generation, fared at least as well in this regard as other neighbourhood

children. This was in large part because, across the province, public provision for education beyond the one-room schoolhouse had
remained dismal for *all* children until the late 1950s. As late as 1952,
fewer than one-third of children then in grade 2 would go on to com-
plete high school; across the country the national average was fifty-
two out of one hundred children.[40] The historic reluctance of poor
school districts to tax themselves in order to provide decent facili-
ties and attract qualified teachers had persisted into the mid-twentieth
century, as had the willingness of a few, usually wealthier, districts to
do what was needful to attract good teachers capable of instructing
and inspiring potential high achievers. Meanwhile, provincial spending per pupil on elementary and secondary education had remained
far below the national average even in 1956: "$92 compared with the
Canadian average of $219."[41] The improved educational opportunities
that became available in the late 1950s meant that Compton children
born in the previous decade as the community era was ending could
attend regional high schools like other Island teenagers. A decade
later, the province also had a technical college and a provincially
funded non-denominational university, replacing a Catholic university and a junior college that had offered the first two years of university.[42] Even with improved educational facilities at last in place, many
rural Island families, former communitarian families included, lacked
the resources or the determination to see that their children benefited
from post-primary schooling. Nevertheless, many children from this
communitarian background were able to take advantage of the new
opportunities, especially as their parents threw off the old community unease with higher education and made new pathways possible.
Meanwhile, even before the advent of new opportunities and changed
attitudes, a few older siblings of these younger, more privileged, communitarian children had somehow contrived to get high school or
vocational training and, as adults, seized opportunities to obtain academic and professional training.

For the first generation with ready access to education beyond the
common-school level, subsequently leaving the Island for broader
horizons was all but taken for granted. Those born later had less reason to go away. As "the garden transformed," there were more possibilities than formerly for rewarding work for both sexes within the
province, particularly in the public sector: in the provincial and federal civil service, in teaching, and even in the growing tourism sector. They could have the cherished Island way of life for themselves
and, in time, for their children without having to settle for a markedly
inferior standard of living. Even if, as many did, they opted to live in

rural areas and commute to their off-farm jobs, they could provide their families with access to modern mass media and such amenities as up-to-date sports facilities and, without much travel, to urban entertainment and cultural venues. Meanwhile, Island-born descendants of community members whose formal education ended before or during their high-school years could likewise be found both among the Compton diaspora (now almost always occurring within Canada) and in their native province, with a small number shuttling between those two worlds, tugged on the one hand by good-paying off-Island jobs and on the other by the lure of home.

As the twentieth century ended, community-descended women and men born in the middle decades of the century (the 1940s, 1950s, and 1960s) were probably as well represented as other Island-born men and women in diverse fields of employment. They worked in a wide array of labouring jobs, and in trades, education, service industries, bureaucracies, and most professions. They had also become entrepreneurs in fields that ranged from updated versions of ancestral occupations such as farming and boat building to new forms of communications media. Occupational diversity was also characteristic of relatives born off-Island. Geographically dispersed and numbering in their hundreds, these community descendants had not, in the end, been significantly delayed or handicapped by their ancestors' unconventional life in a utopian community.[43] Nevertheless, as this chapter has already shown and as the next section further illustrates, there were legacies from that era that were complex and long lasting.

Ties That Bind and Ties That Shamed

In the early post-community days, a strong sense of kinship persisted. Among the Bangor families, as noted, some farm tasks continued to be done on a cooperative basis. And in both settlements, the children were more likely to have cousins rather than other schoolmates as their closest friends. Visits back and forth between Bangor and Belle River were an expected part of many summer Sundays. Until his passing, Hector, in particular, was a living bond between the two groups of families and a reminder of their once strong ties. Following one visit to Bangor-area families in 1959, he wrote a remarkably detailed letter to assorted off-Island kin describing his experiences and the hospitality he had encountered in each household, seemingly with a view to including those living away in the circle of connectedness.[44] Inevitably, as time passed, the kin ties weakened, especially as a result of dispersal within, and particularly beyond, the Island. Unless they were raised in close physical proximity, children born of community-era parents often did not know, or even know about, cousins who were not their first cousins. And yet, as they grew older, some of them made a point of connecting with a larger kin circle, employing such media as Facebook and email to establish and maintain links. Funerals became occasions for establishing personal contact, however briefly, with previously little known relatives and for exploring and valuing common ties in congested blood. As hands were shaken and identities shared ("Simon was my brother"; "Russell was my father"), there remained a sense of bondedness that seemed to exceed even the usual clannishness associated with old-stock Prince Edward Island families.

Genealogical research became another link, both for community-descended women and men raised in the province and for those born and raised elsewhere, particularly in the twenty-first century as such research tools as Ancestry.com and DNA testing became commonplace and affordable. This genealogically inclined subset of Compton community descendants is, of course, part of a vast network of researchers who seek to understand more about themselves and their immediate families by finding out more about those whose ancestral blood they share. Rather than fearing the discovery of less than illustrious forebears, as was once the case,[45] many of these twenty-first-century researchers want to know about their ancestors' flaws and foibles in order to incorporate their new knowledge into a better understanding of the dynamics of their own family life.[46] As Deborah Cohen's anecdotally rich study of family secrets from the Victorians to the present day makes clear, there is a therapeutic, even "spiritual," dimension as well as entertainment value in their quests.[47] Yet online searches and even follow-up visits to archives can take such researchers only so far. Genealogically inclined descendants of the Compton community have discovered that there can be richly rewarding online contacts with others of their kin cohort and the possibility of adding a few new names to the extended family tree. But the challenge that remains for all of them is getting beyond the silences and evasions that were characteristic of their parents' and grandparents' generation.

In the immediate post-community era, there was a decided reluctance on the part of the older generation of former Compton community members to discuss their people's unconventional past. When those with the longest memories got together, aspects of the former community life with its complex kin ties and difficult denouement were sometimes discussed, though typically in hushed tones and just among themselves. One descendant born in the late 1940s observed a furtive attempt by her father and an older cousin to burn a family letter. Rescuing it from the stove, the young woman found the letter, written as the community was nearing its end, to contain nothing salacious or disgraceful but rather evidence of family tensions that preceded the break-up. It was the short, anguished account cited earlier in which one of Hector's brothers described the psychological harm he believed their community had inflicted on himself and the younger generation.[48] While there was clearly no wholesale destruction of documents related to the community era such as took place under Oneida business leaders in the 1940s,[49] neither was there any inclination to pass along even those stories from the heyday of the community era that might have been considered a source of pride for a new generation. One young man who as a university student on Prince Edward Island in the early 1970s was encouraged by his professor to write about the Compton family's utopian community for an Island Studies class met an unmistakable reticence when he approached his beloved grandmother for information. Likewise, outside researchers interested in the Comptons' unusual religious and communitarian history were politely turned away. That history, it seemed clear, was meant to remain confined to the recesses of the family memory bank rather than brought forward even in edited and sanitized form.

Attention to the mid-century context helps to explain alumni unease about revisiting the communitarian era. Before elaborating on that context, however, it is important to emphasize that silences and secrets within families are part of a long and widespread pattern and that, as noted, the attempt to uncover and even publicize them is a fairly recent phenomenon. While the silence is most understandable in connection with what Anna Green calls "extreme historical contexts," that is, matters of "public memory" with potentially serious consequences for individual families (research into problematic family ties related to the Nazi era and the former Soviet Union, for instance),[50] it has been most pervasive in ordinary families keen to hide ancestral embarrassments. As Australian historian Marjorie Theobald observed in 2010 in writing about her own family, many of the matters that were once sources of shame and therefore kept hidden have now "gone completely from our moral handbook."[51] But while they lasted they were deeply troubling for families across the Anglo-Saxon world who valued respectability. In *Family Secrets*, Deborah Cohen includes mixed-race and out-of-wedlock ancestors, "defective" children, homosexuality, and domestic violence as the sorts of things that the Victorian middle class increasingly sought to hide. An entire chapter in *The Family Story: Blood, Contract and Intimacy, 1830–1960* augments Cohen's examples, listing many other matters that families still sought to keep private in the first half of the twentieth century.[52]

While the Victorian era is stereotyped as the time of greatest concern about family propriety and hence obsessiveness with protecting family secrets, Cohen suggests that mid-twentieth-century families may actually have been more inclined than their Victorian forebears to want to hide potentially troubling family matters.[53] Her suggestion, though based on research on British families, accords with popular images of 1950s Cold War North America as an age of conformity, especially when it came to family norms. "Normal" families were idealized, as a bulwark against the inroads of Communism as well as a source of societal well-being and personal fulfilment.[54]

Unfortunately for the families of the former Compton community, it was at precisely this historical moment that they had to engage fully with the outside world. As seen, it was at mid-century that Prince Edward Island was increasingly drawn into a larger national and North American culture and into the modernizing and homogenizing values that prevailed in those larger worlds. Their former way of life as a utopian community now became problematic in a way that it hadn't been previously, certainly not in the 1930s when its communitarian values and practices had been commended by journalists and other outside inquirers, or even in the early 1940s when, according to scholars Enid Charles and Sylvia Anthony, the community was regarded by neighbours with "respect and affection, combined with tolerance of differences in behaviour."[55] Writing in the 1960s on "Varieties of Literary Utopias," Northrop Frye observed that in the western democracies there was "something of a paralysis of utopian thought and imagination" as a result of the "repudiation of Communism." The "straight utopia" gave way to "utopian satire," as in William Golding's *Lord of the Flies*.[56] It may seem to be something of a stretch to link this broad cultural and literary moment to the world of the Comptons. And yet, that world was a microcosmic illustration of its reach: concern and misunderstanding about "Communism" had a spillover effect even in such remote and unlikely corners of Cold War North America as Prince Edward Island. This concern resulted in confusion and unease even about communitarian groups that bore no resemblance to Soviet-style socialism. The same woman who rescued from fire the family letter mentioned above distinctly remembers a conversation in which her father referred to a perception among some locals that their people had been "Communists."

The transition to life in a modernizing rural society was bound to be challenging for older men and women who had lived most or all of their lives in a community informed by unconventional economic and religious practices and helmed by a patriarch whose goal, to the extent possible, was to have its members live apart from the mainstream. In retrospect it is unsurprising that neither they nor the men and women who came to adulthood in the troubled late community era were willing to share reminiscences when in later years their children or others asked them to do so. Nevertheless, the transitional era was also challenging for Compton community descendants who came to adulthood with few or no memories of their people's former way of life. Their families' unconventional past shadowed them, albeit to varying degrees, and left them feeling "other." They wanted to be regarded not as different but rather as conventional, respectable, and "modern." Thus, occasional questions about whether they were related to "those" Comptons were perceived as laden with innuendo and condescension. Such questions were interpreted as harking back to the Compton community's differentness in terms of such matters as "communistic" economic arrangements, educational deficiencies, cousin marriage, and religious practices.

In the third decade of the twenty-first century, when acceptance and embrace of diversity is a hallmark of Canada's aspirational self-image, those long-ago sensitivities may seem positively quaint. But for at least some of those who experienced them, they retain a vividness and poignancy. I was one of "those" Comptons. As an exceedingly self-conscious and conformist-minded teenager when I finished high school in the late 1950s, what most concerned me in terms of fitting in was the matter of our anomalous religious identity.[57] At the time, I knew little about other aspects of my extended family's past beyond the fact that it was unconventional. But I did know that, while religion seemed to matter in our own household in a vague and undemonstrative way (a dusty black Bible in our parents' bedroom; "The Old-Fashioned Revival Hour" on the radio[58] as we ate our Sunday dinner; our father singing snatches of hymn tunes as he went about his work), our family didn't attend church and had never made a practice of doing so. In contrast, all of my high-school classmates, Catholics and Protestants alike, went to church, mostly to the mainstream United Church of Canada in the case of the Protestants. I wanted very much to be part of that, part of Prince Edward Island's church-sanctioned culture of respectability and normalcy.

Perhaps if I had remained on the Island it would have happened. But like several of my siblings, I longed to shed the extended family baggage and move on: to anonymity as well as job opportunities. It would take many decades of living away and a historian's slowly acquired awareness of social and cultural complexity before I concluded that my "embarrassing" past was in fact rich social history. From the safe distance of the twenty-first century, it came to seem like a worthwhile scholarly initiative rather than a source of personal or familial discomfort to revisit my ancestors' religious "otherness" and their attempt to create a godly utopia.

Concluding Reflections

My research for *All Things in Common* unearthed some ongoing patterns and proclivities in the ways that generations of Comptons responded to their changing circumstances from the late eighteenth century onward. Were the recurring family behaviours a result of nature or nurture? Recent research in genetics, and especially in the relatively new field of epigenetics,[1] has made that old, dichotomizing question less useful. Among experts who write for a popular audience there are now lively debates about "the relative contributions of genes and environment ... to the formation of personalities."[2] In *A Brief History of Everyone Who Ever Lived: The Stories in Our Genes*, geneticist Adam Rutherford adopts something of a middle ground in terms of the debate. "Genes change culture, culture changes genes," he writes, later adding that "We swing from genetic determinism to genetic denialism. Both extremes are simplistically wrong."[3] As its title suggests, Christine Kenneally's *The Invisible History of the Human Race: How DNA and History Shape Our Identities and Our Futures* likewise adopts a middle-of-the-road approach, though it leans towards the importance of inheritance. Kenneally draws on the work of a wide range of researchers, historians among them, to make a case for the ability of genealogical and genetic research to help illuminate the sources of who we are and argues that research of this sort is effectively "[b]lurring the boundaries between family history, personal history, and social history."[4]

Given past misrepresentations in genealogy and genetics and the dark uses to which they have been put, most historians remain wary of such research.[5] Nevertheless, like the historians Kenneally cites, other historians in future may be drawn to projects that engage with specialist research on the relative roles of genes and environments in their attempts to detect and understand individuals' and families' patterned responses over time to changing historical circumstances. Especially given the protracted history of intermarriage in one branch of the Compton line, the debates seemed to me both germane and intriguing as I pondered intergenerational patterns of Compton family behaviour, and for that reason worth referencing in these concluding reflections. That said, it is only the patterns, and not their underlying sources, on which I can responsibly comment in the pages that follow.

Some of the patterns, such as a tendency for the men to stick to a limited range of occupations generation after generation, may have been the norm in many if not most North American families until fairly recently. But in other ways these particular Comptons were outliers. Loyalist William's decision not to support the American Revolution provides striking evidence of this. Even in deeply divided and sorely tempted colonial New Jersey, most of William's neighbours and kin ultimately rejected the lure of the Loyalist cause. Yet outlier tendencies went back even further. From the time that Loyalist William's forebears had come to New Jersey in the 1660s, having fled the New World Puritans' theocratic religious control and taken up with the new sect called Baptists, they seem to have been drawn to religious mavericks. That pattern would continue among his descendants in the Maritime provinces, most notably in their gravitation to Prince Edward Island's defiantly unconventional Scottish Presbyterian clergyman Donald McDonald, until, ultimately, they themselves became the mavericks: a fiercely believing people who were, finally, without even a church to call their own.

Nor was the resistance to structure and external authority necessarily confined to the realm of religion. It may explain the inability of Loyalist William's son and namesake to fit into the burgeoning family shipbuilding enterprise of his Vaughan in-laws in St. Martins, New Brunswick, in the early 1800s. From a twenty-first-century perspective, the paths that Loyalist William, his son, and their descendants chose in secular and religious life seem often to have been at odds with their own best interests. Though not without talents and a willingness to take risks, they remained people of, at best, modest means even after the long decades of land insecurity were behind them, and largely invisible and without acclaim until well into their utopian moment.

That moment was, of course, the time of their most obvious "otherness." Yet even in that phase they departed in an important respect from what is often regarded as a normative feature of full-fledged utopian communities: a greater flexibility on gender roles. Hector D.

Compton may have claimed in 1945 that the community over which he presided as secretary-treasurer was just like what Edward Bellamy had envisioned in his celebrated utopian novel *Looking Backward*. But under the patriarchal Hector there was no hint of the enlarged possibilities for women that Bellamy had envisioned and that had led to his novel's being embraced by contemporary women's movement activists.[6] Finally, these Comptons' utopianism prolonged a pattern of very large families and close-cousin marriages well after these phenomena had ceased to be social norms even in "backward" Prince Edward Island.

Generation after generation they seem to have lived and died without much of a relationship to the state in its various manifestations.[7] As refugees, Loyalist William and his family were briefly dependent on imperial officials in New York and New Brunswick for the aid that enabled their precarious existence. But thereafter, their descendants appear to have had only limited and intermittent interaction with the apparatus of the state, even after it transitioned to a liberal order that fostered and was crucial to an emerging democratic capitalist society in nineteenth-century Canada. In this, admittedly, they were but an extreme case of a larger pattern. In an influential article in 2000, Ian McKay portrayed the emergence of a "liberal order framework" that was becoming hegemonic in central Canada in the mid-nineteenth century. Crucially, however, as McKay acknowledged, the emerging liberal order did not succeed in fully eliminating "antithetical traditions" and "aliberal entities."[8] In a follow-up to his article, R.W. Sandwell drew on historiography on Canadian families to illustrate the limits of liberalism's reach. In the nineteenth and even in the first half of the twentieth century, she noted, "many people lived out their lives, or some portion of them" in "aliberal worlds." Families who were poor or rural were particularly unlikely or unable to opt into a liberal order in which progress and individualism were dominant themes and in which, by the early twentieth century, such seemingly egalitarian goals and values as companionate marriage relationships were becoming part of liberalism's broadening agenda. Moreover, "old ties of kinship, hierarchy, collectivism, loyalty, and obedience, though under increasing strain as the twentieth century progressed, continued to shape family relations in many households."[9]

Historians writing about state formation and consolidation in the Maritimes have found that the apparatus of the state had an extremely limited reach in the mid-nineteenth century and, even in the early twentieth century, an *ad hoc* character, particularly in terms of everyday life in rural communities and families.[10] "[R]eligion was a far more powerful influence upon everyday life … than was the influence of the provincial 'state,'" Graham Wynn observed in writing about the earlier period.[11] This was arguably the case throughout the region well into the twentieth century. It was certainly the case for the Comptons and their utopian community.

Even during the Great Depression, neither the federal nor provincial government did much to assist Prince Edward Islanders, as I noted in Chapter 4. As secretary-treasurer of B. Compton Limited, Hector Compton seems not to have expected it to be otherwise, declining to participate in even tentative efforts to seek government aid for potato growers, and providing modest aid to needy individuals and families on behalf of the company as an aspect of his people's civic and Christian duty. When during the following decade he had to deal with unprecedented wartime government intervention in the company's business affairs, he experienced frustration and even anguish, particularly since the new requirements came at a time when his main concern was signs of end times and his people's unreadiness for the Coming Crisis. It was only in the wake of the postwar dissolution of B. Compton Limited, more or less coincident with steps towards Prince Edward Island's modernization via more activist federal and provincial governments, that the families who had been part of the Compton community were in a position to participate in the new order. Even Hector then proved willing to take advantage of the good things on offer, as was shown in his eagerness to qualify for the old age pension.

Despite being an "eccentric group" in Prince Edward Island society,[12] the utopian Comptons were free from outside interference with their way of life. This was not only because there was no strong and intrusive state to coerce them – they were, in any event, breaking no written laws – but also because, as a people, they were deeply rooted in Island society and helmed by a man whose leadership qualities were recognized and valued well beyond Belle River. They were, quite simply, part of the Island's social fabric: hardworking and reliable in their personal conduct, valued for what they provided by way of employment and social support, only mildly gossip-worthy in their unorthodox marital and worship arrangements, and their men only somewhat more noteworthy than their neighbours when it came to a fondness for drink.

Ultimately what seems most salient about this family line, since it helps to account for much else, was the strength and endurance of their kin ties. William Compton may have been unlucky or imprudent in not finding a place among his up-and-coming Vaughan in-laws in early nineteenth-century St. Martins, but there can be no denying the cohesiveness of the large family that he and Mary raised. With the exception of the son who remained in New Brunswick, their children had all been part of the Cape Breton years, and then, by 1841, they had all – adult sons included – become residents of Prince Edward Island. The peculiar circumstances of their fecund descendants' intertwined familial and religious lives had further strengthened the kinship networks even in the decades before some of them became godly utopians. Even the young Mary Compton who fled to Boston from her father's dreary household in the 1920s retained strong, lifelong ties with other Island kin and an inability to reject entirely even those aspects of her people's religious beliefs that she found most problematic.[13] The extensiveness of the elderly Hector's correspondence with off-Island relatives in the post-community years also spoke to the persistence of kin ties. A phrase in Leonore Davidoff's *Thicker Than Water: Siblings and Their Relations, 1780–1920* seemed particularly apposite as I considered the Compton phenomenon of thick blood and enduring ties: a "lattice of kinship created by fertile clan-like families." Davidoff, though, was writing about a very different phenomenon. Her subjects were middle-class families in an increasingly expansive England – the Darwins and the Gladstones are among her exemplars – and their kinship networks had "vital consequences for economic, social, and political organization."[14] One can hardly claim such consequences for the tangled networks of frequently poor and mostly anonymous Comptons. Even their years of comparative prosperity as utopians and their brief moment of fame did not ultimately translate into anything socially transformative, not even on a small scale and in their own province.

And yet families such as these are also worthy of scholarly attention. The broad field of social history has long since demonstrated the value of looking beyond famous names and transformative events as we seek to construct more inclusive and meaningful pasts. In Canada, as elsewhere, family history as part of that field has proven to be instructive and revealing even when it has dealt with families who lived on the margins and only slowly and indirectly shaped larger events, if they did so at all.

As for utopian and intentional communities, they, too, are part of Canada's social fabric, whether based on faith and family like B. Compton Limited or established for other reasons. I wrote about the Compton community at a time when, in their ancestors' homeland, the dystopian dreams of a singular individual were being proffered as the route to renewed American greatness and a cure for the nation's ills. As the disastrous elements of that "cure" unfolded, afflicting even global politics, classic fictional dystopias were rediscovered and took on a new saliency. Like many others, I read, or reread, the best-known works in this genre. They provide a salutary if fictional reminder that even admirable goals such as those of the porcine utopian dreamers in *Animal Farm* can end in disaster.[15] That real-life North American utopias have typically had less fraught and dramatic trajectories does not lessen their importance as subjects for scholarly investigation. It is my hope that *All Things in Common* will prompt historians to explore other instances of Canadian utopias and in so doing uncover the experiences of men and women who, at least for a time, dwelt "a little removed from the highway of ordinary travel"[16] as they sought to live out their dreams of community.

Notes

Introduction

1. Caption under photograph in Flora S. Rogers, "Brotherly Love Rules This Community," *Halifax Chronicle*, 20 June 1935, 1, 2.
2. In practice, the terms utopian, communal, and intentional are often used interchangeably or as synonyms, with the latter term more common in contemporary usage, especially when a more diverse range of associative relationships is being considered, as in Timothy Miller's *The Quest for Utopia in Twentieth-Century America* (Syracuse: Syracuse University Press, 1998). See also Michael Robertson, *The Last Utopians: Four Late Nineteenth-Century Visionaries and Their Legacy* (Princeton: Princeton University Press, 2018), Introduction and Ch. 6.
3. I deal more fully with definitions of utopias and utopian communities and their historiography in Chapter 4.
4. R.W. Sandwell, *Canada's Rural Majority: Household, Environments and Economics, 1870–1940* (Toronto: University of Toronto Press, 2016). In "The Lay of the Land: Four New Books in Canadian Rural History," *Acadiensis* 42, no. 1 (Winter 2008): 204, James Murton contends that Canadian rural history as a "field" does not exist. See also R.W. Sandwell, "Through Local Eyes: The Promise and Problems of Place-Based History," *Acadiensis* 45, no. 1 (Winter/Spring 2016): 187–94.
5. Alison Light, *Common People: The History of an English Family* (London: Penguin/Fig Tree Imprint, 2014).
6. Richard White, *Remembering Ahanagran: Storytelling in a Family's Past* (New York: Hill and Wang, 1998), quoted phrase at 49; Marjorie Theobald, *The Wealth beneath Their Feet: A Family on the Castlemaine Goldfields* (Melbourne: Arcadia, 2010); Light, *Common People*, 57 for "history's losers"; Carolyn Abraham, *The Juggler's Children: A Journey into Family, Legend and the Genes That Bind Us* (Toronto: Random House Canada, 2013). Of these four writers, Light has least to say about evasive relatives, seemingly since the family members she knew personally during her working-class childhood in Portsmouth had scant knowledge of or interest in their ancestry. As discussed later in this book, the twenty-first century

has seen a decline in the longstanding tendency to preserve silence on awkward ancestors.

7. On liberal order Canada, see Ian McKay, "The Liberal Order Framework: A Prospectus for a Reconnaissance of Canadian History," *Canadian Historical Review* 81, no. 4 (2000): 617–45. I reread this article with a new appreciation of its significance for my subjects – in terms of their distance from McKay's "liberal order framework" – after reading R.W. Sandwell's "The Limits of Liberalism: The Liberal Reconnaissance and the History of the Family in Canada," *Canadian Historical Review* 84, no. 3 (2003): 423–50. See also Nancy Christie's "From Interdependence to 'Modern' Individualism: Families and the Emergence of Liberal Society in Canada," *History Compass* 10, no. 1 (2012): 81–104.

8. Timothy Caulfield, "A DNA Test Won't Reveal the Real You," *Globe and Mail*, 5 May 2018, 3; Suzanne Morphet, "The Growth of Genealogy Tourism," *Globe and Mail*, 6 June 2018, A13. See also Margaret Conrad et al., *Canadians and Their Pasts* (Toronto: University of Toronto Press, 2013), 71.

9. Several scholarly works on Canadian Mennonites have set a high standard in this regard. See T.D. Regehr, *Mennonites in Canada, 1939–1970: A People Transformed*, Volume 3 of *Mennonites in Canada* (Toronto: University of Toronto Press, 1996); Royden Loewen, *Diaspora in the Countryside: Two Mennonite Communities and Mid-Twentieth-Century Rural Disjuncture* (Toronto: University of Toronto Press, 2006); Marlene Epp, *Mennonite Women in Canada: A History* (Winnipeg: University of Manitoba Press, 2008). These authors begin by acknowledging their personal and familial connectedness to Mennonite communities but go on to provide thoughtful critical analysis rather than either a glorification or denunciation of a past that they share.

10. Historians who have both contributed to the field of Canadian family history and written about its historiography include award-winning scholars like Bettina Bradbury, whose monographs combine demographic and social history approaches, most notably *Working Families: Age, Gender and Daily Survival in Industrializing Montreal* (Toronto: McClelland and Stewart, 1993). In addition to the specialized overviews of Canadian family history contained in the articles by Sandwell and Christie cited in note 7, see a capacious survey that includes works predating the new social history of the 1960s, Cynthia Comacchio's "'The History of Us': Social Science, History, and the Relations of the Family in Canada," *Labour/Le Travail* 46 (Fall 2000): 167–220, and Bradbury's "Feminist Historians and Family History in Canada in the 1990s," *Journal of Family History* 25, no. 3 (July 2000): 362–83. Relatively few monographs follow a single Canadian family line across generations and changing circumstances, though

two works that do so to excellent effect are Marguerite Van Die's *Religion, Family, and Community in Victorian Canada: The Colbys of Carrollcroft* (Montreal: McGill-Queen's University Press, 2005) and Adele Perry's *Colonial Relations: The Douglas-Connolly Family in the Nineteenth-Century Imperial World* (Cambridge: Cambridge University Press, 2015).

11. Hector D. Compton Collection, privately held and uncatalogued (hereafter HDC Collection). The collection includes some untitled record books, mostly dealing with business matters, and some incoming correspondence, but copies of Hector's outgoing letters make up the bulk of what has survived.

12. Letter from Harriet Stryker-Rodda to Mrs. H.W. Ware, 24 March 1978, copy included in Introduction of Pamela Compton Ware, "The Compton Family in America: The First 200 Years," printed in 2014 and available at Monmouth County Historical Association (MCHA), Freehold, New Jersey. Scattered copies of *Comptonology* can be found at MCHA.

13. For help with these kinds of matters I have relied most frequently on an unpublished genealogy prepared in the 1980s by Pamela Hatton Compton and available in print form as "Compton: Bears; Grant; Hume; Sanders; Martin; Munn; MacDougall," Acc. 4289, Public Archives and Record Office, Charlottetown, PEI.

14. Christine Kenneally, *The Invisible History of the Human Race: How DNA and History Shape Our Identities and Our Futures* (New York: Viking, 2014), 176. While acknowledging the limitations of genealogical approaches as a form of history, Margaret Conrad et al., in *Canadians and Their Pasts*, likewise recognize that the research individuals do on their own families "often serves as a foundation for a broader historical consciousness" (82–3). My sense is that academic historians are no longer as dismissive of genealogical research as they were in the early days of their discipline's professionalization, when historian/archivist D.C. Harvey deplored genealogists' motives and morals; see Ian McKay, "The 'Morals of Genealogy': Liberal Settler Colonialism, the Nova Scotia Archives, and the North American Ancestor-Hunters, 1890–1980," *Acadiensis* 48, no. 1 (Autumn 2019): 43–89.

15. Light, *Common People*, 56.

16. Abraham, *The Juggler's Children*, 74.

17. Nancy F. Cott's *The Bonds of Womanhood: Woman's Sphere in New England, 1780–1835* (New Haven: Yale University Press, 1977) was a pioneering work on this subject.

18. When Comacchio writes in her historiographical article on Canadian families that "we still know far more about women's roles in families than we do about those of men," I understand her to mean this in reference to such matters as parenting, since earlier in the article she challenged

the idea of working-class "family strategies" as a likely exaggeration of "familial consensus" in decision making about the family economy ("'The History of Us,'" 201, 214). See also Leonore Davidoff, *Thicker Than Water: Siblings and Their Relations, 1780–1920* (Oxford: Oxford University Press, 2012), for the point that feminist insights "have contributed to the recognition that so-called family strategies are not necessarily unitary. Rather, they operate in 'a tangle of love and domination' in actual households that are the locus of labour, material, and financial organization, not only emotional interaction" (17).

1 Loyalist William and His Namesake in the Maritime Colonies: "Movement Became a Habit"

1. Maya Jasanoff, *Liberty's Exiles: American Loyalists in the Revolutionary World* (New York: Knopf, 2011).
2. Remarkably, in the 1660s two men named William Compton were pioneer white settlers in New Jersey, one in Woodbridge, Middlesex County, the other in Middletown, Monmouth County. It seems clear, as genealogists of the considerable Compton diaspora believe, that Loyalist William was a descendant of the original Middletown William and that the two pioneer Williams were unrelated.
3. The original Middletown town book is in the Cornell University Library. See online at https://archive.org for "The Town Book of Old Middletown, 1667 to 1700"; "The Records of Quaker Marriages at Shrewsbury, 1667–1731"; "The Burying Grounds of Old Monmouth." The location and allocation of town lots, including William Compton's, is shown on p. 1 of the Town Book. Brendon McConville's *These Daring Disturbers of the Public Peace: The Struggle for Property and Power in Early New Jersey* (Ithaca: Cornell University Press, 1999), provides excellent background; see 15 for quoted passage.
4. *Celebration of the Two Hundredth Anniversary of the First Baptist Church, Middletown, New Jersey, 1688–1888* (Trenton, NJ: MacCrellish and Quigley, 1888), 10–11, available online from https://archive.org.; McConville, *Daring Disturbers*, 14–15.
5. State of New Jersey, Department of State, NJSA, Searchable Data Bases and Record Request Forms, Colonial Marriage Bonds, 1665–1799, for descriptive overview, and Reference C (Part I: 1735–1764):317, Groom Compton, William Jr., Bride Sweed, Sarah, Date 2 Mar 1762. In some references the surname Sweed is rendered Sweet.
6. McConville, *Daring Disturbers*, Ch. 4, quotation at 223. See also Larry R. Gerlach, *Prologue to Independence: New Jersey in the Coming of the American Revolution* (New Brunswick, NJ: Rutgers University Press, 1976).

Gerlach cites a study indicating that, on the eve of the Revolution, "about 30 per cent of the white adult males in the colony were landless" (15).

7. On illiteracy as the norm among Loyalists, see Dennis P. Ryan, "New Jersey's Loyalists," 11, in Pamphlet # 20 in the series *New Jersey's Revolutionary Experience*, ed. Larry Gerlach (New Jersey Historical Commission, 1975).

8. Ruma Chopra, *Choosing Sides: Loyalists in Revolutionary America* (Lanham, MD: Roman and Littlefield, 2013), 1, 3. See also Michael S. Adelberg, *The American Revolution in Monmouth County: The Theatre of Spoil and Destruction* (Charleston, SC: History Press, 2010). Adelberg contends that county residents' decision making about choosing sides was based mainly on local considerations and that many of them changed sides during the course of the war, sometimes more than once, for reasons that included self-interest, even self-preservation.

9. Adelberg, *American Revolution in Monmouth County*, 40, for the comparatively high number of Loyalists; also Adelberg, *Roster of the People of Revolutionary Monmouth County [New Jersey]* (Baltimore: Clearfield Company, 1997), 2, and 56–7 for a list of eighteen adult male Comptons in the county showing that most were associated with patriot activity during the war.

10. British Headquarters Papers (Carleton Papers or American Manuscripts), Item William Compton (10291), Allowances for Loyalists 1783/01/01 to 1783/03/31, document page number 7258 (4), mf M-361, and Item William Compton (10293), Allowances for Loyalists, 1783/04/01 to 1783/06/30, document page number 8253 (2), mf M-363, Library and Archives Canada (hereafter LAC).

11. Ruma Chopra, *Unnatural Rebellion: Loyalists in New York City during the Revolution* (Charlottesville: University of Virginia Press, 2011), 136–7, 181. See also Barnet Schecter, *The Battle for New York: The City at the Heart of the American Revolution* (New York: Walker and Company, 2002), which depicts Carleton's "management style" as "the antithesis of Clinton's" (365).

12. Adelberg, *American Revolution in Monmouth County*, 141–3; Adelberg, *Roster*, 56, for Cornelius Compton of Freehold, New Jersey, signer of an 1883 petition opposing the return of "Tories." Cornelius was a traditional name in Loyalist William's family background. He himself had a brother and a son named Cornelius.

13. Maxine N. Lurie and Richard Veit, eds., *New Jersey: A History of the Garden State* (New Brunswick, NJ: Rutgers University Press, 2012), Ch. 1.

14. Chopra, *Choosing Sides*, 1. See also 16 for an example of someone who switched from Rebel to Loyalist and for Chopra's point that "local on-the-ground realities exerted greater pressures than staunch conviction."

15. See David Bell, *American Loyalists to New Brunswick: The Ship Passenger Lists* (Halifax: Formac Publishing, 2015), 9, for the estimate of refugees from New York to what was then still known as the colony of Nova Scotia.

16. Bell, *American Loyalists to New Brunswick*, 9, 92, 206. For the quoted observation about the landscape, see Christopher Moore, *The Loyalists: Revolution, Exile, Settlement* (Toronto: McClelland and Stewart, 1994), 154. The words were those of Sarah Frost, a pregnant wife and mother who would later give birth in a tent.

17. Esther Clark Wright, *The Loyalists of New Brunswick* (Yarmouth, NS: Sentinel Printing, 1955), Ch. 7, for the establishment of New Brunswick as a separate colony.

18. Bell, *American Loyalists to New Brunswick*, 92–3. In Company # 13, the unit in which Loyalist William and his family were included on the *Duchess of Gordon*, only New Yorkers outnumbered Jerseyites. Wright's *Loyalists of New Brunswick* includes five Compton men as family heads in her list of Loyalists arriving in New Brunswick (271). None has been identified as kin of William and Sarah.

19. Jasanoff, *Liberty's Exiles*. The quoted phrase comes from Linda Colley's review of *Liberty's Exiles*; see https://www.theguardian.com/books/2011/feb/19/libertys-exiles-maya-jasanoff-review.

20. M.A. MacDonald, "Clash or Collaboration? Saint John Loyalists Meet the Planters and Others of the River in 1784–1785," in *Planter Links: Community and Culture in Colonial Nova Scotia*, ed. Margaret Conrad and Barry Moody (Fredericton: Acadiensis Press, 2001), 177 (population estimate); M.A. MacDonald, *Rebels and Royalists: The Lives and Material Culture of New Brunswick's Early English-Speaking Settlers, 1758–1783* (Fredericton: New Ireland Press, 1990), 101 (for Fort Howe); L.F.S. Upton, *Micmacs and Colonists: Indian-White Relations in the Maritimes, 1713–1867* (Vancouver: University of British Columbia Press, 1979, 75–6, 78 (for Malecites).

21. David Bell, *American Loyalists to New Brunswick*, 22–3, and for more detail on the problems connected with the Loyalists' arrival and early settlement, D.G. Bell, *Early Loyalist Saint John: The Origins of New Brunswick Politics, 1783–1786* (Fredericton: New Ireland Press, 1983), Chs. 2 and 3, and p. 99, for the incorporation of Saint John as a "city." See also Wright, *Loyalists of New Brunswick*, Ch. 5, regarding the so-called royal bounty, and Ch. 9 for problems with getting Loyalists settled on land.

22. Bell, *Early Loyalist Saint John*, 48–9.

23. Archives and Research Library, New Brunswick Museum, Saint John, "Plan of the Town on the East Side of the Harbour of Saint John ... From an Original Plan by Paul Bedell," showing William's lots as 1103 and 1104. See also Bell, *Early Loyalist Saint John*, 159. Asher Dunham, who had

captained the militia company (a non-military unit) in which the Comptons were included on the *Duchess of Gordon*, was a near neighbour. See Bell, *American Loyalists to New Brunswick*, 92, for Dunham.

24. Bell, *American Loyalists to New Brunswick*, 206. The Lists had shown four children ten or older in the family at the point of departure from New York (92) Possibly an older child had failed to survive the voyage or had been left behind for some reason. The latter practice was not uncommon. For instance, when Lewis and Mary Barbara Fisher sailed to New Brunswick in the fall of 1783, they left their eldest child behind with grandparents; see Robert C. Fisher, "A Loyalist's War: Private Lewis Fisher in the American Revolution, 1775–1883," *Canadian Military History* 19, no. 4 (Autumn 2010): 65. The names of William and Sarah's five children are given in William's 1804 will, which I discuss below.

25. One genealogist gives 1765 as the birthdate for this William, but a suggested birthdate of c. 1771 in another record is more probable, given the fact that he lived into 1867.

26. There were no fewer than seventy-six carpenters in Saint John at the time of its incorporation, according to a list of occupations of "freemen" prepared at that time. See Wright, *Loyalists of New Brunswick*, 161 (list), 163 ("first boom days"), 188–9 (slackening growth). On the petitioning and surveying processes that were part of land settlement, see Robert Fellows, "The Loyalists and Land Settlement in New Brunswick, 1783–1790: A Study in Colonial Administration," *Canadian Archivist* 2, no. 2 (1970): 5–15.

27. Class and political tensions among Saint John Loyalists both before and after New Brunswick became a separate colony under Governor Thomas Carleton are examined in detail in Chs. 3 and 4 of David Bell's *Loyalist Rebellion in New Brunswick: A Defining Conflict for Canada's Political Culture* (Halifax: Formac Publishing, 2013), a popularized and updated edition of Bell's *Early Loyalist Saint John*. As Bell explains, under Carleton some prominent Loyalists lost ground as government advisors, but elite assumptions about ordinary Loyalists remained, limiting their prospects for upward mobility and for roles in government decision making. Tensions reached a climax when "Lower Covers" rioted during the election of 1785, thereby cementing their image as riff-raff. On Carleton, see also W.G. Godfrey, "Carleton, Thomas," *Dictionary of Canadian Biography Online*, and, on a leading government critic, Ann Gorman Condon, "Hardy, Elias," *Dictionary of Canadian Biography Online*.

28. No evidence has been found to link William Compton personally to the riot that was part of the 1785 election process or to subsequent forms of protest, including petitions, some of which created difficulties for Lower Covers, including, for a few, arrest for "seditious libel"; see Bell, *American Loyalists to New Brunswick*, Ch. 4.

29. Wright, *Loyalists of New Brunswick*, 163, 210, 212.
30. Public Archives of New Brunswick (hereafter PANB), RS 108, land petition of James Hendry et al., 5 May 1802 (mf F1042). In this petition Hendry stated that he and Compton had petitioned together in 1785 for a lot near the entrance to Lake Washadeamock. There is no evidence that the two ever got clear title to the lot. The only land grant to a William Compton listed in the federated data base of PANB for the period 1771–1867 is for 1810 for Loyalist William's namesake son.
31. PANB, RS 108, land petition of John Howard, 23 December 1805 (mf F1040). For reference to the Howard/Compton link in St. Martins, see also Esther Clark Wright, *The Ships of St. Martins: Shipbuilding and a List of Vessels Built at St. Martin's New Brunswick, 1800–1899* (Saint John: New Brunswick Museum, 1974), 6, and, for further details on the locally prominent if unpopular Howard, see Howard Temperley, ed. and intro., *Lieutenant Colonel Joseph Gubbins/New Brunswick Journals of 1811 and 1813* (Fredericton: Heritage, 1980), 67–8, and Ross N. Hebb, *Quaco-St. Martins: A Brief History/The First Hundred Years, 1784–1884* (Fredericton: Quaco/Springhill Press, 1997).
32. Wright, *Ships of St. Martins*, 6; Hebb, *Quaco-St. Martins*.
33. Ann Gorman Condon, *The Envy of the American States: The Loyalist Dream for New Brunswick* (Fredericton: New Ireland Press, 1984), Ch. 8.
34. PANB, RS71A, Saint John County Probate Court Records, William Compton, 1804. Five shillings would probably have amounted to no more than the income from a few days' labour at the time; see Rusty Bittermann, "Farm Households and Wage Labour in the Northeastern Maritimes in the Early 19th Century," *Labour/Le Travail* 31 (1993): 23.
35. Regarding Cornelius, see R. Wallace Hale, *Early New Brunswick Probate Records, 1785–1835* (Bowie, MD: Heritage Books, 1989), 138, for reference to his widow, Eleanor Compton, daughter of Anthony Egbert and executrix of Egbert's will, which included bequests to four of her children, one of them also named Cornelius. The reference to one of Loyalist William's daughters as the wife of a Loyalist and the mother of a John Connolly, an illiterate petitioner, is in PANB, RS108, land petition of John Connolly, 27 November 1823 (mf F4194).
36. A series of conferences on Planter history beginning in the 1990s resulted in several edited collections, including Margaret Conrad, ed., *Intimate Relations: Family and Community in Planter Nova Scotia, 1759–1800* (Fredericton: Acadiensis Press, 1993). It contains Althea Douglas's article on her Vaughan background, "Connectional History: A Gender-Related Approach to Genealogy," 54–61. See also Douglas's "From Mother to Daughter: Some Maritime Family Planter Links," *Nova Scotia Historical Review* 13, no. 1 (June 1993): 139–56, and Wright, *Ships of St. Martins,*

6–8. On Chester as an ill-favoured settlement area, see Julian Gwyn, "Shaped by the Sea but Impoverished by the Soil: Chester Township to 1830," in *The Nova Scotia Planters in the Atlantic World, 1759–1830*, ed. T. Stephen Henderson and Wendy G. Robicheau (Fredericton: Acadiensis Press, 2012), 99–121.

37. Wright, *Ships of St. Martins*, 7–8; PANB, RS71A, Saint John County Probate Records, Daniel Vaughan, 1808. The inventory showed that Daniel Vaughan held a quarter share in the *Rachael* as well as a good deal in the way of livestock and farming and household effects.

38. One of Daniel Vaughan's sons married a Sarah Sweet, sometimes rendered Sweed; see Douglas, "From Mother to Daughter." As shown earlier, Sarah Sweed/Sweet was the name of Loyalist William Compton's wife, who, like the Vaughans, had Rhode Island origins.

39. G.A. Rawlyk, *Ravished by the Spirit: Religious Revivals, Baptists, and Henry Alline* (Montreal: McGill-Queen's University Press, 1984); George E. Levy, ed., *The Diary and Related Writings of the Reverend Joseph Dimock (1768–1846)* (Wolfville, NS: Lancelot Press for Acadia Divinity College and Baptist Historical Committee of the United Baptist Convention of the Atlantic Provinces, 1979), 102, also Barry M. Moody, "Dimock, Joseph," *Dictionary of Canadian Biography Online*; D.G. Bell, ed., *The Newlight Baptist Journals of James Manning and James Innis* (Hantsport, NS: Acadia Divinity College and the Baptist Historical Committee of the Atlantic Provinces, 1984), 210–11, 275–6, 282–3; J.M. Bumsted, ed., "The Autobiography of Joseph Crandall," *Acadiensis* 3, no. 1 (1973–4): 79–96; PANB, Daniel F. Johnson's New Brunswick Newspaper Vital Statistics, vol. 43, no. 2413, for excerpt from *Christian Visitor*, 6 February 1878, on the early days of St. Martins First Baptist Church.

40. Hector D. Compton Collection, privately held and uncatalogued (hereafter HDC Collection), Hector D. Compton (hereafter HDC), brief note on "Compton Genealogy," Belle River, PEI, 16 December 1964.

41. PANB, land grant to Ebenezer Vaughan and twenty-four others, pp. 265–71, registered 5 December 1810, mf F16304; petition in name of Thomas Templeman, 4 February 1803, mf 1043; petition in name of William Grant, 24 July 1815, mf F4177.

42. Regarding the purchase by Thomas Carpenter of one hundred acres from William Compton, see PANB, land petition of Carpenter and others, 1812, mf F4175. Information about the Compton family's movements during this period comes from various sources, including genealogical listings and data from the 1881 census for Prince Edward Island, which recorded individuals' ages and places of birth. While both these sources contain some errors and inconsistences, they are useful, in conjunction

with other primary and secondary sources which I cite later, for following the sojourning of William and Mary.

43. Wright, *Ships of St. Martins*, 25, for William A. Compton as builder of the *Gambia*; Quaco Museum and Archives, File, Shipbuilding Gen. # 1, for builders of the *Talent*, also Family Group Sheet for William Henry Compton and for Rueben Vail, both showing the marriage of William A. Compton to Hannah W.H. Vail.

44. T.W. Acheson, *Saint John: The Making of a Colonial Urban Community* (Toronto: University of Toronto Press, 1985), 16.

45. Lewis R. Fischer, "The Port of Prince Edward Island, 1840–1889," in *Ships and Shipbuilding in the North Atlantic Region*, ed. Keith Matthews and Gerald Panting (St. John's: Memorial University of Newfoundland, 1978), 41–70; Nicholas J. de Jong and Marven E. Moore, *Launched from Prince Edward Island: A Pictorial Review of Sail* (Charlottetown: PEI Heritage Foundation, 1981); Stephen J. Hornsby, *Nineteenth-Century Cape Breton: A Historical Geography* (Montreal: McGill-Queen's University Press, 1992), 58; Phyllis R. Blakeley and John R. Stevens, *Ships of the North Shore (Pictou, Colchester and Cumberland Counties)*, Occasional Paper 11 (Halifax: Maritime Museum of Canada, 1963), 3, 47, 48. Reference to Louisa Compton Bears's birth in Wallace, Nova Scotia, comes from family accounts.

46. Wright, *Ships of St. Martins*, 7. Data on the Vaughans as owners, masters, etc., can be found in "Ships and Seafarers of Atlantic Canada," CD ROM, now digitally available as part of the Atlantic Canadian Shipping Project of the Maritime History Archive, Memorial University of Newfoundland (hereafter, "Ships and Seafarers of Atlantic Canada," ACSP). On the importance of kin involvement in other St. Martins shipbuilding and shipping families, see A. Gregg Finley, "The Morans of St. Martins, NB, 1850–1880: Towards an Understanding of Family Participation in Maritime Enterprise," in *The Enterprising Canadians: Entrepreneurs and Economic Development in Eastern Canada, 1820–1914*, ed. Lewis R. Fischer and Eric W. Sager (St. John's: Maritime History Group, Memorial University of Newfoundland, 1979), 35–54.

47. Hebb, *Quaco-St. Martins*, 73.

48. For the birth of Emily Compton Martin in St. Martins in 1817, see Susan Hornby, ed., *Keepsakes and Memories: Our Belfast* (Belfast, PEI: Belfast Historical Society, 2009), 52. For the birth of the Comptons' second-last son, see PEI census for 1881 showing James Compton of Lot 61 as born on PEI and age sixty-two.

49. Regarding these industries as sources of employment, see Doug Sobey, "The Forests of Prince Edward Island, 1720–1900," Ch. 4 in *Time and a Place: An Environmental History of Prince Edward Island*, ed. Edward

MacDonald, Joshua MacFadyen, and Irené Novaczek (Montreal: McGill-Queen's University Press, and Charlottetown: Island Studies Press, 2016), esp. 92–3, 100–1; also Rusty Bittermann and Margaret McCallum, "From Wine to Wood: The Goslings of London and Prince Edward Island's Early Timber Trade," *Island Magazine* 69 (Spring/Summer 2011): 15–22. On the movement of labourers from PEI to the Bras d'Or Lake area of Cape Breton in 1818, see Bittermann, "Farm Households and Wage Labour," 16.

50. Public Archives of Nova Scotia (hereafter PANS), Cape Breton Island Petitions, 1787–1843, Cape Breton no. 1933, mf 15795 for "1818 Hume, Eli Dawson."

51. PANS, MG3, Vol. 302, account book of Laurence Kavanagh of St. Peters, 1817–24, 49; R.J. Morgan, "Kavanagh, Laurence," *Dictionary of Canadian Biography Online*. Morgan writes that, along with another successful Cape Breton merchant, Kavanagh is thought to have "'owned'" much of the island's population as a result of his control over its commerce. On early white settlement in River Denys, see Rita Heuser Farrell, *Our Mountains and Glens: The History of River Denys, Big Brook and Lime Hill (North Side), Cape Breton, Nova Scotia* (Fredericton: Cummings Imagesetting, 1993), esp. Chs. 1 and 2.

52. For the building of the sawmill and gristmill and the quotation, see an account of early settler history in the Malagawatch area by Neil MacDonald, writing in July 1894 as "Bartimaeus" in the Gaelic periodical *Mac-Talla*. I am most grateful to Pauline L. MacLean of Highland Village Museum for sending an email with this information. Anne Marie MacNeil of the Beaton Institute, University College of Cape Breton, provided further translated excerpts from *Mac-Talla*, entitled "1894 – Bartimaeus' Account" (cited hereafter as "Bartimaeus' Account"). My thanks to Jill Campbell-Miller for providing a copy of "Centennial of the Malagawatch United Church, C.B., July 31–Aug. 3, 1930" (8, for the Compton mill reference).

53. Hornsby, *Nineteenth-Century Cape Breton*, 80.

54. PEI census for 1881, showing B. Joseph Compton, farmer, Lot 61, age fifty-four, born in Cape Breton.

55. Data extracted from "Ships and Seafarers of Atlantic Canada," ACSP.

56. Margaret Conrad, *At the Ocean's Edge: A History of Nova Scotia to Confederation* (Toronto: University of Toronto Press, 2020), 235.

57. Rusty Bittermann, "The Hierarchy of the Soil: Land and Labour in a 19th-Century Cape Breton Community," *Acadiensis* 18 (Autumn 1988): 33–55; Farrell, *Our Mountains and Glens*, Chs. 1 and 2; Beaton Institute, University College of Cape Breton, MG2, 18, "Short Account of the Settlements in Cape Breton," 1820, by Thomas Crawley; Hornsby,

Nineteenth-Century Cape Breton, 23, 52–4; Andrew Parnaby, "The Cultural Economy of Survival: The Mi'kamaq of Cape Breton in the Mid-Nineteenth Century," *Labour/Le Travail* 61 (Spring 2008): 69–98; L.F.S. Upton, *Micmacs and Colonists: Indian-White Relations in the Maritimes, 1713–1867* (Vancouver: University of British Columbia Press, 1979), 88–9.

58. In my 2016 article in *Acadiensis*, written at a time when I still lacked conclusive evidence of a link, I erred on the side of caution in referring to a Cape Breton connection between McDonald and the Comptons as only a probability based on family tradition; see Brouwer, "'Prince Edward Island's Unique 'Brotherly Love' Community': Faith and Family, Communalism and Commerce in B. Compton Limited, 1909–1947," *Acadiensis* 45, no. 1 (Winter/Spring 2016): 3–23.

59. M[urdock] Lamont, *Rev. Donald McDonald: Glimpses of His Life and Times* (Charlottetown: Murley and Garnhum, 1902), Ch. 1; John Murray, *History of the Presbyterian Church in Cape Breton* (Truro: News Publishing, 1921), 41; "Centennial of the Malagawatch United Church," 7, which sanitizes McDonald's brief ministry in Cape Breton.

60. R. MacLean, "McLeod, Norman," in *Dictionary of Canadian Biography Online*; Flora McPherson, *Watchman against the World: The Story of Norman McLeod and His People* (London: Robert Hale, 1962).

61. David Weale, "'The Minister': The Reverend Donald McDonald," *Island Magazine* no. 3 (Fall–Winter 1977): 2 (drinking with Catholics); and M. Lamont, *Glimpses*, 21–4, for Lamont's attempts to deal with unsavoury stories that had followed McDonald from Scotland, especially with regard to drinking. In Lamont's telling, McDonald's weaknesses were exaggerated by the Seceders, a rival sect within Scottish Presbyterianism, and he was among the "Indians" with the object of learning their language rather than because of debauchery. My thanks to David Weale for sharing a letter from Mrs. M., a Cape Breton informant, dated 2 May 1974, in which she recounted family stories of McDonald that went back to her great-grandfather's day as a pioneer settler in the area.

62. Jean M. MacLennan, "MacLennan, John," in *Dictionary of Canadian Biography Online*, and, for more on his work in Cape Breton, Jean A. MacLennan, *From Shore to Shore: The Life and Times of the Rev. John MacLennan of Belfast, P.E.I.* (Edinburgh: Knox Press, 1977), Ch. 9; also, "Centennial of the Malagawatch United Church," 8.

63. J. MacGregor, *Historical and Descriptive Sketches of the Maritime Colonies of British America* (London: Longman, Rees, Orme, Brown, and Green, 1828; reprinted Johnson Reprint Corp, 1968) (13–14 for Belfast district).

64. The monument is in the cemetery in Brooklyn where Mary Vaughan Compton was the first person to be buried. The land for the cemetery had been part of the farm of her son Joseph. See image 1 following page 86.
65. David Weale, "McDonald, Donald," *Dictionary of Canadian Biography Online*; letter of Mrs. M. to Weale.
66. M. Lamont, *Glimpses*, 80–1.
67. M. Lamont, *Glimpses*, 81.
68. Wright, *Loyalists of New Brunswick*, 203.
69. Obituary for Mary Vaughan Compton, *The Islander*, 30 March 1866.

2 The Comptons and Colonial Prince Edward Island: Settlement and Spirituality

1. See John G. Reid, "Imperial-Aboriginal Friendship in Eighteenth-Century Mi'kma'ki/Wulstukwik," in *The Loyal Atlantic: Remaking the British Atlantic in the Revolutionary Era*, ed. Jerry Bannister and Liam Riordan (Toronto: University of Toronto Press, 2012), for the point that the arrival of Loyalists and Scottish immigrants in the late eighteenth century "presented a lethal threat to the aboriginal economy and the environmental balances on which it depended" (87). The impact of the arrival of Loyalists and Scottish immigrants on First Nations' way of life may have been even more devastating on Prince Edward Island than it was in Cape Breton and other parts of the Maritimes, for in PEI there was no back country to which they could retreat. See L.F.S. Upton, *Micmacs and Colonists: Indian-White Relations in the Maritimes, 1713–1867* (Vancouver: University of British Columbia Press, 1979), Ch. 8. See also Andrew Parnaby, "The Cultural Economy of Survival: The Mi'kmaq of Cape Breton in the Mid-Nineteenth Century," *Labour/Le Travail* 61 (Spring 2008): 69–98; David Keenlyside and Helen Kristmanson, "The Paleo-Environment and the Peopling of Prince Edward Island: An Archaeological Perspective," in *Time and a Place: An Environmental History of Prince Edward Island*, ed. Edward MacDonald, Joshua MacFadyen, and Irené Novaczek (Montreal: McGill-Queen's University Press and Charlottetown: Island Studies Press, 2016).
2. J.M. Bumsted, *Land, Settlement, and Politics on Eighteenth-Century Prince Edward Island* (Montreal: McGill-Queen's University Press, 1987) (98 for the number of Loyalists and former soldiers); John Cousins, *New London: The Lost Dream/The Quaker Settlement on P.E.I.'s North Shore, 1773–1795* (Charlottetown: Island Studies Press at the University of Prince Edward Island, 2016).
3. Rusty Bittermann and Margaret McCallum, "Upholding the Land Legislation of a 'Communistic and Socialist Assembly': The Benefits of

Confederation for Prince Edward Island," *Canadian Historical Review* 87, no. 1 (March 2006): 1–28 (3 for the number of proprietors); Bumsted, *Land, Settlement, and Politics*; Ian Ross Robertson, ed., *The Prince Edward Island Land Commission of 1860* (Fredericton: Acadiensis Press, 1988), Introduction, and Robertson, *The Tenant League of Prince Edward Island, 1864–1867* (Toronto: University of Toronto Press, 1996). As Robertson points out in the first of these books, it was not exclusively the self-interest of absentee proprietors that prevented the development of the colony's land. There were other barriers, including the impact of the American Revolution; see Introduction, ix–x.

4. J.M. Bumsted, ed., *The Collected Writings of Lord Selkirk, 1799–1809*, Vol. 1 (Winnipeg: Manitoba Record Society, 1984), Introduction. Bumsted notes that complaints from some of these immigrants had given Prince Edward Island "a bit of an unsavoury reputation" back in Scotland (37).

5. Public Archives and Records Office, Charlottetown (hereafter PARO), "About the 1841 Census," online introduction to the census, which is available on microfilm at PARO.

6. J. MacGregor, *Historical and Descriptive Sketches of the Maritime Colonies of British America* (London: Longman, Rees, Orme, Brown, and Green, 1828; reprinted Johnson Reprints, 1968), 2–3.

7. Robertson, *Tenant League*, 16.

8. J.M. Bumsted, "Lord Selkirk of Prince Edward Island," *Island Magazine* 5 (Fall–Winter 1978): 3–8 (quotation at 8). Lord Selkirk's relatively successful settlement on PEI is much less well known to students of Canadian history than his later, fraught effort to establish a settlement colony at Red River in what is now Manitoba. For background on his several North American settlement schemes, see Bumsted, ed., *Collected Writings of Lord Selkirk*, Introduction. For the Malthus connection, see J. Marc MacDonald, "Lord Selkirk's Succeeding and Flourishing Settlement on 'Prince Edward's Island,'" *Island Magazine* no. 84 (Fall/Winter 2019): 37–47.

9. See Douglas Sobey, "'The Forests of Prince Edward Island, 1720–1900," Ch. 4 in *Time and a Place*, for the attack on the Island's forests, first by farmers intent on land clearing and then for cargoes and materials for the shipbuilding industry, which I discuss below. In the same collection, see also Edward MacDonald and Boyde Beck, "Lines in the Water: Time and Place in a Fishery," for early officials' often negative views about the viability of combining farming and fishing (222–3).

10. PARO, "About the 1841 Census," online introduction to the 1841 census.

11. Bumsted, "Lord Selkirk of Prince Edward Island," 6.

12. Although the settlement was referred to as Belle Creek in nineteenth-century censuses and other documents, in this work I normally refer to it as Belle River, its usual twentieth-century name. As Belle Rivière

in the Acadian era, it had been part of an area of some settlement activity, but within a few years of the Acadians' deportation, the land they had cleared was largely overgrown; see Susan Hornby, ed., *Keepsakes and Memories: Our Belfast/Origins and Times of the People of Belfast, Prince Edward Island* (Belfast, PEI: Belfast Historical Society, 2009), 23, and Earle Lockerby and Douglas Sobey, *Samuel Holland: His Work and Legacy on Prince Edward Island* (Charlottetown: Island Studies Press, 2015), Ch. 6, and table, 91.

13. PARO, microfilm of manuscript census for 1841, for households in Lot 62. Details regarding the Comptons of Lot 62 here and in the next several paragraphs come from this source. The 1841 census, only some of which has survived, is disappointing in that only household heads are listed by full name, but it does provide valuable information on landholding arrangements, crops, livestock, family size, etc.

14. Hornby, ed., *Keepsakes and Memories*, 52, for photo of Emily Compton Martin; Malcolm M. Macqueen, *Skye Pioneers and "The Island"* (np, np [1929]). The copy of *Skye Pioneers* at PARO is accompanied by a detailed index to family names in the book (see 151 for intermarried Martins, Comptons, and Grants).

15. Other, unrelated, Comptons had preceded the Loyalist Comptons. A Compton had been among the ill-fated Quaker settlers in the late eighteenth century, and just after the beginning of the new century, Colonel Harry Compton arrived from England as a landed proprietor to take up much of Lot 17. See Cousins, *New London*, 72, and Hubert G. Compton, "The First Settlers of St. Eleanors," *Prince Edward Island Magazine* 1, no. 1 (July 1899): 167–71.

16. The escheat movement sought to have proprietors' land returned to the state (escheated). The proprietors had failed to meet the legal obligations by which they had originally obtained their lots, the protesters argued. Escheated lands should therefore be made available on a freehold basis to the people who actually lived on and worked those lands. It did not happen then, and it would be a long time in coming. See Rusty Bittermann, *Rural Protest on Prince Edward Island: From British Colonization to the Escheat Movement* (Toronto: University of Toronto Press, 2006); and Robertson, *Tenant League*. As Bittermann points out, "The final solution to the landlord/tenant conflict on the Island only came when the state began using coercion to bring about a comprehensive solution by forcing the last of the landlords to sell their estates to the Island government." This occurred with the Land Purchase Act of 1875 following PEI's entry into Confederation (275).

17. Bittermann, *Rural Protest*, 51. See also Ian Ross Robertson, "Coles, George," *Dictionary of Canadian Biography Online*.

18. For Wellington Compton's lease, dated 21 December 1841, see PARO, Leases and Related Documents of PEI Townships, 61 and 62, mf 99. I am most grateful to Ian Robertson for helping me interpret the 1841 census categories for landholding; email, 1 January 2016.

19. Hornby, ed., *Keepsakes and Memories*, 165–6.

20. Figure cited by Robertson, in "Coles, George."

21. Bumsted, ed., *Collected Writings of Lord Selkirk*, 179. The quotations are from the second edition of Lord Selkirk's *Observations on the Present State of the Highlands of Scotland with a view of the Causes and Probable Consequences of Emigration*, published in 1806.

22. For early exports, see PARO, mf census for 1841, Lot 44 description. See also Andrew Hill Clark, *Three Centuries and the Island* (Toronto: University of Toronto Press, 1959), Ch. 6, for landholding patterns, rural productivity, and export patterns in the mid-nineteenth century; and Joshua MacFadyen, "The Fertile Crescent: Agricultural Land Use on Prince Edward Island, 1861–1971," in *Time and a Place*, esp. 161–2, 167.

23. PARO, mf census of 1841 for Lot 62.

24. PARO, mf census for 1841, Lot 62 description; Rusty Bittermann, "Farm Households and Wage Labour in the Northeastern Maritimes in the Early Nineteenth Century," *Labour/Le Travail* 31 (1993):13–45; Lewis R. Fischer, "The Port of Prince Edward Island, 1840–1889: A Preliminary Analysis," in *Ships and Shipbuilding in the North Atlantic Region*, ed. Keith Matthews and Gerald Panting (St. John's: Memorial University of Newfoundland, 1978), 41–70.

25. Katherine F.C. MacNaughton, *The Development of the Theory and Practice of Education in New Brunswick, 1784–1900* (Fredericton: University of New Brunswick Historical Studies No. 1, 1947).

26. "Bartimeus' Account," *Mac-Talla*, 14 July 1894, as provided by Anne Marie MacNeil, Beaton Institute, University College of Cape Breton; Sir Andrew Macphail, *The Master's Wife*, introduction by Ian Robertson (Toronto: McClelland and Stewart, 1977; orig. ed. 1939), 25. Although Sir Andrew claimed that his father had taught in Cape Breton at age eight, he may actually have been closer to twelve at the time; see PARO, William Macphail Papers, Acc. 4871, file 13, fragment of letter dated 15 May 1843, undertaking to hire William.

27. PARO, *Journal of the Legislative Assembly of Prince Edward Island*, 1841, Appendix (G), "Report of the Visitor of District Schools for the year ending January 28, 1841," 17 (majority not attending school), 21 (Belle Creek school), 22 (quoted remark about Ewen Lamont's school); Macphail, *The Master's Wife*, 24–5. Belle River already had a teacher in 1837–8, and William Lamont was teaching there in 1840–1; see Anna K. Riley, *Belle River, 1800–1900 (a short social history)* (np: Belle River Women's Institute,

1972), 11, copy at PARO. For the 1852 Education Act, see Ian Ross Robertson, "Reform, Literacy and the Lease: The Prince Edward Island Free Education Act of 1852," *Acadiensis* 20, no. 1 (Autumn 1990): 52–71.

28. David Weale, "The Ministry of the Reverend Donald McDonald on Prince Edward Island, 1826–1867," doctoral dissertation in history, Queen's University, 1976, 227, for statistic on followers.

29. *Summerside Progress*, 4 March 1867, mf copy at PARO.

30. See below, p. 162, n. 24, and p. 163, n. 31.

31. Jean M. MacLennan, *From Shore to Shore: The Life and Times of the Rev. John MacLennan of Belfast, P.E.I.* (Edinburgh: John Knox Press, 1977), and her entry "MacLennan, John," in *Dictionary of Canadian Biography Online*.

32. Riley, *Belle River*, 9–10; Macqueen, *Skye Pioneers*, 82–4.

33. M[urdock] Lamont, *Rev. Donald McDonald: Glimpses of His Life and Times* (Charlottetown: Murley and Garnhum, 1902), 170–6, for a detailed account of a communion service at DeSable; Weale, "The Ministry of the Reverend Donald McDonald." See also Weale, "McDonald, Donald," *Dictionary of Canadian Biography Online*, and John MacLeod, *History of Presbyterianism on Prince Edward Island* (Chicago: Winona Publishing, 1904), esp. Ch. 21.

34. M. Lamont, *Glimpses*, Ch. 6; Nathan Mair, ed., *Word and Spirit: Reports on the Life and Work of the Remarkable Reverend Donald McDonald of Prince Edward Island*, printed 1993, copy obtained from Maritime Conference Archives, United Church of Canada. In 1858, local officials in what remained of the established Church of Scotland on PEI again courted McDonald, this time at a synod meeting in Charlottetown, but, as in past years, some of those present were sharply critical of his style of ministry; see Mair, *Word and Spirit*, 16–21.

35. M. Lamont, *Glimpses*, 154.

36. William Gregg, *History of the Presbyterian Church in the Dominion of Canada* (Toronto: Presbyterian Printing and Publishing Company, 1885), 276–7; Weale, "McDonald, Donald"; Duncan Campbell, *History of Prince Edward Island* (Charlottetown: Bremner Brothers, 1875), 189–93. A McDonaldite hymn was sung at a funeral as recently as 2013 by a musically gifted group of sisters who, like the deceased, were descendants of McDonald's followers.

37. Weale, "McDonald, Donald." On ten lost tribes theories, see Zvi Ben-Don Benite, *The Ten Lost Tribes: A World History* (New York: Oxford University Press, 2009).

38. MacLeod, *History of Presbyterianism*, Ch. 21; Weale, "Ministry of the Reverend Donald McDonald," 244, for Montgomery's mockery of McDonaldites.

39. M. Lamont, *Glimpses*, which tacitly acknowledges inconsistencies and contradictions in McDonald's theology; and John Webster Grant, "Presbyterian Revivals," in *The Contribution of Presbyterianism to the Maritime Provinces of Canada*, ed. Charles H.H. Scobie and G.A. Rawlyk (Montreal: McGill-Queen's University Press, 1997), 118–27, quotation at 122. See also John Webster Grant, *Divided Heritage: The Presbyterian Contribution to the United Church of Canada* (Yorkton, SK.: Gravelbooks, 2007), where Grant observes that McDonald and the Reverend Norman McLeod, a fellow maverick minister of the Kirk, far from being "aberrations ... represented aspects of Highland Presbyterianism that only needed encouragement to come to the surface" (130).

40. A.B. Warburton, *A History of Prince Edward Island* (Saint John: Burnes and Co., 1923), 403. McDonald's *A Treatise on the holy ordinance of baptism* was published in 1845. A major issue was the Baptists' practice of adult baptism by total immersion rather than infant baptism.

41. See, for instance, Paul Boyer, *When Time Shall Be No More: Prophecy and Belief in Modern American Culture* (Cambridge, MA: Harvard University Press, 1992). For Millerites and Mormons and other millenarian sects in Upper Canada in the first half of the nineteenth century, see William Westfall, *Two Worlds: The Protestant Culture of Nineteenth Century Ontario* (Montreal: McGill-Queen's University Press, 1989), Ch. 6.

42. Campbell, *History*, 190–1; Macphail, *The Master's Wife*, 64.

43. See George A.Rawlyk, *Ravished by the Spirit: Religious Revivals, Baptists, and Henry Alline* (Montreal: McGill-Queen's University Press, 1988), 84–5, for concerns that some followers of Henry Alline were libertines sexually as well as theologically. Campbell's profile of McDonald in his chapter on "Eminent Islanders" presents him as the epitome of a learned, respected, and loved clergyman (*History*, 189–93).

44. M. Lamont, *Glimpses*, 176. The number of communicants (808) was even higher two weeks earlier at DeSable (175).

45. M. Lamont, *Glimpses*, Ch. 5 (93 for quoted passage on delight in McDonald's visits; 99 for his role in organizing relief), and 152–4 for McDonald's antipathies. Lamont does not dwell on possible scriptural reasons for his objections to pigs and pictures. Pigs, left to roam by farmers, and underfed, were a major nuisance on the Island and much loathed by McDonald. Lamont explains the most eccentric of McDonald's antipathies, his objection to cradles, as based on a fear that a cradle could injure the infant brain. Admonitions related to the hiring of teachers and to candidates for election reflected the important role that religion played in Island electoral and educational politics. On McDonald's visits to his followers and his sociability, see also Weale, "The Ministry of the Reverend Donald McDonald," Ch. 9 (204 for no home of his own). Further information on

McDonaldites' involvement in community relief is provided in C.C. Ince, *Old DeSable* (np, 1975), 15–17.

46. M. Lamont, *Glimpses*, 63–6, 81–9, 123. Lamont considered that McDonald's decision to ordain men to eldership without the participation of another ordained clergyman, as was the norm in the Church of Scotland, "practically singled him out as the founder of a new sect" (63). For physical descriptions of some McDonaldite churches, see Ince, *Old DeSable*, 15–17, and PARO, Acc. 4332, James Harvey Bishop fonds, undated newspaper clipping with photograph and details about the Churchill Presbyterian Church.

47. Westfall, *Two Worlds*, 167, 177.

48. Weale, "The Ministry of the Reverend Donald McDonald," Ch. 8, esp. 185; M. Lamont, *Glimpses*, 141–2. Lamont here challenged the assumption held by some Islanders that McDonald's failure to save for his old age was because of his belief in the impending end of the world.

49. Ian Ross Robertson, "The 1850s: Maturity and Reform," Ch. 15 in *The Atlantic Region to Confederation: A History*, ed. Phillip Buckner and John G. Reid (Toronto: University of Toronto Press, 1994); Daniel Sampson, "Introduction: Situating the Rural in Atlantic Canada," in *Contested Countryside: Rural Workers and Modern Society in Atlantic Canada, 1800–1950*, ed. Daniel Sampson (Fredericton: Acadiensis Press, 1994); Edward MacDonald, "Economic Dislocation and Resiliency on Prince Edward Island: Small Producer, Distant Markets," *London Journal of Canadian Studies* 31 (2016): 19–34; Alan A. Brookes, "Islanders in the Boston States," *Island Magazine* no. 2 (Spring/Summer 1977): 11–15.

50. Eric W. Sager and Gerald E. Panting, *Maritime Capital: The Shipping Industry in Atlantic Canada, 1820–1914* (Montreal: McGill-Queen's University Press, 1990), 88.

51. Lewis R. Fischer, "The Shipping Industry in Nineteenth Century Prince Edward Island," *Island Magazine* no. 4 (Spring/Summer 1978): 15–21 (15 for "golden years"), and Fischer, "The Port of Prince Edward Island, 1840–1889"; MacDonald, "Economic Dislocation," for the reference to more than 176 locations (20). See also Nicholas de Jong and Marven E. Moore, *Launched from Prince Edward Island: A Pictorial Review of the Age of Sail* (Charlottetown: PEI Heritage Foundation, 1981). In "The Shipping Industry," Fischer notes that, despite the period encompassed in his "golden years," the industry was already beginning to "founder" by the late 1860s (16).

52. For James Compton and the *Dolphin*, see Hornby, ed., *Keepsakes and Memories*, 120, and, for details, data found in "Ships and Seafarers of Atlantic Canada," CD ROM, now digitally available as part of Atlantic

Canadian Shipping Project (ACSP) of the Maritime History Archive, Memorial University of Newfoundland.

53. Clark, *Three Centuries*, 116–19; Robertson, "The 1850s," 336–7.

54. PARO, mf census for Lot 62, Prince Edward Island, for 1861.

55. John's household, for instance, where seven of the nine children were females, showed more cloth production than some neighbouring households. His eldest daughter would show up in a later census as a tailoress. Regarding cloth, butter, and cheese production on PEI during the nineteenth century, see Clark, *Three Centuries*, 118, 186–7. Cloth production on the Island was still largely home- rather than mill-based in the mid-nineteenth century, and a good deal of butter making remained home-based even after creameries and cheese factories began to develop in the 1880s. See also Marjorie Griffin Cohen, *Women's Work, Markets, and Economic Development in Nineteenth-Century Ontario* (Toronto: University of Toronto Press, 1988), Ch. 5, which deals with changes in women's roles in dairying in several Canadian provinces.

56. PARO, *Journal of the House of Assembly of Prince Edward Island/Fourth Session of the Twenty-first General Assembly*, Appendix A, Report on Lot 61 by Duncan Fraser; Robertson, *The Tenant League*, 48.

57. For the involvement of the sheriff in rent collecting in Lot 61 and for the dramatic local resistance that was part of Tenant League activism in the colony, see Robertson, *The Tenant League*, 48–9.

58. Handwritten account of elder George Bears's ministry, background, and familial connections obtained from The Croft House, Selkirk Heritage and Cultural Centre, Wood Islands, PEI, June 2014.

59. Obituary for Mary Compton Vaughan in the *Islander*, 30 May 1866. The monument erected in the Brooklyn cemetery in 2006 in honour of William and Mary states that Mary was the first person to be buried there. See *Illustrated Historical Atlas Province of Prince Edward Island*, originally published in 1880 by J.H. Meacham and Co., reprinted by Mika Publishing Company, Belleville, ON, 1977, where the cemetery on Joseph's property is identified as an Episcopal Church cemetery (123). This perhaps had something to do with the fact that his wife had been born in England.

60. M. Brook Taylor, "Worrell, Charles," *Dictionary of Canadian Biography Online*.

61. Data on MacDougalls and Comptons in Bangor come from the 1861 and 1881 census. The building of the church in Bangor is discussed below.

62. *Illustrated Historical Atlas*, 123, 127–8, and "Patron's Directory" section, unpaged, for Comptons as patrons in Lots 40 and 63; *Frederick's Prince Edward Island Directory and Book of Useful Information for 1889–90* (Charlottetown: Frederick's Publishing, 1889), 528, 560. On the importance and frequency of occupational pluralism as a strategy in the rural

Maritimes for obtaining household security, see Sampson, "Introduction," in *Contested Countryside*.

63. The quotation comes from the first page of the Directory [164], located in the last section of the *Illustrated Historical Atlas*. The number of advance subscribers (3,579) and the price are given in "Meacham's 1880 Atlas: A Brief History," *Island Magazine* no. 74 (Fall/Winter 2013): 35–8.

64. For the Belfast district success stories mentioned here, see "A Belfast PEI Scrapbook" at http://www.islandregister.com/belfastscrapbook.html and Hornby, ed., *Keepsakes and Memories*, 124. The school at Uigg, one of the few "First Class Schools" in the province, was located in this region; see *Frederick's Prince Edward Island Directory*, 663. Regarding William Macphail and his remarkable family, see Ian Ross Robertson, "Macphail, William," *Dictionary of Canadian Biography Online*, and Robertson's Introduction to Sir Andrew Macphail's *The Master's Wife*.

65. Focusing on specific circumstances and localities in the nineteenth-century Maritimes, Rusty Bittermann and others have shown how difficult it could be to get ahead even after more than a generation if one began with little or no capital, and how mythic the long-held notion of "an essentially egalitarian social structure" was. See Bittermann, "Farm Households and Wage Labour," and Bittermann, Robert A. MacKinnon, and Graeme Wynn, "Of Inequality and Interdependence in the Nova Scotian Countryside, 1850–1870," *Canadian Historical Review* 74, no. 1 (March 1993): 1–44 (2 of latter for quotation).

66. For Coles, the "father" of responsible government on PEI, among numerous other achievements, see Ian Ross Robertson, "Coles, George," *Dictionary of Canadian Biography Online*.

3 On the Road Again: Sojourners and Religious Renegades in the Post-Confederation Era

1. Alan A. Brookes, "Out-Migration from the Maritime Provinces, 1860–1900: Some Preliminary Considerations," *Acadiensis* 5, no. 2 (Spring 1976): 26–55; Patricia A. Thornton, "The Problem of Out-Migration from Atlantic Canada, 1871–1921," *Acadiensis* 15, no. 1 (Autumn 1985): 3–34, which included Newfoundland for comparative purposes and emphasized "pull" as well as "push" factors (16 for "epic proportions"); Margaret Conrad, "Chronicles of the Exodus: Myths and Realities of Maritime Canadians in the United States, 1870–1930," in *The Northeastern Borderlands: Four Centuries of Interaction*, ed. Stephen J. Hornsby, Victor A. Conrad, and James J. Herlan (Fredericton: Acadiensis Press, 1989), 97–119. For an overview of the region in the 1880s, including out-migration, see Judith Fingard, "The 1880s: Paradoxes of Progress," in *The Atlantic Provinces in*

Confederation, ed. E.R. Forbes and D.A. Muise (Toronto: University of Toronto Press, 1993), Ch. 3.

2. Thornton, "The Problem of Out-Migration," 18; Edward MacDonald, *If You're Stronghearted: Prince Edward Island in the Twentieth Century* (Charlottetown: Prince Edward Island Museum and Heritage Foundation, 2000), 30.

3. Michael Bliss, "Party Time in Malpeque," *Island Magazine* no. 36 (Fall/ Winter 1994): 13–19.

4. Alan A. Brookes, "Islanders in the Boston States: 1850–1900," *Island Magazine* no. 2 (Spring/Summer 1977): 11–15 (quotation at 13). See also Andrew Robb, "Michael A. McInnis, the *Maple Leaf* and Migration from Prince Edward Island," *Island Magazine* no. 67 (Summer 1985): 15–19. Island-born McInnis published the *Maple Leaf* monthly out of his new home in Oakland, California, from 1907 to 1947.

5. Gerald Friesen, *The Canadian Prairies: A History* (Toronto: University of Toronto Press, 1987), 203; Kenneth S. Coates and William R. Morrison, eds., *"My Dear Maggie …" Letters from a Western Manitoba Pioneer/ William Wallace* (Regina: University of Regina, 1991), xii (hereafter Coates and Morrison, eds., *"My Dear Maggie …"*.

6. HDC, "Subject Water," nd, in Hector D. Compton Collection, privately held and uncatalogued (hereafter HDC Collection).

7. Friesen, *Canadian Prairies*, 183, and Ch. 9; Douglas Francis and Chris Kitzan, eds., *The Prairie West as Promised Land* (Calgary: University of Calgary Press, 2007), Introduction, xii.

8. Coates and Morrison, eds., *"My Dear Maggie …"*, Introduction, and 100 for "old highlandman."

9. HDC, "Subject Water," nd, and "P.S.," undated fragment of letter to unnamed family members, probably written in the early 1940s, both in HDC Collection.

10. Coates and Morrison, eds., *"My Dear Maggie …"*, 119. Wallace mentions "Compton" in a letter dated 23 February 1883.

11. HDC to Mr. A.D. Nicholson, 9 October 1951, and "P.S.," nd, both in HDC Collection; Coates and Morrisons, eds., *"My Dear Maggie …"*, 112. A Mr. Butcher, whom Hector remembered as a harsh teacher, turns up in Wallace's correspondence as a friend and fellow immigrant.

12. Coates and Morrison, eds., *"My Dear Maggie …"*, 169.

13. HDC, "P.S.," HDC Collection.

14. Susan Hornby, ed., *Belfast People: An Oral History of Belfast, Prince Edward Island* (Charlottetown: Tea Hill Press, 1992), 94–5. A tape of the interview with Elizabeth – Libby – Compton, held at Public Archives and Records Office, Charlottetown (hereafter PARO), contains fuller details of her reminiscences.

15. Duncan Campbell, *History of Prince Edward Island* (Charlottetown: Bremner Brothers, 1875), 192–3; also M[urdoch] Lamont, *Rev. Donald McDonald: Glimpses of His Life and Times* (Charlottetown: Murley and Garnhum, 1902), Ch. 9, for an account of his last days, death, and funeral, and for the monument.

16. "In Memoriam," reproduced in, for instance, J.H. Bishop, *Church of Scotland in Prince Edward Island (MacDonaldite Section)* (np, nd [1991]), 76–7. There, Lydia is identified as Lydia Hume, though she married the widower Peter Hume only in 1887.

17. Ewen Lamont, Elder, *A Biographical Sketch of the Late Rev. Donald McDonald* (Charlottetown: John Coombs, 1892), Appendix, 34–7 (quotation at 36); also M. Lamont, *Glimpses*, 169–70, 182–3. The minority's warning against choosing an unconverted man was a direct echo of a leading evangelical's warning to a New England congregation more than a century earlier that it should not choose a minister "no matter how learned, who had not undergone a conversion experience"; see Frances Fitzgerald, *The Evangelicals: The Struggle to Shape America* (New York: Simon and Schuster, 2017), 19.

18. Copy of "Macdonaldite Minute Book" of Belle Creek and Brooklyn congregations, minutes of 27 December 1867 (hereafter Copy of "Macdonaldite Minute Book"). Dr. David Weale kindly shared his handwritten copy of this minute book, lent to him in 1972 by Nathan Bears. It later became part of J.H. Bishop Fonds, Accession 4332, PARO.

19. A similar pattern seems to have prevailed among Canadian Mennonites before the Second World War; see T.D. Regehr, *Mennonites in Canada, 1939–1970: A People Transformed* (Toronto: University of Toronto Press, 1996), 21, for the quoted passage on the traditional way of selecting religious leaders, and Chs. 9, 10, and 11 on changing attitudes and practices regarding youth training and higher education after the war.

20. Copy of "Macdonaldite Minute Book," 29 February 1868 (authorizing Bears to baptize); 23 January 1869 (two other elders authorized to baptize elsewhere); 14 June 1869 (authorization to administer communion); 15 April 1871 (appointing Bears to full ministry); 13 May 1876 (for the term "ministering elder").

21. University of Prince Edward Island, Robertson Library, Prince Edward Island Collection, Lamont, Murdoch [Murdock], Diary, 1885–8, entry for 24 April 1886, regarding the fractious meeting that voted for church union (hereafter Lamont, Murdoch, Diary); also Ewen Lamont, Elder, *Biographical Sketch of the Late Rev. Donald McDonald*, 38–42, 43; and Bishop, *Church of Scotland in Prince Edward Island*, 49–50. Ewen Lamont does not mention his own opposition to union with the national church or his role in a later rupture, which I discuss below.

22. William Lawson Grant and Frederick Hamilton, *Principal Grant* (Toronto: Morang and Company, 1904), 124–8 (quotations at 125 ["chiefly women ..."], 126 ["primitive" and "... Highland"], and 128 ["... a pleasure ..."]). Grant's estimate of the number gathered inside the DeSable church is surely too large: H.M. Scott Smith's account of the church's architecture (in *The Historic Churches of Prince Edward Island* [Erin, ON: Boston Mills Press, 1986], 79) puts its seating capacity at five hundred people. It is likely that congregants entered in separate groups to be served communion. Grant was not a newcomer to PEI. He had served briefly in the Church of Scotland ministry on the Island in the early 1860s, but, while McDonald lived, Grant would probably have had had no opportunity to preach to his followers. For a valuable overview of Grant's career, see D.B. Mack, "Grant, George Monro," *Dictionary of Canadian Biography Online.*

23. Boyde Beck, *Country Churchyards/Églises de campagne: Historic Churches of Prince Edward Island/Églises Historique de l'Île-du-Prince-Edouard* (Charlottetown: Prince Edward Island Museum and Heritage, 2002), cover, 31, 32; Bangor Free Church of Scotland Record Book, in possession of the church secretary, examined 1 July 2014; J. Angus MacLean, *Making It Home: Memoirs of J. Angus MacLean,* written with the assistance of Marion Bruce (Charlottetown: Ragweed Press, 1998). MacLean's grandfather was an elder in the church at Caledonia, and his son Murdock was for a time precentor for the Gaelic singing (16). For photographs and information about the church at Coleman see http://peiheritagebuildings.blogspot.ca/2012/09/church-of-scotland-coleman.html, accessed 26 July 2017 On the Cambridge congregation, see Bishop, *Church of Scotland in Prince Edward Island,* 15–16, 17–18.

24. Copy of "Macdonaldite Minute Book," minutes for 15 April 1871 (my italics on "Unattached"). Representatives were in attendance from Belle River, Brooklyn, Orwell, Murray Harbour, Lot 48, and Nine Mile Creek. The group seems not to have been successful in obtaining a distinctive religious identity for themselves in the 1871 census. Most of that census has not survived, but the census superintendent's summary, which has survived, makes no separate reference to the group in its overview of religious denominations; see "Report of the Superintendent of the Census Returns, Charlottetown, August 23, 1871," reproduced online in islandregister.com.

25. Information about Bears comes from a brief handwritten account held at the Croft House, Selkirk Heritage and Cultural Centre, Wood Islands, PEI.

26. Copy of "Macdonaldite Minute Book," minutes for 15 June 1872 and 2 May 1874 (early disputes), 17 April and 13 May 1876 (deed arrangements and George's statement of their beliefs).

27. Copy of "Macdonaldite Minute Book," minutes for 13 May 1876, second resolution containing "a list of the names of those who have separated themselves from us and [to] have no fellowship with them as the Scriptures direct."

28. HDC to Our Dear Helen and Peter, 11 and 12 May 1964, HDC Collection. John Henry Compton's name was not on the list of those identified in the May 1876 minutes as holding dissident beliefs, perhaps because he had not yet expressed himself forcefully, or to avoid embarrassing elder John. Significantly, in the 1881 census John Henry chose not to identify his family as McDonaldite.

29. See, for example, *Presbyterian Witness and Evangelical Advocate* 22, no. 31 (31 July 1869): 241. An unnamed "correspondent" had written about a communion service in Lot 61 involving "no fewer than 240 communicants" and conducted "in a disorderly manner." The *Witness* added, "Presbyterians in the Island who can influence Mr. McDonald's people for good should do so." A year earlier, the journal of the established Church of Scotland for the Maritimes had depicted the McDonaldite minority as a group at odds with "all Christian order"; see *Monthly Record*, June 1868, 112; also November 1869, 135.

30. Copy of "Macdonaldite Minute Book," minutes for 28 March 1879 (last will and testament of George Bears); 21 June 1879 (interim appointment); 21 July 1879 (permanent appointment as ministering elder).

31. "Church of Scotland (Rev. Donald McDonald, Baptisms)/Baptisms 1868–1894 (Brooklyn and Belle Creek Section)," mf, Acc. 3145, PARO. Most of the baptisms in this record were performed by Bears and Compton. For arrangements to publish Bears's hymns, and for the decision to use the term "McDonaldite" in the census, see copy of "Macdonaldite Minute Book," minutes for 21 July 1879 and 29 March 1881. See 1881 and 1891 censuses for Lot 62, PEI (mf, PARO) for entries for John Compton showing his occupation as ministering elder.

32. Ewen Lamont, Elder, *Biographical Sketch of the Late Rev. Donald McDonald*, Appendix, 42.

33. Ewen Lamont, Elder, *Biographical Sketch of the Late Rev. Donald McDonald*, 8–10, 41; Harold S. MacLeod, *The Lamonts of Lyndale* (self-published, 2003). For references to Ewen Lamont and his family in the *Guardian*, see, for instance, 22 November 1905, 1; 17 May 1929, 3; 4 October 1952, 4.

34. Copy of "Macdonaldite Minute Book," minutes for 29 September 1883 and 27 June 1885. It is noteworthy that the elders in the Brooklyn-Belle River congregations styled themselves a presbytery and were recognized as such by Lamont, since it signified their desire to adhere to standard Presbyterian church organization despite the absence of involvement by

any ordained clergy. The diary kept by Ewen's son Murdock in the mid- to late 1880s indicates that his father and John Compton did in fact interact frequently, visiting and writing about church matters and sharing preaching duties, with Ewen often preaching in Gaelic. The diary occasionally refers to concerns about John's preaching but is not explicit; Lamont, Murdoch, Diary, 1885–8.

35. Ewen Lamont, Elder, *Biographical Sketch of the Late Rev. Donald McDonald*, Appendix, 42–3.

36. See, for instance, D. Bruce Hindmarsh, "'I Am a Sort of Middle-Man': The Politically Correct Evangelicalism of John Newton," in *Amazing Grace: Evangelicalism in Australia, Britain, Canada and the United States*, ed. George A. Rawlyk and Mark A. Noll (Montreal: McGill-Queen's University Press, 1994), 29–55.

37. Early draft of Bishop manuscript, 79, J.H. Bishop fonds, Acc. 4332, PARO, for Bishop's portrayal of John Compton as a ministering elder who did not measure up by comparison with George Bears and Ewen Lamont. Bishop's ancestors had been part of the minority McDonaldite group.

38. M. Lamont, *Glimpses*, 233–4. Hymnody likewise played an important role in the evangelical ministry of Henry Alline, and his hymns became an important part of his legacy; see George A. Rawlyk, *Ravished by the Spirit: Religious Revivals, Baptists, and Henry Alline* (Montreal: McGill-Queen's University Press, 1988), Ch. 2, and Rawlyk, ed., *The New Light Letters and Spiritual Songs, 1778–1793* (Hantsport, NS: Lancelot Press, 1983).

39. M. Lamont, *Glimpses*, 80–1.

40. "Church of Scotland … Baptisms, 1868–1894," showing that the eighty-first baptism by Senior Elder John Compton was that of Robert, son of Louisa Compton and George Compton, born 19 July 1877, baptized 24 June 1883, entry followed by parenthetical abbreviation "Adul." I discuss the matter of sexual relations and close intermarriage among Comptons in Chapter 5.

41. Andrew Macphail, *The Master's Wife*, introduction by Ian Robertson (Toronto: McClelland and Stewart, 1977; orig. ed. 1939), 45, for the reference to "infirmity" – this in a context of a tongue-in-cheek discussion of the antinomian heresy said to flourish in the community, and 49, for William's decision to give up alcohol.

42. For instance, HDC Collection, HDC to Our Dear Helen and Peter, 11 and 12 May 1964.

43. HDC Collection, HDC to Our Dear Helen and Peter, 11 and 12 May 1964 (contains quotation), and HDC to Dear Nephew David, 26 November 1965.

4 The Founding and Growth of an Island Utopia

1. Hector D. Compton Collection, privately held and uncatalogued (here-after HDC Collection), untitled large grey business record book, 344, for "Memoranda of time service by all male members of Benjamin Compton Co. between January 1, 1909 and March 12, 1921." Founder Ben was the son of Daniel/Donald Compton. The others listed by Hector were grand-children of Daniel/Donald or of John Compton. The "Memoranda" can-not be taken as a fully reliable guide to those involved at the beginning. Some of the males listed were still young children when the company began. On the other hand, neither Hector's father, John Henry, nor Ben's brother George shows up on the list, though both were still living when it was drawn up.

2. HDC Collection, fragment of a letter by HDC marked "P.S." but lacking salutation and date. Although the founding date given here and else-where in Hector's writing is 1909, there had, as shown, been some joint economic activity among them before the founding members made an agreement to pool their resources and operate as a community; see HDC and James M. Compton, liquidators (unsigned draft), to Provin-cial Secretary and the Director of Income Tax, 24 April 1948, where Hector writes, "We worked together under various stages for Thirty-Six years before we asked for Incorporation." In discussing the community in what follows, irrespective of time period, I refer interchangeably to the Compton community or Compton company and to B. Compton Limited.

3. HDC Collection, HDC and James M. Compton to Provincial Secretary and the Director of Income Tax, 24 April 1948.

4. HDC Collection, HDC to Dear George, Sybil and All, 21 January 1963, for reference to having begun typing and keeping copies of business cor-respondence in 1923. By contrast, the nominal leader of the satellite set-tlement in Bangor for much of the Compton community's existence, "Big John" Compton, left no paper trail, with the exception of a handwritten note on the back of another letter. Drawing on Hector's correspondence and family memories, I deal with John's role in later chapters.

5. Flora S. Rogers, "Brotherly Love Rules This Community," *Halifax Chron-icle*, 20 June 1935, 1, 2; Enid Charles and Sylvia Anthony, "The Com-munity and the Family in Prince Edward Island," *Rural Sociology* 3, no. 1 (1943): 37–51 (46 for the reference to the Compton community as a utopian community).

6. Edward Bellamy, *Looking Backward 2000–1887*, Oxford World's Classics edi-tion, ed. and intro. Matthew Beaumont (New York: Oxford University Press, 2007); HDC Collection, HDC to Dear Brother George, 29 November 1945.

7. Beaumont, Introduction, *Looking Backward*, xii (for religious sensibility); George E. Connor, "The Awakening of Edward Bellamy: Looking Backward at Religious Influence," *Utopian Studies* 11, no. 1 (January 2000): 38–50. See also Michael Robertson, *The Last Utopians: Four Late Nineteenth-Century Visionaries and Their Legacies* (Princeton: Princeton University Press, 2018), Ch. 2.

8. Gregory Claeys, *Searching for Utopia: The History of an Idea* (London: Thames and Hudson, 2011), for publication figure; Beaumont, Introduction, *Looking Backward*, vii.

9. A.W. Rasporich, "Utopia, Sect, and Millennium in Western Canada, 1870–1940," *Prairie Forum* 12, no. 2 (Fall 1987): 217–43; Ian McKay, *Reasoning Otherwise: Leftists and the People's Enlightenment in Canada, 1890–1920* (Toronto: Between the Lines, 2008), 88.

10. E.D.S. Sullivan, ed., *The Utopian Vision: Seven Essays on the Quincentennial of Sir Thomas More* (San Diego: San Diego University Press, 1983), 6 ("bright vision"); Donald E. Pitzer, ed., *America's Communal Utopias* (Chapel Hill: University of North Carolina Press, 1997), Introduction by Pitzer, 4.

11. For instance, Laurence Foster, *Religion and Sexuality: Three American Communal Experiments of the Nineteenth Century* (New York: Oxford University Press, 1981); John A. Hostetler, *Communitarian Societies* (New York: Holt, Rinehart and Winston, 1974); Rosabeth Moss Kanter, *Commitment and Community: Communes and Utopias in Sociological Perspective* (Cambridge, MA: Harvard University Press, 1972); Louis J. Kern, *An Ordered Love: Sex Roles and Sexuality in Victorian Utopias* (Chapel Hill: University of North Carolina Press, 1981). American writers' fascination with their own utopian tradition continues. For a review of five recent works, see Christopher Benfey, "Building the American Dream," *New York Review of Books*, 6 April 2017, 18–20.

12. Andrew Scott, *The Promise of Paradise: Utopian Communities in British Columbia*, 2nd ed. (Madeira Park, BC: Harbour Publishing, 2017; orig. ed. 1997); Katheleen Rogers, *Welcome to Resisterville: American Dissidents in British Columbia* (Vancouver: University of British Columbia Press, 2014); Sharon Ann Weaver, "Making Place on the Canadian Periphery: Back-to-the-Land on the Gulf Islands and Cape Breton," PhD dissertation in history, University of Guelph, 2013.

13. Scott, *Promise of Paradise*; Rasporich, "Utopia, Sect, and Millennium"; Mikko Saikklu, "Utopians and Utilitarians: Environment and the Economy in the Finnish-Canadian Settlement of Sointula," *BC Studies* no. 154 (Summer 2007): 3–38; Kevin Wilson, *Practical Dreamers: Communitarianism and Co-operation on Malcolm Island* (Victoria, BC: Institute for Co-operative Studies, 2005). Both Scott and Rasporich include Sointula in

their surveys. As Wilson's title suggests, there has been a lasting and vibrant communitarian ethos at Sointula, despite the failed vision of its eccentric utopian founder.

14. Colin M. Coates, "Is There a Canadian Utopian Tradition?" (paper presented to Canadian Historical Association Annual Meeting, Fredericton, May 2011); "Canadian Utopias Project/Built Utopian Settlements to 1945," canadianutopiasproject.ca; last accessed 26 November 2020. I am grateful to Coates and Milroy for sharing information about their research.

15. John Cousins, *New London: The Lost Dream/The Quaker Settlement on P.E.I.'s North Shore, 1773–1795* (Charlottetown: Island Studies Press at the University of Prince Edward Island, 2016).

16. In *Mennonites in Canada, 1939–1970: A People Transformed* (Toronto: University of Toronto Press, 1996), T.D. Regehr indicates that some leaders of early Mennonite communities in Canada started out with utopian aspirations for their settlements, but he does not discuss what such aspirations would have involved (14). E.K. Francis's *In Search of Utopia: The Mennonites of Manitoba* (Altona: D.W. Friesen and Sons, 1955), despite its title, is a study of his subjects as an ethnic and religious group; it does not provide an explication of what a Mennonite utopia would have looked like. But see Carlos D. Colorado and Susan Fisher Stoerz, "Utopia Enacted: The Exodus of 'Kanadier' Old Colony Mennonites," in *Prophéties et utopies religieuses au Canada*, ed. Bernadette Rigal-Cellard (Bordeaux: Presses Universitaires de Bordeaux, 2011), 217–37, regarding a Mennonite group that moved to Mexico in the 1920s in order to preserve their conservative way of life.

17. Nathaniel Hawthorne's *The Blithedale Romance* (New York: A.L. Burt, 1852) drew on Hawthorne's personal experience at Brook Farm. Barbara Kingsolver's *Unsheltered* (New York: HarperCollins, 2018) imaginatively recreates Vineland, New Jersey, as the setting for her nineteenth- and twenty-first-century characters' lives. Canada is, of course, best known for Margaret Atwood's fictional dystopias, especially *The Handmaid's Tale* (1985) and *The Testaments* (2019).

18. Ruth Levitas, *The Concept of Utopia* (Hemel Hempstead: Phillip Allan, 1990), 7. See also Robertson, *The Last Utopians*, 6, who in describing utopianism as *"the envisioning of a transformed, better world"* (his italics) acknowledges that it is "a capacious definition."

19. James M. Morris and Andrea L. Krass, *Historical Dictionary of Utopianism* (Langham, MD: Scarecrow Press, 2004), 309. See also Toby Widdicombe, James M. Morris, and Andrea L. Krass, *Historical Dictionary of Utopianism*, 2nd ed. (Langham, MD: Roman and Littlefield, 2017), 411, 414, where the definition I have quoted is not much changed. Newer

entries, however (including the Orange Revolution and the Arab Spring), and an enlarged bibliography make the second edition far too capacious to be a useful guide to any meaningful understanding of utopianism.

20. On the Amish in the US, see Dorothy Schwieder, "Utopia in the Midwest: The Old Order Amish and the Hutterites," *Palimpsest* 54, no. 3 (1973): 9–23, downloaded 9 December 2019, and Donald B. Kraybill, ed., *The Amish and the State*, 2nd ed. (Baltimore: Johns Hopkins University Press, 2003); for Canada, Orland Gingerich, *The Amish of Canada* (Waterloo: Conrad Press, 1972). Another good example of a weak fit with this definition would be Upper Canada's the Children of Peace, a "backwoods utopia"; see Albert Schrauwers, "'I was a stranger and ye took me in': Charity, Moral Economy, and the Children of Peace," *Canadian Historical Review* 80, no. 4 (December 1999): 624–40.

21. Pitzer, Introduction, *America's Communal Utopias*, 5.

22. Morris and Krass, *Historical Dictionary*, xxx; Kanter, *Commitment and Community*, 7; Peyton E. Richter, ed., *Utopias: Social Ideals and Communal Experiments* (Boston: Holbrook Press, 1971), 5; Michail Barkunin, *Crucible of the Millennium* (Syracuse, NY: Syracuse University Press, 1986), 2–3.

23. *Census of the Commonwealth of Massachusetts, 1895*, Vol. 2, Population and Social Statistics (Boston: Wright and Potter Printers, 1897), 672, showing 1,186 males and 1,972 females from PEI in Boston at the time of the census.

24. Sam B. Warner, Jr., *Streetcar Suburbs: The Process of Growth in Boston, 1870–1900* (Cambridge, MA: Harvard University Press, 1962). Warner quotes a common phrase of the day used to refer to suburban contractors: "Nova Scotia hatchet and saw men" (129). It probably applied to Maritimers in general. Although he may have been bragging, one Prince Edward Islander interviewed by oral historian Gary Burrill told him that over time, men from the Island built up such a good name in the building trades that Boston-area contractors would seek them out; see Gary Burrill, *Away: Maritimers in Massachusetts, Ontario, and Alberta – An Oral History of Leaving Home* (Montreal: McGill-Queen's University Press, 1992), 52.

25. Annie Griffin Tennyson's success as a lodging-house operator is mentioned above, p. 40. Lodging houses, overwhelmingly run by women, were cheaper places to live than boarding houses, but they did not provide the family-like ambiance that moral reformers regarded as necessary to keep young workers from going astray; Mark Peel, "On the Margins: Lodgers and Boarders in Boston, 1860–1900," *Journal of American History* 12, no. 4 (1986): 813–84.

26. HDC Collection, undated letter fragment by HDC marked P.S.

27. Susan Hornby, ed., *Belfast People: An Oral History of Belfast, Prince Edward Island* (Charlottetown: Tea Hill Press, 1992), 92–9. An oral transcript of the full interview with Libby Compton is available at Public Archives and Records Office, Charlottetown (hereafter PARO).

28. "Death of Mr. Benjamin Compton, Victim of Mill Accident," *Guardian*, 14 March 1921, 1.

29. HDC Collection, untitled large grey business record book, 345–8, meeting of 15 March 1921, and 350, meeting of 17 August 1924. In a letter to his son George, written 25 July 1964, Hector stated that he had served as company secretary from the beginning and also as treasurer from the time of Ben's death.

30. In 2020 the purchasing power of $103,000.00 was $1,994,718.30, according to the Bank of Canada Inflation Calculator; http://www.bankofcanada.ca/rates/related/inflation-calculator/

31. HDC Collection, HDC and James M. Compton, liquidators (unsigned draft), to Provincial Secretary and the Director of Income Tax, 24 April 1948. A redrafted version, dated 7 June 1948, signed by Hector, contains additional details, including the company's reason for incorporating and arrangements made then that complicated the dissolution process.

32. HDC Collection, portion of letter (probably to son George and family), marked "Extra Sheet," 29 June 1964, describing the grade 8 graduation exercises in which he and his cousin Dan had been involved in Chicago and at which they had received diplomas to enter high school. Hector's contribution to the graduation exercises was to recite the Gettysburg Address.

33. HDC Collection, Hector D. Compton, untitled statement, 3 April 1948.

34. It is not clear that John received the official designation of company president as successor to Dan. I have found no record of a meeting to appoint him following Dan's death. Hector tended to speak of John mainly in terms of spiritual leadership.

35. The claim that William Grant Compton of Bangor was persuaded by his second wife "to leave the Compton Cooperative to protect her inherited land" comes from Margo Redmond's "The Compton History in Historical Context," unpublished three-page typescript, nd. It is not, clear, however, that William had ever been a part of B. Compton Limited. He is not included in the group of participants listed by Hector Compton at the time of founder Ben's death in 1921. Another Bangor relative who did not join the community was also named Hector Compton.

36. For the Jardine connection, see *Jardines of Atlantic Canada*, written and compiled by Donald E. Jardine, published 1997 by the Atlantic Provinces Branch of the Jardine Clan Society, Vol. 1, 353–8. Albert Jardine, husband of elder John Compton's daughter Martha, was the son and the

nephew of immigrant Jardines. His devout uncle, an Edinburgh-trained doctor, became an MLA and a justice of the peace as well as a farmer on PEI. Other families directly linked to B. Compton Limited as a result of (sometimes generational) marriage ties included Grants, Bears, and Humes.

37. Kathleen Stuart, "Two Centuries of Energy on PEI," in *Time and a Place: An Environmental History of Prince Edward Island*, ed. Edward MacDonald, Joshua MacFadyen, and Irené Novaczek (Montreal: McGill-Queen's University Press and Charlottetown: Island Studies Press, 2016), 273.

38. A now elderly informant who was part of the Bangor settlement recalls making this trip as a child.

39. Regarding the railway, see Allan Graham, *A Photo History of the Prince Edward Railway* (np, 2000), 48, 125. HDC to Dear John and All, 14 May 1933, in HDC Collection, refers to a truck from Bangor bringing an engine to Belle River and returning with flooring, flour, molasses, etc. In a brief unpublished memoir, Hector's son George (b. 1925) shared nostalgic memories of growing up on "the hill." He recalled, as an eleven-year-old, taking a company truck to race against a younger brother in another vehicle; George H. Compton, "Some of my recollections and memories of bye-gone days," nd.

40. Ruby MacMillan Matheson with Marian Bruce, *Echoes of Home: Stories of Bygone Days in Wood Islands* (Summerside: Williams and Crue, nd [2001 or earlier]), 128.

41. Edward MacDonald and Boyde Beck, "Lines in the Water: Time and Place in the Fishery," in *Time and a Place*, 226–36 (229 for "beads" reference), and Edward MacDonald, "Economic Dislocation and Resiliency on Prince Edward Island: Small Producer, Distant Markets," *London Journal of Canadian Studies* 31 (2016): 19–34.

42. MacDonald and Beck, "Lines in the Water," 228–9.

43. HDC Collection, for Hector D. Compton, untitled statement dated 3 April 1948, and "AGREEMENT," dated 28 March 1927, signed by M[alcolm] F. Riley and H.D. Compton.

44. MacDonald and Beck, "Lines in the Water," 236 (marketing live lobster), and Edward MacDonald, *If You're Stronghearted: Prince Edward Island in the Twentieth Century* (Charlottetown: Prince Edward Island Museum and Heritage Foundation, 2000), 174, caption under photograph (for decline in canneries).

45. MacDonald and Beck, "Lines in the Water," 230.

46. "Libby Compton" in Hornby, ed., *Belfast People*, 93–8 (quotations at 96).

47. An amateur drawing of the windmill, with information by Hector Compton on the reverse detailing sources of mill power and work sites, is contained in Pamela Hatton Compton's unpublished genealogy, prepared in

the 1980s and held at PARO as "Compton: Bears; Grant; Hume; Sanders; Martin; Munn; MacDougall," Acc. 4289 (hereafter Pamela Hatton Compton, "Compton," PARO. Relevant details are also in HDC Collection, HDC, "Subject Water," nd, and HDC, "Records," a small grey booklet from the 1930s.

48. Information here and elsewhere about the community's business activities is derived from Hector D. Compton's correspondence and untitled record books, from contemporary published articles about the community, from the recollections of now elderly former community members, and from recent local histories. Rural general stores often took in butter and eggs from local farmers as part of their routine business; see Matheson and Bruce, *Echoes of Home*, 58.

49. David Frank, "The 1920s: Class and Region, Resistance and Accommodation," in *The Atlantic Provinces in Confederation*, ed. E.R. Forbes and D.A. Muise (Toronto: University of Toronto Press, 1993), 234.

50. HDC Collection, HDC to Mrs. S.M., 24 June 1926, regarding the death of her husband in the mill.

51. HDC Collection, untitled large grey business record book, 385, for Statement of Assets, 30 December 1918, and 346, for listing of assets at meeting of 15 March 1921.

52. HDC Collection, HDC, untitled statement, 3 April 1948; also HDC Collection, untitled business record books for transactions and other entries for the second and third decades of the twentieth century.

53. In the HDC Collection, in a letter fragment marked only "P.S.," for which no date or recipient is shown, Hector observed, "The depression hit us fairly hard in Investments." Also, HDC to Crown Trust Company, Toronto, 2 December 1955, regarding investments that became virtually worthless "[f]ollowing the slump."

54. HDC Collection, HDC to Dear John and All, 10 November and 24 November 1932, and 11 July 1933.

55. Rogers, "Brotherly Love Rules This Community"; "Compton Community Not Supporting Tuber Bonus Plan," unsigned article, *Guardian*, 21 June 1935, 3; HDC Collection, HDC to Dear John and All, 10 November 1932 and 11 July 1933, and HDC to Dear Brother George and Hector [Jardine], 28 November 1938.

56. HDC Collection, HDC to Dear Folks, 22 June 1933; also untitled small grey record book, 14, recording the sale in 1933 of 10,880 butter shooks to Central Creameries and 6,380 to "Other."

57. HDC Collection, HDC to Mr. George Tilley ("good orders") and to Rev. Fr. J.P. McKenna, both 6 December 1936; HDC to Aage Timm (former employee who had returned to Denmark), 7 December 1938; and HDC to Dear Brother George, and Hector [Jardine], 28 November 1938.

58. George H. Compton, "Some of my recollections," 4; "Unique PEI Colony Makes Progress," *Guardian*, 3 January 1935; HDC Collection, HDC, "Subject Water," nd ("active petitioning" for the branch line); Stuart, "Two Centuries of Energy," 275–6 (includes 1941 statistic). As Maritime Electric's power lines extended into rural areas in the late 1930s and early 1940s, it experienced a lack of the necessary generating capacity to meet all the new needs. This may explain why at the end of the 1930s the Compton community in Belle River was again relying on its own power supply; see A. Kenneth Bell, *Getting the Lights: The Coming of Electricity to Prince Edward Island* (Charlottetown: Prince Edward Island Heritage Foundation, 1989), 17, and, for the community's own power source, Helen Jean Champion, *Over on the Island* (Toronto: Ryerson Press, 1939, reprinted 1946), 117.

59. HDC Collection, HDC to Alvadore Grant, Bremerton, Washington, 3 February 1938; Champion, *Over on the Island*, 116.

60. Hector had the widow sign a paper acknowledging with thanks the company's "gift" of $200.00 to her and her children and exonerating the company from any legal responsibility for her husband's death. Having heard a rumour that she was preparing to seek more money, he wrote an icy letter reminding her of the absence of any legislation requiring compensation in such cases and castigating her for her own "unexcusable idleness" and for her daughter's unreliability and lack of gratitude as an employee in their lobster cannery; HDC Collection, notice of exoneration signed by Mrs. S.M., 17 December 1925, and HDC to Mrs. S.M., 24 June 1926.

61. HDC Collection, HDC to Brother George, 5 May 1933, regarding a Danish sailor directed to Belle River by the Nova Scotia-based George, looking for work and unwilling to take the $5.00 offered him until he had earned it.

62. Rogers, "Brotherly Love Rules This Community."

63. HDC Collection, untitled large green record book, 20, for payments to Louisa Jardine of Bangor.

64. HDC Collection, untitled large grey record book, 344. Later in 1923, both women married company men. It is likely that agitation to have their contributions recognized came from their future husbands. I return to the subject of women's roles in the Compton community in later chapters.

65. HDC Collection, HDC and James M. Compton, liquidators (unsigned draft), to Provincial Secretary and the Director of Income Tax, 24 April 1948.

66. See, for instance, Betsy Beattie, *Obligation and Opportunity: Single Maritime Women in Boston, 1870–1930* (Montreal: McGill-Queen's University Press, 2000), Epilogue and Conclusion.

67. HDC Collection, HDC to Dear John, 14 May 1941. While this occurrence took place during the war years, the desperation to keep a job

would have been even greater during the Depression. See Matheson and Bruce, *Echoes of Home*, for several references to Wood Islands-area men being employed by B. Compton Limited.

68. Henning Bender and and Birget Flemming Larsen, eds., *Danish Emigration to Canada* (Aalborg: Danes Worldwide Archives, 1991), 140, 141, 144. Hector corresponded in a friendly way with at least one former worker who returned to Denmark; HDC Collection, HDC to Aage Timm, 7 December 1938. I discuss the Danish workers' ongoing connections to the community, including marital connections, in Chapter 5.

69. HDC Collection, HDC to Miss Ada C. Harris, 15 January 1924; "The Sanitorium [*sic*] Campaign," *Guardian*, 2 December 1929, 9; B. Compton Limited contributed $100.00 to the campaign. On the high rate of tuberculosis, see Douglas O. Baldwin, *She Answered Every Call: The Life of Public Health Nurse Mona Gordon Wilson (1894–1981)* (Charlottetown: Indigo Press, 1997), 178.

70. Leonard John Cusack, "The Prince Edward Island People and the Great Depression, 1900–1935," MA thesis, University of New Brunswick, History Department, 1972; 17 for the reference to the WI.

71. MacDonald, *If You're Stronghearted*, Ch. 5 (182 for Campbell government and ending relief); E.R. Forbes, "Cutting the Pie into Smaller Pieces: Matching Grants and Relief in the Maritime Provinces during the 1930s," *Acadiensis* 17, no. 1 (Autumn 1987): 34–55.

72. Heidi Macdonald, "Doing More with Less: The Sisters of St. Martha (PEI) Diminish the Impact of the Great Depression," *Acadiensis* 33, no. 1 (Autumn 2003): 21–46.

73. George H. Compton, "Some of my recollections," 3–4, and George's notation on a photograph of a pile of logs brought to the mill.

74. HDC Collection, HDC to Dear John, 27 January 1935 (help to kin), and HDC to Dear George and Hector, 28 November 1938 (the casket).

75. Charles and Anthony, "The Community and the Family," 46.

76. J.T. Croteau, *Cradled in the Waves: The Story of a People's Co-operative Achievement in Economic Betterment on Prince Edward Island, Canada* (Toronto: Ryerson Press, 1951); John G. Reid, "Health, Education, Economy: Philanthropic Foundations in the Atlantic Region," *Acadiensis* 14, no. 2 (Autumn 1984): 64–83. See also MacDonald, *If You're Stronghearted*, 173–8.

77. MacDonald, *If You're Stronghearted*, 176; Croteau, *Cradled in the Waves*. For an instance of a newspaper article claiming positive Catholic and Protestant responses to Croteau's work, see "Rev. Dr. Murphy Reviews Adult Education," *Guardian*, 24 July 1936, 5. See also Marion Bruce and Elizabeth Cran, *Working Together: Two Centuries of Co-operatives on Prince Edward Island* (Charlottetown: Island Studies Press, 2004).

78. Rogers, "Brotherly Love Rules This Community."
79. Charles and Anthony, "The Community and the Family," 46; Kathleen Compton, "The Compton's" [*sic*], unpublished typescript, November 1983. Kathleen recounted what her grandmother, an outsider, told her about neighbourhood reactions to the community Comptons: "although you went to school with them and played with them, you never dated a Compton because it just wasn't done" (6). Hector's involvement with the car ferry committee is shown in two front-page *Guardian* articles, 20 and 27 January 1937, and recalled by his son George in "Some of my recollections," 2–3. For background and detail on the building of the ferry, see Marian Bruce, *Saltwater Road: Tales of Travel on the Northumberland Strait* (np: Wood Islands and Area Development Corporation, 2014).
80. For a vivid account of Oneida and Noyes's leadership by an insider/ scholar, see Ellen Wayland-Smith, *Oneida: From Free Love Utopia to the Well-Set Table* (New York: Picador, 2016).

5 Living in Community: Family, Faith, and Fame

1. The kinds of interactions mentioned here are based on my reading of the correspondence and business records of Hector D. Compton as contained in Hector D. Compton Collection, privately held and uncatalogued (hereafter HDC Collection). See also Ruby MacMillan Matheson with Marian Bruce, *Echoes of Home: Stories of Bygone Days in Wood Islands* (Summerside: Williams and Crue, nd [2001 or earlier]).
2. Hector's account of the large funeral for community member Simon Grant indicates that it was unusual in terms of size and the mixed group of people in attendance; HDC Collection, HDC to Emily Grant, 18 August 1936.
3. HDC Collection, HDC to Dear Cousin Belle, 15 December 1944, 2.
4. Public Archives and Records Office of Prince Edward Island (hereafter PARO), Series 3, Subseries 2, RG22, Attorney General Fonds, Inquest, 1932, Compton, George Emerson.
5. Details about George's peripatetic existence come mainly from the inquest into his death. Hector's comment about "weaker minds" is in HDC Collection, HDC to Dear John and All, 10 November 1932, referencing the recent suicide attempt of another kinsman or acquaintance.
6. "Skipper Lost When Island Ship Grounds," *Guardian*, 9 November 1936.
7. HDC Collection, HDC to Emily Grant, 18 August 1936, regarding death and funeral of Simon Grant; HDC to John Hays Hammond Jr., 17 December 1936, for details of Oliver's drowning, a reference to his death as the third recent loss of Belle River partners, and for the sale of the *Hatavan* "to have it off our minds."

8. In old age, Hector wrote fondly about this period in an uncharacteristically light-hearted article that he submitted unsuccessfully to the *Reader's Digest*; HDC Collection for typescript of the story "It Worked."

9. HDC Collection, HDC to Dear Cousin Belle, 15 December 1944.

10. "Sad fatality at Belle River yesterday, Mary Jardine wades beyond depth, drowns," *Guardian*, 9 August 1937.

11. A pattern of problem drinking was one of many aspects of her extended family background that Mary Compton Gerrard pondered during her long life in the US. I am most grateful to her son Keith for numerous emails about Mary's reflections on her Island upbringing and for sharing his own knowledge of family history.

12. Adam Rutherford, *A Brief History of Everyone Who Ever Lived: The Stories in Our Genes* (London: Weidenfeld and Nicholson, 2016), 257.

13. Greg Marquis, "Prohibition's Last Outpost," *Island Magazine* no. 57 (Spring/Summer 2005): 2–9; Julie V. Watson, *Shipwrecks and Seafaring Tales of Prince Edward Island* (Halifax: Nimbus Press, 2001), 137–43; Edward MacDonald, *If You're Stronghearted: Prince Edward Island in the Twentieth Century* (Charlottetown: Prince Edward Island Museum and Heritage Foundation, 2000), 138–44. On the purchase of liquor-laced cooking products for consumption from a general store near Belle River, see Matheson and Bruce, *Echoes of Home*, 59–61. See also Robert E. Mennel, *Testaments and Secrets: The Story of a Nova Scotia Family, 1844–1977* (Toronto: University of Toronto Press, 2013), for the same phenomenon in early twentieth-century Nova Scotia (188).

14. HDC Collection, HDC to Dear John and All, 24 November 1932.

15. HDC Collection, HDC to Dear Brother George, 5 May 1933. See also HDC to Dear George and Family, 1 August 1964, where he acknowledges that although he, too, had been a drinker in his youth, he had come to recognize its harmful effects and "stood out against it."

16. David G. Stewart Jr., "Growth, Retention, and Internationalization," in *Revisiting Thomas F. Odea's "The Mormons": Contemporary Perspectives*, ed. Cardill K. Jacobson, John P. Hoffman, and Tim B. Heaton (Salt Lake City: University of Utah Press, 2008), 352–3; Andrew Scott, *The Promise of Paradise: Utopian Communities in British Columbia*, 2nd ed. (Madeira Park, BC: Harbour Publishing, 2017; orig. ed. 1997), Ch. 4. As A.W. Rasporich observed, in western Canada in the late nineteenth and early twentieth centuries, the banning of alcohol was part of the practice of a number of utopian communities, including the Doukhobors, as well as the Finns of Sointula; "Utopia, Sect and Millennium in Western Canada, 1870–1940," *Prairie Forum* 12, no. 2 (Fall 1987): 217–43. The banning of alcohol in Vineland, New Jersey, the utopian community founded by Charles K. Landis in the 1860s and featured in Barbara Kingsolver's novel

Unsheltered, seems to have been based on business rather than moral considerations: Vineland's grape production resulted in the emergence of the Welch's grape juice company.

17. HDC Collection, HDC, "Compton Geneaology [*sic*]," 16 December 1964; also HDC to nephew Arthur, 19 March 1963, where he explained that the men in the family had had "such intense natures, such spiritual thirst and such proneness to revert to alcohol when the true Spirit seemed lacking."

18. M[urdock] Lamont, *Rev. Donald McDonald: Glimpses of His Life and Times* (Charlottetown: Murley and Garnhum, 1902), 170–6. People who came from long distances to participate in the communion events often lodged with families who lived near the church.

19. William Pfaff, "Challenge to the Church," review of *Why Priests? A Failed Tradition* by Gary Wills, in *New York Review of Books*, 9 May 2013, 8 (for quotation). Howard Clark Kee et al., *Christianity: A Social and Cultural History*, 2nd ed. (Upper Saddle River, NJ: Prentice Hall, 1998), Ch. 4, provides an account of the transition "From Charismatic Movement to Institution."

20. For instance, HDC Collection, HDC to Dear Nephew David, 26 November 1965.

21. MacDonald, *If You're Stronghearted*, 17; H.M. Scott Smith, *The Historic Churches of Prince Edward Island* (Erin, ON: Boston Mills Press, 1986); Boyde Beck, *Country Churchyards/Églises de campagne, Historic Churches of Prince Edward Island/Églises historiques de l'Île-du-Prince Edouard* (Charlottetown: Prince Edward Island Museum and Heritage, 2002).

22. HDC Collection, HDC to Dear Son George, 25 July 1964. A letter from Hector to brother George W., 9 December 1945, recalls how "the spiritual condition of our own little society" had "in the past" been "uppermost and talked [of] on every occasion" along with readings from McDonald's writings as well as the Bible. But this may not have been typical of the Sunday gatherings: Hector was writing to his Nova Scotia-based brother at a time when he was deeply concerned about what he saw as spiritual declension within the community.

23. M. Lamont, *Glimpses*, 87.

24. HDC Collection, undated letter fragment marked P.S., where Hector wrote that Ben had "kept us keyed up to anticipate the fulfilment of the many Promises of the Bible"; also HDC to Dear Son George, 25 July 1964.

25. HDC Collection, HDC to Cousin Rose, 28 March 1934, where Hector remembered Dan as "abler and stronger in many ways than I"; letters of tribute to Dan's character and ability in the *Patriot* newspaper, April 1923, by Mrs. William D. MacEwen, St. Peter's Harbour, and by Robert Mooney, Ruskin, as copied in Pamela Hatton Compton's unpublished genealogy, prepared in the 1980s and held at PARO as "Compton: Bears;

Grant; Hume; Sanders; Martin; Munn; MacDougall," Acc. 4289 (hereafter Pamela Hatton Compton, "Compton," PARO). The letter writers remembered Dan as the high-principled business leader of the Compton community in Bangor and for unshowy acts of charity that went well beyond the immediate kin circle.

26. HDC Collection, HDC to Dear Brother George, 5 May 1933 ("stress"); to Dear Son George, 25 July 1964, and 1 August 1964, regarding other family members' negative memories about John; HDC to a niece, John's eldest daughter, 18 August 1964, sharing anecdotes that an elderly doctor had related in a kindly way about John and some of his "queer stunts"; and HDC to nephew Arthur, 19 March 1963, for the sending of McDonald's book on the millennium to Bennett. Regarding the latter, Hector believed that "some of its views were quite noticeable in his public Addresses after ward."

27. HDC Collection, HDC to Dear Son George, 25 July 1964, for John as their "recognized spiritual leader" following the deaths of Ben and Dan.

28. HDC Collection, HDC to Our Dear Helen and Peter, 11 and 12 May 1964. On Hector's claim that McDonald had believed in salvation only for the elect, see also HDC to nephew Arthur, 19 March 1963. M. Lamont's *Glimpses* indicates that there was, in fact, a good deal of inconsistency in McDonald's statements on doctrinal matters. Nor would a strict interpretation of Calvinist doctrine have fitted easily with McDonald's encouragement of revivals.

29. HDC Collection, HDC to Our Dear Helen and Peter, 11 and 12 May 1964.

30. HDC Collection, HDC to Dear John and All, 11 July 1933.

31. My observation in this paragraph about sketchy and unhappy memories of the Sunday worship services is based on conversations with several people who were children or teenagers in the last years of the community. The more positive memory quoted in the paragraph is found in HDC Collection, William (Bill) Bears to HDC, writing from his home in Maine, 3 December 1962 and copied ("Word for Word") by Hector, 25 January 1963. Typed copies of the original handwritten letter were prepared to be sent to relatives.

32. HDC Collection, HDC in undated "P.P.S" to Emma for "Universal Salvation"; to Our Dear Helen and Peter, 11 and 12 May 1964, and to Dear Nephew David, 26 November 1965.

33. Zvi Ben-Dor Benite, *The Ten Lost Tribes: A World History* (New York: Oxford University Press, 2009), describes Anglo- or British Israelism as "the belief that Anglo-Saxons (and related Europeans) are the descendants of the ten lost tribes, a superior chosen race, destined to rule the world" (187). I discuss the myth of Anglo-Israelism and the elderly

Hector's increasing interest in it in Chapter 7. It perhaps bears clarifying that Anglo/British Israelites are not British Jews, much less citizens of Israel.

34. For his statement to an audience of kin in Boston that "a Seed, the Seed of the House of Israel," had been planted in Prince Edward Island (the clear implication was that it was among his own people), see HDC Collection, "Dear People/Belle River & Bangor," 26 December 1936. His community's connection to "The House of Israel" is also implied, though more gloomily, in HDC to Dear George and Hector, 28 November 1938. In another gloomy letter, he refers to the Compton community as having been a "chosen" people, though now sadly fallen from righteousness; HDC to Harold Grant, 29 August 1947. Hector's belief in his people's chosen-ness was, if anything, stronger in his old age, as shown, for instance, in HDC to son George and family, 21 January 1963. See also David Compton, *Leaving Home: PEI Farm Boy ... CNN News Anchor* (Charlottetown: Retro-Media Publishing, 2010), 48–9, for Hector's belief in old age that a young family member who was then a professional broadcaster might have a role to play in heralding end-times events.

35. Perhaps the most eccentric such thinker was the widow of an English vicar who, with her interwar followers, came to believe that she was a female messiah figure, that their society's very British garden was the original Garden of Eden, and that, if they could keep themselves sinless, Christ would return to their very community; see Jane Shaw, *Octavia, Daughter of God: The Story of a Female Messiah and Her Followers* (London: Jonathan Cape, 2011). I am grateful to Professor Pamela Walker for drawing my attention to this book.

36. Paul Boyer, *When Time Shall Be No More: Prophecy Belief in Modern American Culture* (Cambridge, MA: Harvard University Press, 1992), 10.

37. A.N. Wilson used the term in his historically well grounded novel in reference to the intergenerational intermarried kin of potter Josiah Wedgwood; see *The Potter's Hand* (London: Atlantic Books, 2012), 492. See also M.A. MacDonald, "Clash or Collaboration? Saint John Loyalists Meet the Planters and Others of the River, 1784–1785," in *Planter Links: Community and Culture in Colonial Nova Scotia*, ed. Margaret Conrad and Barry Moody (Fredericton: Acadiensis Press, 2001), 180.

38. Rutherford, *A Brief History*, Part One; Adam Kuper, *Incest and Influence: The Private Life of Bourgeois England* (Cambridge, MA: Harvard University Press, 2009); Leonore Davidoff and Catherine Hall, *Family Fortunes: Men and Women of the English Middle Class, 1780–1850* (Chicago: University of Chicago Press, 1999), 219–21; Leonore Davidoff, *Thicker Than Water: Siblings and Their Relations, 1780–1920* (Oxford: Oxford University Press, 2012), Ch. 9.

39. Allan Greer, *The People of New France* (Toronto: University of Toronto Press, 1997), 95; Elizabeth Fox-Genovese, *Within the Plantation Household: Black and White Women of the Old South* (Chapel Hill: University of North Carolina Press, 1988), 299, 315. See also Brian Connolly, *Domestic Intimacies: Incest and the Liberal Subject in Nineteenth Century America* (Philadelphia: University of Pennsylvania Press, 2014), where Connolly notes that "[t]he contiguity of incest and interracial marriage prohibitions in legal codes and the broader discourse was common in antebellum America" (95).

40. Mary Henley Rubio, *Lucy Maud Montgomery: The Gift of Wings* (Toronto: Doubleday, 2008), 87; J. Angus MacLean with the assistance of Marian Bruce, *Making It Home: Memoirs of J. Angus MacLean* (Charlottetown: Ragweed Press, 1998).

41. Thomas D. Hamm, *The Quakers in America* (New York: Columbia University Press, 2003), 32. Colonial Quakers did, though, like their British counterparts, seek to prevent close-kin marriage; see J. William Frost, *The Quaker Family in Colonial America: A Portrait of the Society of Friends* (New York: St. Martin's Press, 1973), 160–1, and Davidoff, *Thicker Than Water*, 234–5. For the Amish, see Dorothy Schwieder, "Utopia in the Midwest: The Old Order Amish and the Hutterites," *Palimpsest* 54, no. 3 (1973): 9–23, downloaded 9 December 2019.

42. Stirling F. Delano, *Brook Farm: The Dark Side of Utopia* (Cambridge, MA: Harvard University Press, 2004); Louis J. Kern, *An Ordered Love: Sex Roles and Sexuality in Victorian Utopias* (Chapel Hill: University of North Carolina Press, 1981).

43. John G. Turner, *Brigham Young: Pioneer Prophet* (Cambridge, MA: Harvard University Press, 2012), 88, for quotation; Leonard J. Arrington, *Brigham Young: American Moses* (New York: Alfred A. Knopf, 1985), 334, for number of Young's children; Laurel Thatcher Ulrich, *A House Full of Females: Plural Marriages and Women's Rights in Early Mormonism, 1835–1870* (New York: Alfred A. Knopf, 2017), for the early days of plural marriage and Mormon women's mixed responses.

44. Kern, *Ordered Love*, 208 (for his definition of complex marriage), 217 (for "scientific breeding"); Ellen Wayland-Smith, *Oneida: From Free Love Utopia to the Well-Set Table* (New York: Picador, 2016) 70 (for "spiritually accomplished"). Wayland-Smith elaborates on "Sticky Love" in Ch. 4. Noyes advocated even more intense "inbreeding" than was ultimately practised at Oneida, she writes. Even so, "following his own precept of 'breeding in and in,' Noyes fathered ten of the sixty-two Community children born during the eugenics experiment between 1869 and 1879, while another nineteen were his blood relatives" (128).

45. The crowded living quarters of the urban and rural poor were regarded as literal breeding grounds for all kinds of sexual immorality. As Leonore

Davidoff notes in *Thicker Than Water*, "in an era of crowded sleeping and sanitary arrangements … much that went on was not named" (76). See also Deborah Cohen, *Family Secrets: Living with Shame from the Victorians to the Present* (London: Viking, 2013), xiii.

46. Pamela Hatton Compton, "Compton," PARO, contains a page for George listing children said to be from his two marriages. George's paternity of a child not listed there but thought to have been his oldest is confirmed by a PEI baptismal record; see above, p. 164, n. 40. While some details may have differed, stories of George's sexual excesses were familiar to relatives who grew up in different countries and remained largely unknown to each other until the early twenty-first century. One of his grandsons, born and raised in the Boston area, knew two of George's "illegitimate" offspring as half-siblings of his mother, George's youngest daughter.

47. G.A. Rawlyk, *Ravished by the Spirit: Religious Revivals, Baptists, and Henry Alline* (Montreal: McGill-Queen's University Press, 1988), 85, and D.G. Bell, ed., *The Newlight Baptist Journals of James Manning and James Innis* (Hantsport, NS: Acadia Divinity College and the Baptist Historical Committee of the Atlantic Provinces, 1984), 15–16. Both these works suggest that antinomian excesses in the realm of sexuality and morals were in some way related to resistance to religious "forms, orders and externals" (Bell, 19). On antinomianism in the McDonaldite religious world of his austere father, the Master, see Sir Andrew Macphail, *The Master's Wife* (Toronto: McClelland and Stewart, 1977), 45.

48. It is possible that the women who bore – or, in the case of Ben, may have borne – children by these two brothers did so as an outcome of shared sexual appetites or Bible-based religious beliefs about the importance of procreation, or even a combination of these two factors. But it seems to me likely that the women's physical vulnerability was the most decisive factor.

49. On Hector's seeming pride in the fecundity of an older generation of male kin, see HDC Collection, "Compton Geneaology [*sic*]," 16 December 1964, one page, written by Hector for a relative who had requested some details of family history. For his concern in 1938 that none of the community women in Belle River was then bearing children, see HDC to brother George W. and Hector [Jardine], 28 November 1938, 2. His worries seem to have been unnecessary: in this period, Compton community families in Belle River were reportedly even larger on average than the high neighbourhood average. See Enid Charles and Sylvia Anthony, "The Community and the Family in Prince Edward Island," *Rural Sociology* 3, no. 1 (1943): 46.

50. Kuper, *Incest and Influence*, 40, 249 (for quotations); Davidoff, *Thicker Than Water*, Ch. 9. As Davidoff points out, understandings of what

constitutes "incest" have historically been and remain problematic, with even anthropologists, "the once defining experts," unable to reach common ground (197–8). Geneticist Adam Rutherford notes that Charles Darwin *did* eventually worry that his and Emma's consanguineous marriage was responsible for their children's health problems. See his *A Brief History*, 195–6, 200.

51. Connolly, *Domestic Intimacies*. By the end of the twentieth century, views like Morgan's would, in turn, be challenged by new genetic research. See, for instance, Martin Ottenheimer, *Forbidden Relatives: The American Myth of Cousin Marriage* (Urbana: University of Illinois Press, 1996), Davidoff, *Thicker Than Water*, 246–7, and the views of Rutherford, discussed below.

52. See Gary Burrill, *Away: Maritimers in Massachusetts, Ontario, and Alberta – An Oral History of Leaving Home* (Montreal: McGill-Queen's University Press, 1992), for an instance of a PEI sojourner who, living in Roxbury, Massachusetts, had learned to ridicule cousin marriage back home (72). There were situations in which a family history of cousin marriage led to readily understandable fears. For instance, New Brunswick-born Stanley Alexander Saunders, the son of first cousins, was concerned that he might pass along his blindness, the result of an inherited and incurable eye disease, and decided that he and his wife should not take the risk of having children; see S.A. Saunders, *The Economic History of the Maritime Provinces*, ed. and intro. T.W. Acheson (Fredericton: Acadiensis Press, 1984), Introduction, 5, 12 (originally published 1939 as part of Royal Commission on Dominion-Provincial Relations).

53. Rutherford, *A Brief History*, 206.

54. It was probably Hector who served as chief gatekeeper in initially forbidding and then allowing the marriages of the two half-sibling couples mentioned above.

55. HDC Collection, HDC to George W. [Compton] and Hector [Jardine], 28 November 1938, 2; to Grover, 24 November 1947; and to George, 23 November 1962. As noted above, p. 86, even in the late twentieth century, Old Order Amish in the American Midwest continued to practise close endogamy in order to maintain their religious beliefs and values, despite knowing the genetic risks.

56. Charles and Anthony, "The Community and the Family," 46.

57. HDC Collection, HDC to Dear Brother George, 5 May 1933.

58. Burrill, *Away*, first section; Betsy Beattie, *Obligation and Opportunity Obligation and Opportunity: Single Maritime Women in Boston, 1870–1930* (Montreal: McGill-Queen's University Press, 2000).

59. HDC Collection, HDC to "Dear People/Belle River & Bangor," 26 December 1936, writing from the home of a relative in Everett, Massachusetts.

60. HDC Collection, HDC to Gladys and Household, 4 April 1945, in which he draws on a letter he wrote about the visit just afterwards, on 31 December 1936.

61. "Co-operative P.E. Island Community/MacDonaldite Community at Bangor, P.E.I. Cited As Example of Successful Co-operation," 21 February 1933, 3 "(Special to the Guardian)"; "Bangor, P.E.I., Cited As Shining Example," 5 June 1933, 4 "(The New York Sun)."

62. "Unique PEI Colony Makes Progress/Mr. Compton Interviewed on Success of Community Movement," *Guardian*, 3 January 1935, 3. Business record books and the comments of other observers contradict the claim that no records were kept of community families' purchases or of monies paid.

63. Flora S. Rogers, "Brotherly Love Rules This Community," *Halifax Chronicle*, 20 June 1935, 1, 2; Tom Crowthers and Betty Rogers Large, *Out of Thin Air: The Story of CFCY/"The Friendly Voice of the Maritimes"* (Charlottetown: Applecross Press, 1989), 45 (for the reference to Ewen). See MacDonald, *If You're Stronghearted*, 152–4, for CFCY as a local success story.

64. See Gene Allen, *Making National News: A History of Canadian Press* (Toronto: University of Toronto Press, 2013) on CP wire, established in 1917, as "the first organization to provide systematic, regular coverage of domestic and international news to newspapers across Canada." See also "Compton Colony Not Supporting Tuber Bonus Plan," unsigned article, *Guardian*, 21 June 1935, 3, regarding the role of CP in publicizing "Comptonism."

65. HDC Collection, Earl W. Miller of the National Sociological Survey to Hector Compton, 21 January 1935, and Roland T. Patten for the *Packer*, to John Compton, 10 February 1936. The article to which Patten referred, "Some Interesting Sidelights on Co-operative Experiment in Prince Edward Island," appeared in *P.E. Island Agriculturalist*, 6 February 1936, based on information supplied by John, whose handwritten 16 February note on the back of the Patten letter asks Hector to "make some formal reply."

66. HDC Collection, Leonard L. Bass, for "We the People," to Dear Mr. Compton, 4 August 1937. See https://en.wikipedia.org/wiki/Phillips_Lord, accessed 13 November 2017, for "Phillips Lord," a minister's son, broadcaster, and actor, and his long-running radio character Seth Parker. See www.otrcat.com, for the *Time* magazine reference to "We the People."

67. HDC Collection, HDC to John Hays Hammond, Jr., 17 December 1936. On Hammond, see Wikipedia for overview article and reference to related works, including John Dandola's *Living in the Past, Looking to the Future: The Biography of John Hays Hammond, Jr.* (Glen Ridge, NJ, 2004).

68. HDC Collection, HDC to Dear John, 27 January 1935. He identified the authors of the unsigned 3 January 1935 article as "Murley and Morton."

69. HDC Collection, HDC to Our Dear Helen and Peter, 11 and 12 May 1964 (for the reference to some forty letters), and to Dear Bro. Jas and All, 16 April 1946 (regarding media and other inquiries); also Helen Jean Champion, *Over on the Island* (Toronto: Ryerson Press, 1939, reprinted 1946), 118.

70. "Compton Colony Not Supporting Tuber Bonus Plan" (includes quotations).

71. Champion, *Over on the Island*. On Champion's background and the favourable reception for her book, see *Guardian*, 1 December 1936, 1; 27 May 1939, 4; 30 May 1939.

72. Champion, *Over on the Island*, 117.

73. Champion, *Over on the Island*, 159–60.

74. See discussion below, pp. 125–6.

75. Champion, *Over on the Island*, 119; Enid Charles, "The Trend of Fertility on Prince Edward Island," *Canadian Journal of Economics and Political Science* 8, no. 2 (May 1942): 239–40 (quotation), and Charles and Anthony, "The Community and the Family," 46 (access to media).

6 Restiveness Within, Pressures from Without: The Road to Dissolution

1. Rosabeth Moss Kanter, *Commitment and Community: Communes and Utopias in Sociological Perspective* (Cambridge, MA: Harvard University Press, 1972), 127–9, 245. For criticism of Kanter's use of communal longevity as the criterion for determining success or failure in utopias, see Donald E. Pitzer, ed., *America's Communal Utopias* (Chapel Hill: University of North Carolina Press, 1997), Introduction by Pitzer, 13.

2. Ellen Wayland-Smith, *Oneida: From Free Love Utopia to the Well-Set Table* (New York: Picador, 2016); Stirling F. Delano, *Brook Farm: The Dark Side of Utopia* (Cambridge, MA: Belknap Press of Harvard University Press, 2004); Andrew Scott, *The Promise of Paradise: Utopian Communities in BC*, 2nd ed. (Madeira Park, BC: Harbour Publishing, 2017; orig. ed. 1997).

3. Ernest R. Forbes, "Consolidating Disparity: The Maritimes and the Industrialization of Canada during the Second World War," *Acadiensis* 15, no. 2 (Spring 1986): 3–27; Edward MacDonald, *If You're Stronghearted: Prince Edward Island in the Twentieth Century* (Charlottetown: PEI Museum and Heritage Foundation, 2000), Chs. 6 and 7 (quotation at 210).

4. Hector D. Compton Collection, privately held and uncatalogued (hereafter HDC Collection), HDC to Our Dear Helen and Peter, 11 and 12 May 1964; New Testament, King James Version.

5. "Unique PEI Colony Makes Progress," *Guardian*, 3 January 1935, 3.
6. HDC Collection, HDC and James M. Compton, liquidators (unsigned draft), to Provincial Secretary and the Director of Income Tax, 24 April 1948.
7. Information about Mary is based chiefly on correspondence with the older of her two sons, who recalled her stories of removal from the church as one of her "most scarring memories" (20 April 2013, email). Mary seems not to have returned to Prince Edward Island for visits until some years after her father died, but she maintained close connections with Island kin, including Hector. For her siblings' baptisms, see Public Archives and Records Office, Charlottetown (hereafter PARO), Index of Baptisms, for Annie Elizabeth Compton (Record Book #8, 101), George Emerson Compton (Record Book #8, 25), and Elizabeth Louisa Compton.
8. HDC Collection, HDC to John Hays Hammond, 17 December 1936; "Skipper Lost When Island Ship Grounds," *Guardian*, 9 November 1936.
9. Even decades later, his oldest sister reportedly spoke of seeing someone who looked just like Oliver on a street in one of Canada's large cities.
10. For instance, Laurence Foster, *Religion and Sexuality: Three American Communal Experiments of the Nineteenth Century* (New York: Oxford University Press, 1981); Chris Jennings, *Paradise Now: The Story of American Utopianism* (New York: Random House, 2016); Delano, *Brook Farm*; Wayland-Smith, *Oneida*. Even at Oneida, though, Wayland-Smith notes, women were never part of the "upper echelons of business management" (178–9).
11. Laurel Ulrich Thatcher, *A House Full of Females: Plural Marriage and Women's Rights in Early Mormonism, 1835–1870* (New York: Alfred A. Knopf, 2017).
12. Decades later, as an old man, her father apologized to her for not having said no to Hector's request. Meanwhile, in the late 1940s when she was preparing to marry an outsider, she believed that she needed to seek Hector's approval even though the community was then in the process of being wound up; private communication.
13. Michele Stairs, "Matthews and Marillas: Bachelors and Spinsters in Prince Edward Island in 1881," in *Mapping the Margins: The Family and Social Discipline in Canada, 1700–1975*, ed. Nancy Christie and Michael Gauvreau (Montreal: McGill-Queen's University Press, 2004), 247–67.
14. In the 1911 census for Lot 41, PEI, elder John's daughters Louisa Compton, age sixty-six, and Phebe Compton, age fifty-nine, show up as aunts in the Bangor household of Dan Compton and his wife Mary.
15. For the WI and the two churches, see Enid Charles and Sylvia Anthony, "The Community and the Family in Prince Edward Island," *Rural Sociology* 3, no. 1 (1943): 45, and Ruby MacMillan Matheson with Marian

Bruce, *Echoes of Home: Stories of Bygone Days in Wood Islands* (Summerside: Williams and Crue, nd [2001 or earlier]), 71. In 1960, more than a decade after the Compton community had been dissolved, a now elderly Hector Compton, writing to his Halifax-based son, would describe a WI meeting held in the home he now shared with his son and daughter-in-law as "a new departure for this place"; HDC Collection, HDC to son George, 8 April 1960.

16. HDC Collection, untitled black record book with entries for expenditures and purchases from August 1919 to July 1926 and showing purchase of corsets on 7 February and 4 June 1920, and 30 May 1921. Probably if a community woman needed to go to town for another reason, such as a trip to the dentist, she would have been given responsibility for shopping for women's items. Much women's clothing, though, would have been made at home.

17. Susan Hornby, ed., *Belfast People: An Oral History of Belfast, Prince Edward Island* (Charlottetown: Tea Hill Press, 1992), 97, for Libby's neighbourhood medical services. Memories of her acts of resistance were recounted by some of her nieces and a grandson. Among community women in Bangor, Big John's wife seems sometimes to have accompanied him on business trips to the city; see HDC Collection, HDC to Dear Brother George, 5 May 1933.

18. Charles and Anthony, "The Community and the Family," 37. Ruth Sandwell and others have pointed to this period as a turning point for rural Canada overall; see R.W. Sandwell, *Canada's Rural Majority: Household, Environments and Economies, 1870–1940* (Toronto: University of Toronto Press, 2016), 26–7. "After 1940," she writes, "wartime labour shortages disrupted many patterns, and then fossil fuels dramatically expanded transportation, agricultural production, and new forms of resource extraction."

19. MacDonald, *If You're Stronghearted*, Ch. 6; HDC Collection, HDC to Donald Bears, 28 September 1941 (business orders and reduced crew), and HDC to Commanding Officer, Royal Canadian Navy, Halifax, 6 October 1945 (for prewar employee numbers and the importance of founder Ben's son to the company).

20. HDC Collection, HDC to Donald Bears, 28 September 1941.

21. HDC Collection, HDC to brother George, 27 and 28 July 1942, including part of report to RCMP. The fire had threatened nearby buildings; Libby's home was only narrowly saved. The reference to lack of fire insurance on the mill is contained in Matheson and Bruce, *Echoes of Home*, 133.

22. Paul Boyer, *When Time Shall Be No More: Prophecy Belief in Modern American Culture* (Cambridge, MA: Harvard University Press, 1992), esp. 10, 112.

23. HDC Collection, HDC to brother George, 27 and 28 July 1942 (for the reference to receiving *Destiny* as providential), and HDC, P.S. to Mr. Beaton, undated fragment (regarding Russia), probably 1943.
24. HDC Collection, HDC to brother George, 9 December 1945.
25. HDC Collection, HDC to cousin Belle, 13 December 1944.
26. Charles and Anthony, "The Community and the Family," 45, 46. See also Matheson and Bruce, *Echoes of Home*, regarding the attractions of a dance hall in nearby Wood Islands where young men employed in the Compton community mill provided the music for what were sometimes raucous events (54).
27. HDC Collection, HDC to brother George, 12 and 13 January 1946. See also HDC to brother George, 29 November 1945, where he wrote of "extremes of neglect and even defiance of all we ever lived for."
28. For example, HDC Collection, HDC to brother George, 9 December 1945: "It is not a disputation over different faiths as happened in former stages of our people, but a total disregard of all we held sacred and it has come about in a brief space of time."
29. HDC Collection, untitled large grey record book, 357–9, for minutes of general meeting of directors of B. Compton Limited, held at Belle River, 31 December 1943. Two of Hector's sons and one son of Big John Compton were named as directors for 1944, as was an older bachelor relative from Bangor who was considered intellectually incapable of living or working independently. Hector's sister Libby, founder Ben's widow, was also listed as one of the directors, but since there was no further meeting until 1947, when a decision was taken to terminate the company, none of these directorial appointments bore much significance. One change that did take place as a result of this meeting was that separate accounting was henceforth kept "on each Farm or other line of activity"; see HDC and James M. Compton to Provincial Secretary and Income Tax Office, writing as liquidators of B. Compton Limited, 7 June 1948, a rewritten version of the 24 April 1948 draft.
30. HDC Collection, HDC to brother George, 12 and 13 January and 5 July 1946, and to Dear Mary, 6 April 1945. In the July letter to George, Hector wrote despairingly about the recent marriage of founder Ben's youngest daughter to a local non-kinsman and explained that at their wedding reception he had given an end-times message rather than words of congratulation: "I was in that frame of mind where I did not care a whit what anyone thought but still not disrespectful to anyone." Hector was hospitalized in 1947 for what turned out to be a stress-related ailment; see HDC to Our Dear Helen and Peter, 11 and 12 May 1964.
31. HDC Collection, HDC to brother George, 3 April 1946.

32. HDC Collection, HDC to Dear Friends All, 29 November 1944, and to cousin Belle, 15 December 1944, regarding John's final days and visitors, including "the Irish ... with their impulsive words of praise and with tears in their eyes." On Hector's involvement in hospital fundraising, see above, p. 72. Regarding his role in supporting a new ferry service from Wood Islands to Nova Scotia, see "Meeting of Trade Board," *Guardian*, 20 January 1937, 1, 9, and 27 January 1937, 1.

33. Marion Bruce and Elizabeth Cran, *Working Together: Two Centuries of Co-operatives on Prince Edward Island* (Charlottetown: Island Studies Press, 2004), Ch. 4. The Morell cooperative included a store, potato warehouse, creamery, lobster factory, chicken hatchery, and credit union. "The National Film Board of Canada even featured the village in a documentary about the Antigonish Movement" (122).

34. HDC Collection, HDC to brother George, 3 April 1946, and to "Dear Brother Jas. and All," 16 April 1946. W.R. Shaw, deputy minister of agriculture and a future premier, had been serving on a regional committee for the resettlement of returned servicemen. He had written to Hector, enclosing a 1935 article about the company from the *Toronto Star*, and asking for more information about its operation and structure. Hector later met with Shaw and gave him information about the company. Reference to Shaw's interest is contained in both these letters.

35. HDC Collection, HDC to Royal Canadian Navy, 16 October 1945, seeking early release from service of founder Ben's son and detailing problems for the company resulting from manpower shortages; HDC to brother George, 6 September 1946 (machine shop losses); HDC and James M. Compton, liquidators (unsigned draft), to Provincial Secretary and the Director of Income Tax, 24 April 1948 (reference to barn fire).

36. Copy of J.L. (Jack) Compton to H.D. Compton, 20 September 1945. This copy, evidently removed from the HDC Collection sometime after the writer's death in 1972, was rescued and saved by a niece after his son and his youngest brother made a failed attempt to burn it.

37. HDC Collection, untitled large grey record book, 361, Minutes of Meeting held at Belle River, 7 August 1947.

38. HDC Collection, untitled statement by HDC, 3 April 1948, for his response to real and perceived criticisms.

39. HDC Collection, HDC and James M. Compton, liquidators (unsigned draft), to Provincial Secretary and the Director of Income Tax, 24 April 1948. The rewritten version, dated 7 June 1948, and bearing Hector's signature, is largely the same in substance except that there is no longer a specific reference to self-sacrifice by "the Bangor Section."

40. HDC Collection, HDC and James M. Compton, liquidators, to Provincial Secretary and Income Tax Office, rewritten version, 7 June 1948.

Hector was later paid by former shareholders in B. Compton Limited for his work in calculating division of company assets, completing official reports, etc.; see HDC Collection, Minutes of Meeting, 17 March 1950.

41. Raymond B. Blake, "Mackenzie King and the Genesis of Family Allowances in Canada," in *Social Welfare Policy in Canada: Historical Readings*, ed. Raymond B. Blake and Jeff Keshen (Toronto: Copp Clark, 1995), 244–54; Dominique Marshall, "The Language of Children's Rights, the Formation of the Welfare State, and the Democratic Experience of Poor Families in Quebec, 1940–55," *Canadian Historical Review* 78, no. 3 (September 1997): 409–41.

42. I deal more fully with the post-community experiences of former members in Belle River and Bangor in Chapter 7.

43. HDC Collection, "Bangor/Assets of B. Compton Limited as [of] Dec. 31, 1947"; HDC to Donald Jardine, Bangor, 23 July 1948; HDC to Dun & Bradstreet of Canada & The Packer Produce Mercantile Agency, 22 May 1951.

44. Gary Burrill, *Away: Maritimers in Massachusetts, Ontario, and Alberta – An Oral History of Leaving Home* (Montreal: McGill-Queen's University Press, 1992), Introduction, for Maritime patterns of migration. By the early 1950s, daughters as well as sons of former community members were leaving the province in search of work, and from Bangor as well as Belle River.

45. HDC Collection, HDC to brother George, 6 September 1946, for threatened depopulation, and to son George, 13 October 1949, for quotation.

7 Life beyond Community: Diverse Paths in an Era of Change

1. Ellen Wayland-Smith, *Oneida: From Free Love Utopia to the Well-Set Table* (New York: Picador, 2016). Anthony Wonderley's *Oneida Utopia: A Community Searching for Human Happiness and Prosperity* (Ithaca: Cornell University Press, 2017) also carries the Oneida story forward into its post-utopia existence.

2. Albert Schrauwers, *Awaiting the Millennium: The Children of Peace and the Village of Hope, 1812–1889* (Toronto: University of Toronto Press, 1993), 81; Enid Charles and Sylvia Anthony, "The Community and the Family in Prince Edward Island," *Rural Sociology* 3, no. 1 (1943): 46.

3. Hector D. Compton Collection, privately held and uncatalogued (hereafter HDC Collection), HDC to brother George, 28 July 1942.

4. HDC Collection, HDC to son Elmer, 16 May 1950 (age, lack of income, appreciation of aid from sons), and to Mr. A. Nicholson, Regional Director, 9 October 1951 (providing documentation to establish his age).

5. HDC Collection, HDC to Dear Cousins, 5 October 1955 (house renovations); Sadie Inman to HDC, 10 March 1957 (condolence on death

of Bessie); HDC to cousin Sarah, 16 April 1958, and to cousin Marion, 7 March 1960 (living arrangements and grandchildren); HDC to Charlie Hancock, 23 January 1965 (declining further work for a would-be workshop customer).

6. HDC Collection, HDC to cousin Marion, 7 March 1960, and for a similar statement, HDC to Dear Mary, 16 March 1963. See also HDC to three of his sons, 19 February 1965, where he tells them he is on his fourteenth reading of the Bible.

7. HDC Collection, HDC to Dear Cousin Sarah, 16 April 1958; to *American Mercury Magazine*, 26 February 1958; and to Cousin Marion, 7 March 1960 ("am getting 10 magazines and even more books"); "Remarks," 13 September 1966, in untitled brown record book.

8. HDC Collection, "1959 Tithes": a list of publications and individuals in North America and elsewhere to which Hector was then subscribing or to whom he was sending donations. On at least one occasion he was evidently the victim of a fraud in connection with one publication and asked a New York-based relative to investigate; see Philip E. Wilcox to Dear Uncle Hector, 19 May 1959. See also A. Rutherford to HDC, 25 August 1954. Rutherford's particular speciality was pyramidology. Here he was writing en route back to England, thanking Hector for hospitality and financial help. Proud references to the brotherly salutations were made in several letters, including HDC to Cousin Marion, 7 March 1960.

9. Zvi Ben-Dor Benite, *The Ten Lost Tribes: A World History* (New York: Oxford University Press, 2009), esp. Ch. 6; Tudor Parfitt, *The Lost Tribes of Israel: The History of a Myth* (London: Weidenfeld and Nicolson, 2002), referring to British Israelism as "unblessed with even a scintilla of evidence" (47) and noting its growing hostility to modern-day Jews (56); H.L. Goudge, *The British Israel Theory* (London: A.R. Mobray, 1933), analysing its lack of grounding in scientific biblical scholarship and linking it to religious fundamentalism; and O. Michael Friedman, *Origins of the British Israelites: The Lost Tribes* (San Francisco: Mellen Research University Press, 1993), describing the theory as a problem for evangelical Christianity and "a delusion of Satan" (48).

10. As Oxford divinity professor H.L. Goudge observed in 1933, Anglo-Israelism, in addition to being "profoundly un-Christian," fostered "a pride and self-complacency which come only too easily to us Englishmen" (*The British Israel Theory*, iii).

11. For instance, HDC Collection, HDC to Herbert Sanders, 8 April 1954, and HDC to Cousin Sarah, 10 March 1960 ("great Minds").

12. HDC Collection, HDC to Dear Mr. MacLean, 8 December 1954.

13. Andrew Preston, *Sword of the Spirit, Shield of Faith: Religion in American War and Diplomacy* (New York: Anchor Books, 2012), esp. 402–3, 554–5;

Mark Hutchinson and John Wolffe, *A Short History of Global Evangelicalism* (Cambridge: Cambridge University Press, 2012), 166–7.

14. HDC Collection, MacLean to HDC, 13 December 1954.

15. HDC Collection, HDC to Cousin Sarah, 10 March 1960, quoting Sarah's rebukes.

16. HDC Collection, Elmer to Dear Daddy, 19 February 1963. If Hector wrote a reply to this letter, no copy has survived in this collection.

17. HDC Collection, HDC to Herbert Sanders, 8 April 1954, and to Cousin Sarah, 11 March 1960 ("Israel beliefs").

18. See Edward MacDonald, *If You're Stronghearted: Prince Edward Island in the Twentieth Century* (Charlottetown: Prince Edward Island Museum and Heritage Foundation, 2000): "In the late 20th century, Prince Edward Island remained the most ethnically homogeneous province in Canada. Its population was overwhelmingly white, Christian, and Western" (355).

19. HDC Collection, HDC to Dear Cousins, 5 October 1955, for "heathen hordes." The *Guardian* in this period carried very negative stories about the nationalist Mau Mau in eastern Africa (e.g., 28 March 1953, 1, and 20 December 1954, 8). A decade later there was somewhat more awareness of valid reasons for unrest in Africa, but the emphasis was still on the continent's violent character; see "White Men in Africa," *Guardian*, 10 December 1964, 4.

20. HDC Collection, HDC to son John and Family, 17 December 1962 (organized religion); HDC to Herbert Sanders, 8 April 1954 ("coddled"); to Dear Friends Abroad, 8 October 1962; to Dear Son George, 23 November 1962 (a daughter whose churchgoing was perceived as an act of defiance); to Dear Marion and Cousins, 21 December 1962 ("Christianity has become Churchianity").

21. HDC Collection, HDC to Pastor Neesor, June 1958, on his opposition to celebrating Christmas and in particular the setting up of a tree in the household in which he was living.

22. HDC Collection, HDC to George, Sybil and Boys, 5 December 1956, and to Dear Cousin Sarah, 16 April 1958, for instances of his love and appreciation for grandchildren. One woman, now in her sixties, remembers being read to by her grandfather, tears in his eyes as he read *Lassie Come Home*, her copy of which she still treasures.

23. On this, see David Compton, *Leaving Home: PEI Farm Boy ... CNN News Anchor* (Charlottetown: RetroMedia, 2010), 48.

24. My thanks to Liz Salmis for providing a copy of the booklet recording information on officiants and others in attendance at her grandfather's funeral service at his home.

25. HDC Collection, HDC, "Copied from B- I- Radio Addresses of March 1957," 25 April 1957, which also contains Hector's own observations on

world events, and on Bessie's funeral. Regarding the latter, he explained that although the Compton community had "disdained the creeds and formalities of the churches around us" for some forty years and always conducted their own funerals, it was no longer "feasible" to do so.

26. MacDonald, *If You're Stronghearted*, esp. Chs. 7–9 (227 for quotation; 296 for standard of living), and Satadal Dasgupta, "The Island in Transition: A Statistical Overview," in *The Garden Transformed: Prince Edward Island, 1945–1980*, ed. Verner Smitheram, David Milne, and Satadel Dasgupta (Charlottetown: Ragweed Press, 1982), 243–68.

27. Brian Clarke and Stuart Macdonald, *Leaving Christianity: Changing Allegiances in Canada since 1945* (Montreal: McGill-Queen's University Press, 2017), esp. Ch. 1 for the mainstream Protestant denominations, and Ch. 3 for Roman Catholics; MacDonald, *If You're Stronghearted*, 365–6, for the continued saliency of religion. On divides between Maritimers and national leaders in the United Church of Canada on the matter of evangelism, see Phyllis Airhart, *A Church with the Soul of a Nation: Making and Remaking the United Church of Canada* (Montreal: McGill-Queen's University Press, 2014), 236–7. See also G.A. Rawlyk, *Is Jesus Your Personal Saviour? In Search of Canadian Evangelicalism in the 1990s* (Montreal: McGill-Queen's University Press, 1996) for data from a 1993 survey showing residents of the Atlantic Region as more traditional in their faith views than those in other regions of Canada and as more likely to be weekly churchgoers (77). In the case of Islanders, it is likely that a pattern of continuing to live in their rural communities even as they increasingly commuted to non-farm jobs contributed to the ongoing strength of their religious observances; see Dasgupta, "The Island in Transition," 265.

28. HDC Collection, HDC to his sons and others, 5 February 1958, describes a small Sunday gathering in Bangor at the home of the late "Big John" Compton at which scripture was read and psalms were sung. Hector makes it clear that this was a singular event, "the first community of minds we had for so long a time," and he had to be convinced by his sister, John's widow, that it had not been inspired and "defiled" by alcohol. I have seen no evidence that such gatherings were still being held in Hector's own home. A gathering of some immediate family members for Bible reading and hymn singing on a Thanksgiving weekend in 1956 was likewise described in Hector's letter to his son George on 9 October 1956, as an unusual gathering. The daily Bible reading that Hector, his sister Libby, and some others of the elder generation engaged in was a private matter. Curiously, though, one of the Danish labourers who had married a daughter of founder Ben and moved his family to Toronto in the 1950s held Sunday worship for them in their home rather than taking them to church. My thanks to one of his daughters for telling me about this.

29. For background on the Free Church of Scotland on Prince Edward Island, see J.H. Bishop, *Church of Scotland in Prince Edward Island (MacDonaldite Section)* (np, nd [1991]), Preface. For Ted, see obituary for the Reverend Ted MacDougall, *Monthly Record: The Edinburgh Magazine of the Free Church of Scotland*, August 2003, 10. Information about his outreach to the Comptons of Bangor comes from the author's conversation with Ada Compton, 1 July 2014, and emails from several other Comptons, including Dr. Anne Compton, who as young adults knew him personally and in different contexts. Information about who began attending church and when comes from these and other family sources.

30. They had evidently had occasional involvement in the local Presbyterian church even before Hector died in 1970. Writing to his son George on 27 January 1960, following the funeral of a neighbour, Hector had observed, "It felt strange to see [daughter] Joyce and [son] Russell taking seats in the Choir"; letter in HDC Collection.

31. Information on both men comes from email communications and from church-linked websites. A Toronto-born cousin of the two men also came under MacDougall's influence for a time in the 1970s in a youth commune setting, and while he ultimately developed a secular outlook, he continued to admire MacDougall for his intellect and kindness; conversation with Brian MacLaren, 13 January 2018.

32. https://www.youtube.com/watch?V=W14fSWaFpnY; MacKenzie Sisters, Belfast, PEI, 14 August 2011; viewed 18 October 2018.

33. I am most grateful to this respondent for her 1 February 2018, response to a short questionnaire which I sent to members of her cohort of descendants of Compton community alumni.

34. Secularization, regarded for decades as a problematic and "promiscuous concept," has come to be seen by historians as most applicable to the 1960s. See Callum G. Brown and Michael Snape, "Introduction: Conceptualizing Secularisation, 1974–2010," in *Secularisation in the Christian World: Essays in Honour of Hugh McLeod*, ed. Brown and Snape (Farnham, Surrey: Ashgate Publishing, 2010), 1 ("promiscuous concept"), and 9–10, citing McLeod's observation (in *The Religious Crisis of the 1960s*) that "'In the religious history of the West these years may come to be seen as marking a rupture as profound as that brought about by the Reformation.'"

35. Clarke and Macdonald, *Leaving Christianity*, 70.

36. HDC Collection, HDC to son George and family, 1 August 1964, summarizing his conversation with Libby.

37. Copy of J.L. Compton to H.D. Compton, 20 September 1945. See earlier reference to this letter above, p. 110.

38. See Blair Weeks, ed., *Minding the House: A Biographical Guide to Prince Edward Island MLAs, 1873–1993* (Charlottetown: Acorn Press, 2002), for profile of Daniel James Compton (1915–1990), a Conservative MLA in the 1970s and House Speaker in the early 1980s (38). Information about the role of faith in helping Dan Compton achieve sobriety comes from email correspondence with his son. Interestingly, in their 1990s national survey of how ordinary Americans understood and used their pasts, Roy Rosenzweig and David Thelen heard from "several respondents" about the positive role that AA had played in helping them overcome their addictions; see their *The Presence of the Past: Popular Uses of History in American Life* (New York: Columbia University Press, 1998), 196 (part of Thelen's "Afterthoughts").

39. MacDonald, *If You're Stronghearted*, Ch. 7. The number of farms on Prince Edward Island declined from 12,230 in 1941 to 3,677 in 1976; see William Janssen, "Agriculture in Transition," in *The Garden Transformed*, 120. Analogous patterns of agricultural modernization along with rural out-migration were happening around mid-century in other parts of North America, affecting even traditionally distinctive ethnic and faith communities. See, e.g., Jane Marie Pederson, *Between Memory and Reality: Family and Community in Rural Wisconsin, 1870–1970* (Madison: University of Wisconsin Press, 1992) and Royden Loewen, *Diaspora in the Countryside: Two Mennonite Communities and Mid-Twentieth-Century Rural Disjuncture* (Toronto: University of Toronto Press, 2006).

40. MacDonald, *If You're Stronghearted*, 271, for statistic.

41. MacDonald, *If You're Stronghearted*, Ch. 8; Verner Smitheram, "Development and the Debate over School Consolidation," in *Garden Transformed*, 177–202 (181 for statistic on comparative educational expenditures).

42. MacDonald, *If You're Stronghearted*, 292; Dasgupta, "The Island in Transition," in *Garden Transformed*, 261.

43. In regard to educational and occupational changes, their experiences in some ways paralleled transitions in Canadian Mennonite communities in the same era; see T.D. Regehr, *Mennonites in Canada, 1939–1970: A People Transformed* (Toronto: University of Toronto Press, 1996), Part 4.

44. HDC Collection, HDC to "Dear Folks, Bedford, Bangor, Quincey, etc.," 1 October 1959.

45. François Weil, *Family Trees: A History of Genealogy in America* (Cambridge, MA: Harvard University Press, 2013). Weil dates the transition from a search for "pedigree" to a search for "identity" in the US to the last half of the twentieth century, with the television series *Roots*, Alex Haley's hugely popular account of his enslaved African ancestors, as a crucial stimulus to the new turn. Nevertheless, in his book *Researching Your Ancestors in New Brunswick, Canada*, self-published in 1979

(Fredericton, NB), archivist Robert F. Fellows took it for granted that genealogists were still "pedigree hunters" and noted approvingly that their twin motivations were "a curiosity about the past, and a healthy pride in their ancestors" (8).

46. See Paul Jones, "Coming Clean," *Canada's History* 92, no. 5 (October/ November 2012), on twenty-first-century researchers' openness to exploring their family past wherever it takes them. See also Elizabeth Yakel and Deborah A. Torres, "Genealogists as a 'Community of Records,'" *American Archivist* 70 (Spring/Summer 2007): 93–113, for the point that some genealogists are eager to get beyond "simply establishing the facts" of their family past and are engaged in a "search for meaning" (108).

47. Deborah Cohen, *Family Secrets: Living with Shame from the Victorians to the Present Day* (London: Viking, 2013), esp. "Epilogue: Genealogy and Confessional Culture," 241–53. A recent, moving example is Métis scholar and author Jesse Thistle's *From the Ashes: My Story of Being Métis, Homeless, and Finding My Way* (Toronto: Simon and Schuster, 2019), particularly 225–30, for the chapter called "Indian Turned Métis."

48. See above, p. 110 and p. 124, where I quote from the letter.

49. I make this statement with a good deal of confidence, given the extent and variety of materials that have survived in what I refer to in this book as the H.D. Compton Collection.

50. Anna Green, "Intergenerational Family Stories: Private, Parochial, Pathological?" *Journal of Family History* 38, no. 4 (2013): 387–402 (particularly 387–8).

51. Marjorie Theobald, *The Wealth beneath Their Feet: A Family on the Castlemaine Goldfields* (Melbourne: Arcadia, 2010), 219.

52. Cohen, *Family Secrets*; Leonore Davidoff, Megan Doolittle, Janet Fink, and Katherine Holden, *The Family Story: Blood, Contract and Intimacy, 1830–1960* (London: Longman, 1999), Ch. 9.

53. Cohen, *Family Secrets*, xx, and Ch. 7, "The Repressive Family."

54. Elaine Tyler May, *Homeward Bound: American Families in the Cold War Era* (New York: Basic Books, 2008, orig. ed. 1988), and, for a Canadian overview, Doug Owram, *Born at the Right Time: A History of the Baby Boom Generation* (Toronto: University of Toronto Press, 1997), Ch. 1. See also Mona Gleason, *Normalizing the Ideal: Psychology, Schooling and the Family in Postwar Canada* (Toronto: University of Toronto Press, 1999), and Mary Louise Adams, *The Trouble with Normal: Postwar Youth and the Making of Heterosexuality* (Toronto: University of Toronto Press, 1997).

55. Charles and Anthony, "The Community and the Family," 46.

56. Northrop Frye, "Varieties of Literary Utopias," in *Utopias and Utopian Thought*, ed. Frank E. Manuel (Boston: Houghton Mifflin, 1966),

quotations on 28, 29; William Golding, *Lord of the Flies: A Novel* (London: Faber and Faber, 1954).

57. On the desire to conform as traditionally "one of the most important drawing cards for the churches," see Nancy Christie and Michael Gauvreau, Introduction: "'Even the hippies were only very slowly going secular': Dechristianization and the Culture of Individualism in North American and Western Europe," in *The Sixties and Beyond: Dechristianization in North America and Western Europe, 1945–2000*, ed. Christie and Gauvreau (Toronto: University of Toronto Press, 2013), 21, where they cite British historian Jeffrey Cox. My father's binge drinking had also been a source of my youthful personal shame – respectable Island people didn't drink – but by the late 1950s he had achieved lasting sobriety.

58. On the importance and longevity of Charles E. Fuller's "The Old Fashioned Revival Hour" in popularizing fundamentalist and end times messages, see, for instance, Matthew Avery Sutton, *American Apocalypse: A History of Modern Evangelicalism* (Cambridge, MA: Harvard University Press, 2014).

Concluding Reflections

1. Adam Rutherford's *A Brief History of Everyone Who Ever Lived: The Stories in Our Genes* (London: Weidenfield and Nicholson, 2016) provides an accessible discussion of epigenetics for a lay audience and a helpful historical illustration (344–51).

2. Steven Mithen, online review in the *Guardian* (UK), 24 October 2018 (accessed 28 October), of Robert Plomin's *Blueprint* (Cambridge, MA: MIT Press, 2019), which argues for the overwhelming power of DNA rather than nurture to determine who we are. "Genetics," Plomin writes, "explains more of the psychological differences between us than everything else put together" (viii).

3. Rutherford, *A Brief History*, 90, 317.

4. Christine Kenneally, *The Invisible History of the Human Race: How DNA and History Shape Our Identities and Our Futures* (New York: Viking, 2014), 135, for the quotation, which refers specifically to an Australian historian's research project on the backgrounds and descendants of Tasmanian convicts. The goal of the project "is to build detailed biographies of Tasmania's nineteenth-century convicts in order to chart the variety of paths they took and to discover patterns in the population as a whole" (135–6).

5. See Sadie Bergen, "What Are You? Historians Confront Race, Genealogy, and Genetics," *Perspectives on History* 56, no. 2 (February 2018): 23–5 (downloaded 15 December 2019), which summarizes the concerns

of several historians. Bergen notes that "Genetic testing services like Ancestry DNA bring a veneer of scientific objectivity to racial and ethnic identity, cementing what many people intuitively believe." She concludes that historians must push back against the lure of such services and their potential for reinforcing dangerous ideas about race and genetics, "while honoring the roles that heritage, genealogy, and geographical origins play in determining 'who we are.'"

6. Michel Robertson, *The Last Utopians: Four Late Nineteenth-Century Visionaries and Their Legacies* (Princeton: Princeton University Press, 2018), 59, Ch. 5; Hector D. Compton Collection (privately held and uncatalogued; hereafter HDC Collection), HDC to Brother George, 29 November 1945.

7. The discussion of the state that follows relies on the work of specialists on the state and state formation to refer to something larger than just the institutions and political parties making and administering law at any given period. See Allan Greer and Ian Radforth, eds., *Colonial Leviathan: State Formation in Nineteenth-Century Canada* (Toronto: University of Toronto Press, 1992), Introduction, 10, for an understanding that goes beyond the executive and legislative branches in any given jurisdiction to include also "the constellation of agencies and officers sharing in the sovereign authority."

8. Ian McKay, "The Liberal Order Framework: A Prospectus for a Reconnaissance of Canadian History," *Canadian Historical Review* 81, no. 4 (December 2000): 617–45 (631 for "state hegemony," 630 for "antithetical traditions," 636 for "aliberal entities"). For a collection of articles that came out of a 2000 symposium on McKay's liberal order construct, see Jean-François Constant and Michel Ducharme, eds., *Liberalism and Hegemony: Debating the Canadian Liberal Revolution* (Toronto: University of Toronto Press, 2009). The collection begins with McKay's original article and concludes with a longer piece by him that engages with other essayists in the volume.

9. R.W. Sandwell, "The Limits of Liberalism: The Liberal Reconnaissance and the History of the Family in Canada," *Canadian Historical Review* 84, no. 3 (September 2003): 423–50 (quotations at 434 and 442). See also Nancy Christie, "From Interdependence to 'Modern Individualism': Families and the Emergence of Liberal Society in Canada," *History Compass* 10, no. 1 (2011): 81–104. Christie argues that families, while unquestionably marching to their own drummers, contributed to the making of liberal order Canada. Yet "if there was one group which stood outside the liberal order and outside modernity for much longer, it was farm families" (87).

10. Graeme Wynn, "Ideology, Society, and the State in the Maritime Colonies of British North America, 1840–1860," in *Colonial Leviathan*, 284–328;

Janet Guildford and Suzanne Morton, eds., *Making Up the State: Women in 20th-Century Atlantic Canada* (Fredericton: Acadiensis Press, 2010), for Introduction, 9–18, and for Sharon Myers, "The Apocrypha of Minnie McGee: The Murderous Mother and the Multi-Vocal State in 20th-Century Prince Edward Island," 19–33.

11. Wynn, "Ideology, Society, and State," in *Colonial Leviathan*, 320.

12. Enid Charles and Sylvia Anthony, "The Community and the Family in Prince Edward Island," *Rural Sociology* 3, no. 1 (1943): 46.

13. For Mary's departure for Boston, see above, p. 101. The idea propounded by Hector Compton that their people were somehow "special" in terms of the role they were called to play in God's millennial plan was, according to Mary's older son, something she never entirely dismissed even as she moved on in her religious life to conventional denominational practice. I am most grateful to Keith Gerrard for numerous emails reflecting on the legacy that her communitarian and millenarian upbringing played in his mother's life.

14. Leonore Davidoff, *Thicker Than Water: Siblings and Their Relations, 1780–1920* (Oxford: Oxford University Press, 2012), quoted passages at 45. For a fascinating, albeit imperfect, parallel, see Adele Perry, *Colonial Relations: The Douglas-Connolly Family and the Nineteenth-Century Imperial World* (Cambridge: Cambridge University Press, 2015).

15. George Orwell, *Animal Farm: A Fairy Story* (London: Secker and Warburg, 1945), subsequently reprinted in numerous editions without the subtitle.

16. This quotation comes from Nathaniel Hawthorne's Preface to his fictional account of Brook Farm, *The Blithedale Romance* (New York: A.L. Burt, 1852).

Index

An *f* after a number denotes an image in the photo section.

THE CANADIAN SOCIAL HISTORY SERIES

Kathryn McPherson,
Bedside Matters: The Transformation of Canadian Nursing, 1900–1990, 1996.
ISBN 978-0-8020-8679-2

Edith Burley,
Servants of the Honourable Company: Work, Discipline, and Conflict in the Hudson's Bay Company, 1770–1870, 1997.
ISBN 0-19-541296-6

Mercedes Steedman,
Angels of the Workplace: Women and the Construction of Gender Relations in the Canadian Clothing Industry, 1890–1940, 1997.
ISBN 978-1-4426-0982-2

Angus McLaren and Arlene Tigar McLaren,
The Bedroom and the State: The Changing Practices and Politics of Contraception and Abortion in Canada, 1880–1997, 1997.
ISBN 0-19-541318-0

Kathryn McPherson, Cecilia Morgan, and Nancy M. Forestell, Editors,
Gendered Pasts: Historical Essays in Femininity and Masculinity in Canada, 1999.
ISBN 0-978-0-8020-8690-7

Gillian Creese,
Contracting Masculinity: Gender, Class, and Race in a White-Collar Union, 1944–1994, 1999.
ISBN 0-19-541454-3

Geoffrey Reaume,
Remembrance of Patients Past: Patient Life at the Toronto Hospital for the Insane, 1870–1940, 2000.
ISBN 978-1-4426-1075-0

Miriam Wright,
A Fishery for Modern Times: The State and the Industrialization of the Newfoundland Fishery. 1934–1968, 2001.
ISBN 0-19-541620-1

Judy Fudge and Eric Tucker,
Labour before the Law: The Regulation of Workers' Collective Action in Canada, 1900–1948, 2001.
ISBN 978-0-8020-3793-0

Mark Moss,
Manliness and Militarism: Educating Young Boys in Ontario for War, 2001.
ISBN 0-19-541594-9

Joan Sangster,
Regulating Girls and Women: Sexuality, Family, and the Law in Ontario 1920–1960, 2001.
ISBN 0-19-541663-5

Reinhold Kramer and Tom Mitchell,
Walk towards the Gallows: The Tragedy of Hilda Blake, Hanged 1899, 2002.
ISBN 978-0-8020-9542-8

Mark Kristmanson,
Plateaus of Freedom: Nationality, Culture, and State Security in Canada, 1940–1960, 2002.
ISBN 0-19-541866-2 (cloth)
ISBN 0-19-541803-4 (paper)

Robin Jarvis Brownlie,
A Fatherly Eye: Indian Agents, Government Power, and Aboriginal Resistance in Ontario, 1918–1939, 2003.
ISBN 0-19-541891-3 (cloth)
ISBN 0-19-541784-4 (paper)

Steve Hewitt,
Riding to the Rescue: The Transformation of the RCMP in Alberta and Saskatchewan, 1914–1872, 2006.
ISBN 978-0-8020-9021-8 (cloth)
ISBN 978-0-8020-4895-0 (paper)

Robert K. Kristofferson,
Craft Capitalism: Craftworkers and Early Industrialization in Hamilton, Ontario, 1840–1871, 2007.
ISBN 978-0-8020-9127-7 (cloth)
ISBN 978-0-8020-9408-7 (paper)

Andrew Parnaby,
Citizen Docker: Making a New Deal on the
Vancouver Waterfront, 1919–1939, 2008.
ISBN 978-0-8020-9056-0 (cloth)
ISBN 978-0-8020-9384-4 (paper)

J.I. Little,
Loyalties in Conflict: A Canadian Borderland
in War and Rebellion, 1812–1840, 2008.
ISBN 978-0-8020-9773-6 (cloth)
ISBN 978-0-8020-9525-1 (paper)

Pauline Greenhill,
Make the Night Hideous: Four English
Canadian Charivaris, 1881–1940, 2010.
ISBN 978-1-4426-4077-1 (cloth)
ISBN 978-1-4426-1015-6 (paper)

Rhonda L. Hinther and Jim Mochoruk,
Re-imagining Ukrainian-Canadians:
History, Politics, and Identity, 2010.
ISBN 978-1-4426-4134-1 (cloth)
ISBN 978-1-4426-1062-0 (paper)

Reinhold Kramer and Tom Mitchell,
When the State Trembled: How A.J.
Andrews and the Citizens' Committee
Broke the Winnipeg General Strike, 2010.
ISBN 978-1-4426-4219-5 (cloth)
ISBN 978-1-4426-1116-0 (paper)

Barrington Walker,
Race on Trial: Black Defendants in Ontario's
Criminal Courts, 1858–1958, 2010.
ISBN 978-0-8020-9909-9 (cloth)
ISBN 978-0-8020-9610-4 (paper)

**Lara Campbell, Dominique
Clément, and Greg Kealey,**
Debating Dissent: Canada and the 1960s, 2012.
ISBN 978-1-4426-4164-8 (cloth)
ISBN 978-1-4426-1078-1 (paper)

Janis Thiessen,
Manufacturing Mennonites:
Work and Religion in Post-War
Manitoba, 2013.
ISBN 978-1-4426-4213-3 (cloth)
ISBN 978-1-4426-1113-9 (paper)

Don Nerbas,
Dominion of Capital: The Politics
of Big Business and the Crisis of
the Canadian Bourgeoisie,
1914–1947, 2013.
ISBN 978-1-4426-4545-5 (cloth)
ISBN 978-1-4426-1352-2 (paper)

Kirk Niergarth,
"The Dignity of Every Human Being":
New Brunswick Artists and Canadian
Culture between the Great Depression and
the Cold War, 2015.
ISBN 978-1-4426-4560-8 (cloth)
ISBN 978-1-4426-1389-8 (paper)

Dennis G. Molinaro,
An Exceptional Law: Section 98
and the Emergency State, 1919–1936,
2017.
ISBN 978-1-4426-2957-8 (cloth)
ISBN 978-1-4426-2958-5 (paper)

Ruth Bleasdale,
Rough Work: Labourers on the Public
Works of British North America and
Canada, 1842–1982, 2018.
ISBN 978-1-4875-0248-5 (cloth)
ISBN 978-1-4875-2199-8 (paper)

Ruth Compton Brouwer,
All Things in Common: A Canadian
Family and Its Island Utopia, 2021.
ISBN 978-1-4875-0797-8 (cloth)
ISBN 978-1-4875-2556-9 (paper)

www.ingramcontent.com/pod-product-compliance
Lightning Source LLC
Chambersburg PA
CBHW020252030426
42336CB00010B/722